UNDERSTANDING THE ROOTS OF VOLUNTARY ACTION

D1340538

UNDERSTANDING THE ROOTS OF VOLUNTARY ACTION

Historical Perspectives on
Current Social Policy

Edited by Colin Rochester, George Campbell
Gosling, Alison Penn and Meta Zimmeck

sussex
ACADEMIC
PRESS
Brighton • Portland • Toronto

2 4 6 8 10 9 7 5 3 1

First published 2011 in Great Britain by
SUSSEX ACADEMIC PRESS
PO Box 2950
Brighton BN2 5SP

and in the United States of America by
SUSSEX ACADEMIC PRESS
920 NE 58th Ave   Suite 300
Portland, Oregon 97213–3786

and in Canada by
SUSSEX ACADEMIC PRESS (CANADA)
90 Arnold Avenue, Thornhill, Ontario L4J 1B5

British Library Cataloguing in Publication Data
A CIP catalogue record for this book is available from the British Library.

Library of Congress Cataloging-in-Publication Data
Understanding the roots of voluntary action : historical perspectives on
current social policy / edited by Colin Rochester ... [et al.].
p. cm.
Includes bibliographical references and index.
ISBN 978-1-84519-424-6 (pbk. : alk. paper)
  1. Voluntarism—Great Britain—History. 2. Social service—Great
Britain—History. 3. Great Britain—Social policy. I. Rochester, Colin.
HN400.V64U53 2011
302′.14—dc22

Typeset and designed by Sussex Academic Press
Printed by TJ International, Padstow, Cornwall.
This book is printed on acid-free paper.

Contents

The Contributors

The Editors

Colin Rochester is one of the founders and was the first chair of the Voluntary Action History Society. He has spent more than forty years working in and with the voluntary sector and undertaken research and postgraduate teaching at the LSE and Roehampton University where he founded and directed the Centre for the Study of Voluntary and Community Activity. He is academic adviser to the Institute for Volunteering Research and Vice-Chair of the Voluntary Sector Studies Network. Colin co-edited *An Introduction to the Voluntary Sector* (Routledge, 1995) and *Voluntary Organisations and Social Policy* (Palgrave, 2001) and co-authored *Volunteering and Society in the 21ˢᵗ Century* (Palgrave Macmillan, 2010).

George Campbell Gosling is a research student in the history of medicine and teaching associate in modern British history at Oxford Brookes University. His research interests focus on cultures of welfare before and after the classic welfare state, and he has particular interest in the role of the voluntary sector. He has published and spoken widely on the history of medicine and charity in early-twentieth century Britain, often focusing on the southern provincial city of Bristol.

Alison Penn has 25 years experience of working in the voluntary sector. She has a DPhil in history on the post Second World War voluntary sector, focusing on national-local relationships. She currently combines a half-time post at the Open University as a staff tutor in the south-east region with freelance research and training. Alison is also a research fellow at the University of Brighton and Secretary of the Voluntary Action History Society. Her publications include: *From the Rescue of Fallen Women to the Support of Vulnerable Families: The History of St Michael's Fellowship, 1903–2003* (2005).

Meta Zimmeck trained as a historian and has worked in social policy research for over twenty years. She was head of the Voluntary and Community Research Section in the Home Office; public affairs strategist at Volunteering England; and head of the Secretariat for the Commission on the Future of Volunteering. She is a visiting fellow at the Centre for the Study of Voluntary and Community Activity at Roehampton University and Treasurer of the Voluntary Action History Society. Her most recent publications are an article on the Compact in the new *Voluntary Sector Review* and a chapter on the history of government's approach to volunteering in Rochester et al.'s *Volunteering and Society in the 21st Century* (Palgrave Macmillan, 2010).

The Contributors

Beth Breeze is a co-founder of the Centre for Philanthropy at the University of Kent and also works within the ESRC Centre for Charitable Giving and Philanthropy. She began her career as a fundraiser for a youth homelessness charity, and spent a decade working in a variety of fundraising, research and charity management roles before moving into academia. Her main research interests are major donors, new philanthropy and gift theory.

Jenny Cronin completed her PhD thesis on the *Origins and Development of Scottish Convalescent Homes* in 2003, undertaken at the Centre for the History of Medicine at Glasgow University. Since then she has continued to research and write on various aspects of convalescence and related institutions.

Jonathan Fowler is Professor of History and Dean of Liberal Arts at Pellissippi State Community College where he teaches modern world history. He has published articles on philanthropy in late eighteenth- and early nineteenth-century Britain and is currently working on a biography of Sir Thomas Bernard, *Toward a Science of Philanthropy: Thomas Bernard and the Society for Bettering the Condition of the Poor.*

Anne Logan is a lecturer in Social History at the University of Kent. She has written several articles and chapters about the first women magistrates in England and Wales and on the involvement of women volunteers in the construction of criminal justice policy in the period c.1920–1970. Her book, *Feminism and Criminal Justice: A Historical Perspective* was published by Palgrave in 2008. She is currently working on a biography of S. Margery Fry.

Pat Starkey is an honorary research fellow in the School of History, at the University of Liverpool, where she has taught since the 1980s. Her research interests are primarily in the history of voluntary social work agencies working with families and women's history, particularly the way that religion has impacted on women's lives. Pat is a former Chair of the Voluntary Action History Society.

John Stewart is Professor of Health History at Glasgow Caledonian University; and Director of the Centre for the Social History of Health and

Healthcare, a research collaboration between Glasgow Caledonian and Strathclyde Universities. His research interests include the history of child psychiatry; municipal health care in inter-war England and Wales; and the development of health and welfare services in modern Scotland. He is a Fellow of the Royal Historical Society and an Academician of the Academy of Social Sciences.

Shurlee Swain is a professor at the Australian Catholic University and a senior research fellow in the School of Historical Studies at the University of Melbourne. She has published widely in the area of child welfare history, her latest book being *Child, Nation, Race and Empire* (Manchester University Press, 2010).

Steven Thompson is a lecturer in modern history at Aberystwyth University and has carried out research on health, medicine and the labour movement in industrial south Wales during the nineteenth and twentieth centuries. He has authored a monograph entitled "Unemployment, Poverty and Health in Interwar South Wales" that was published by the University of Wales Press in 2006, in addition to a number of articles and essays on related themes. He is currently one of the editors of Llafur, the journal of the Welsh People's History Society.

Brenda Weeden read history at St Hugh's College, Oxford and then trained as an archivist. In 1994 she was appointed to establish the Archive Service at the University of Westminster. In 2005 she began to research the early history of the University. The results were published as *The Education of the Eye: A History of the Royal Polytechnic Institution, 1838–1881* (Grant Editions, 2008).

Alexandra Wright is an associate professor and Dean of the Undergraduate Program in the Faculty of Social Work at the University of Manitoba. She was awarded her PhD by the University of Glasgow for a thesis on *the Origins and Development of Scottish Convalescent Homes, 1860–1939*. Her research interests are human services organzations and effectiveness, efficiency, culture and climate while her publications include *Children in Need: An Examination of Policy Formulation in Scottish Social Work* (Saarbrucken, Germany: VDM Dr Muller Publishers, 2008).

Bridget Yates is a former museum practitioner currently working towards a PhD at the University of Gloucestershire looking at volunteer-led museums in market towns and villages in England. Between 1998 and 2010 she was a visiting tutor in museology at the University of East Anglia. She is a trustee of two independent museums in rural East Anglia.

Abbreviations

ACEVO	Association of Chief Executives of Voluntary Organisations
CGLI	City and Guilds of London Institute
CIN	Children in Need
COS	Charity Organisation Society
CSP	Children's Services Plans
DPAS	Discharged Prisoners' Aid Societies
HLPR	Howard League for Penal Reform
JP	Justice of the Peace
LSE	London School of Economics and Political Science
NAMH	National Association for Mental Health
NCSS	National Council of Social Service
NCVO	National Council for Voluntary Organisations
NIB	National Institute for the Blind
NSPCC	National Society for the Prevention of Cruelty to Children
NUSEC	National Union of Societies for Equal Citizenship
OSCR	Office of the Scottish Charity Regulator
PRL	Penal Reform League
PSEC	Prison System Enquiry Committee
SBCP	The Society for Bettering the Condition and Increasing the Comforts of the Poor
SED	Scottish Education Department
SHHD	Scottish Home and Health Department
SWD	Social Work Department
VAHS	Voluntary Action History Society
WFL	Women's Freedom League

UNDERSTANDING THE ROOTS OF VOLUNTARY ACTION

Introduction:
Today's Debate and the
Experience of the Past

COLIN ROCHESTER

The Need for Historical Understanding

One of the key factors that has shaped contemporary debates on public and social policy has been the rediscovery of what is currently termed the "third" sector by successive governments since the 1980s when Margaret Thatcher led the initial attempt to roll back the frontiers of the state. Since then, discussion of the role of what has also been variously described as the voluntary, nonprofit or nongovernmental sector or civil society in meeting social need has contributed a significant thread – or set of themes – to the discussion of the design and delivery of social welfare, broadly defined, in an age when the welfare state is no longer seen as the best or only means of tackling Beveridge's "five giants" of Want, Ignorance, Disease, Squalor and Idleness.

We have moved a long way from the world of 1978 when the Wolfenden Report on the Future of Voluntary Organisations could reflect a consensus view that the contribution of the voluntary sector to the delivery of welfare, while important, was essentially supplementary or complementary to the role of the state's "welfare bureaucracies" – to use the term coined by David Billis.[1] The Wolfenden Committee could also characterize the nature of the voluntary sector's approach in terms which were uncontroversial:

in the space between the loosely structured informal system and the more strictly organised statutory system, people can use the medium of the voluntary organisation to join with others in devising means to meet their own needs or those of others they wish to help.[2]

Some thirty years on, the expectation of what the voluntary sector can and should contribute to what is now described as a "mixed economy of welfare" has changed radically: voluntary agencies were increasingly enlisted by the Conservative administrations of the 1980s and 1990s as contractors whose services could be commissioned in place of direct provision by statutory bodies while the election of New Labour in 1997 ushered in an era of "partnership" in which voluntary sector organizations were expected to take their place alongside both government and the private, for-profit, sector in addressing a wide range of social need.[3]

These dramatic changes have been accompanied by a growing debate about the desirability of the new arrangements and about their impact. The case for a greatly extended and enhanced role for third sector organizations is based on a belief that they uniquely embody virtuous qualities. These attributes have been listed in a variety of government policy documents and include: "providing services and care, mobilising communities, helping to identify and solve new needs as well as old ones, campaigning for social change, focusing on the needs of service users, tackling complex needs and difficult social issues, being flexible and offering joined up services, capable of earning users' trust, promoting volunteering and mentoring, building stronger and connected communities, and to help transform public services".[4]

There have been growing concerns, however, on the part of academics and practitioners alike, about the ability of voluntary sector organizations to meet these high expectations and about the unintended consequences of the attempt to cast them in this new role. Many of the perceived advantages of voluntary organizations tend, it is suggested, to evaporate as they grow; it is comparatively easy for small organizations to develop close relations with the communities and user groups with whom they work and to respond to their expressed needs in a flexible and "holistic" way. Growth brings increased formality and more bureaucratic forms of organization and management which entail a more systematic, but also more standardized, approach to delivering services. The impact of the new "partnership" arrangements on voluntary agencies may exacerbate the processes associated with growth as government commissioners impose detailed specifications and accountability requirements to meet their own need to show they have accounted properly for the expenditure of public funds. Under these conditions, the third sector is no longer seen as occupying the space between the loose informality of the personal sphere of families and friends and the "more strictly organised statutory system" which Wolfenden saw as its habitat.

At the same time, observers suggest, the sector has lost – or is losing –

its independence. From this point of view It has bartered its very "soul" for access to substantial sums in government funding – which enable it to provide more services for those its exists to benefit – and for some influence on the design of services and the shaping of policy. At the level of the individual agency, there may be implications for its ownership and accountability and its governance. At the sector level, there is a real risk that:

> the cumulative impact of the pursuit of individual voluntary agency advantage is to the detriment of the survival of a distinctive voluntary sector in welfare. If the third sector has no distinctive organizational features, no separate voice or voices, no alternative responses to social need, no different ways of doing things, what will be the rationale for its inclusion within a mixed economy of welfare in the future?[5]

Others take a more optimistic view. The leaders of the highest profile organizations which claim to represent the interests of the sector – the National Council for Voluntary Organisations (NCVO) and the Association of Chief Executives in Voluntary Organisations (ACEVO) – both take this approach although their views are expressed in somewhat different styles, Steven Bubb of ACEVO argues that the growth of the large, formally organized voluntary agencies which are equipped to bid successfully for public funds can only be to the benefit of their users and takes an explicitly pragmatic view of the need to "compromise on certain issues in order to deliver on other objectives".[6] The optimism displayed by NCVO's Stuart Etherington is tinged with caution and hemmed around with conditions; provided that voluntary organizations are well governed and well managed and the contracts into which they enter are not flawed, they can combine an independent stance with the delivery of public services.[7]

This is an important debate which hinges on some key questions:

- What are the respective roles of the state, the market and the voluntary sector in meeting social needs – or what should they be?
- What is the nature of the "competitive advantage" enjoyed by voluntary organizations and how could or should this be best deployed?
- What kinds of "rules of the game" should define how the relationship between the government and the voluntary sector can best be negotiated and ordered?

and:

- To what extent does the voluntary sector provide a separate space for and a distinctive approach to providing social welfare?

Yet the discussion, as well as being muted, is curiously deracinated. The key protagonists seem to have no interest in – let alone any understanding of – the history of voluntary action. Few, if any, of the politicians, civil servants, social policy academics and commentators, leaders of the sector's representative bodies and those who manage and lead voluntary agencies who participate in the discussion of policy are aware of the background to the current debate and the lessons that might be learned from what has gone before. This vacuum exists despite the outstanding work of some individual scholars (such as Jane Lewis, Geoffrey Finlayson, Frank Prochaska and Bernard Harris). It has also been addressed by the foundation – in 1992 – of the Voluntary Action History Society (VAHS) by a small group of researchers and practitioners who were scandalized by the voluntary sector's neglect of its own history and the lack of an historical dimension to the discussion of its role and its contribution to society. Marx's view that "those who don't understand history are condemned to repeat it, the first time as tragedy, the second time as farce"[8] may now be regarded as a dramatic overstatement and oversimplification of a complex relationship. The group of contemporary scholars who formed the *History and Policy* group at the Institute of Historical Research in 2002, argue nonetheless that "too often policy reflects unexamined historical assumptions and cliches" and that "at best, policy without history fails to learn past lessons and, at worst, repeats past mistakes".[9] Like them, the editors of this book believe that there can be little doubt that a lack of knowledge and understanding of past experience represents a serious gap in the armoury of the policy-maker and the social analyst as well as voluntary sector leaders.

This book is the most recent initiative on the part of the Voluntary Action History Society to make a contribution to the continuing struggle to ensure that the contemporary discussion and debate about voluntary action is informed by an understanding of its history. The chapters that follow started life as papers presented to the Society's Third International Conference on the History of Voluntary Action but have subsequently undergone substantial revision to ensure that they make the maximum possible contribution to four key themes which are discussed below. They deal with various aspects of the history of voluntary action in the nineteenth and twentieth centuries and range across a variety of fields of activity, geographical areas and organizational forms. They are concerned with the welfare of children and young people; the relief of poverty; education and employment; health; the criminal justice system; and culture. Some of the studies are UK-wide; others deal with England and Wales or Scotland; and a further number are more local in their scope – a single village in Yorkshire; the South Wales coalfield; the West of Scotland; and London. And they feature the work of individual social entrepreneurs and philan-thropists; working class voluntary action; the role of women; faith-based organizations; the growth of professionalism; and issues of organizational growth and development.

Four Key Themes

Like the best historical writing of any kind, the strength of the individual chapters is in their clear focus on particular manifestations of voluntary action and the detailed consideration they can give to these. On the other hand, the book as a whole represents something that is greater than the sum of these individual parts and the next section of this introductory chapter will attempt to show how they contribute to our knowledge and understanding of four broad themes. These are:

- The "moving frontier" between the state and voluntary action; the distribution of roles and functions between them; and the nature of their inter-relationship;
- The "springs" of voluntary action – what makes people get involved in voluntary organizations or support them financially?
- Organizational challenges for voluntary agencies; including growth; cleaving to their missions and values; and survival;

and

- Issues of continuity and change; how and to what extent has the nature of voluntary action and its role in society remained essentially the same despite the changing context within which voluntary agencies exist and carry out their functions?

The moving frontier

Three of the chapters in this book deal with the shifting relationship between the state and the world of voluntary action. In his study of child guidance in twentieth-century Britain (chapter 3) John Stewart argues that, while a superficial reading of its development would reflect the common view of the way welfare provision has developed from its origins in voluntary efforts to statutory provision by way of a "mixed economy", the reality is far more complex. The relationship can best be categorized – in the phrase used by Beveridge and popularized by Geoffrey Finlayson – as a "moving frontier". Stewart suggests that the history of child guidance can be seen, in Julie Grier's words, as representing "the voluntary-state boundary at its most plastic" and allowing a considerable degree of autonomy, activism and influence.

While the local state increasingly stepped in to fill the gap left by the withdrawal of philanthropic funding and to meet the need for additional resources to meet rising demand for child guidance services in the 1930s and beyond, government's involvement was cautious and piecemeal. This, together with the uneven availability of charitable funds, meant that the circumstances of individual clinics were very different. While many of them led a precarious, hand-to-mouth existence, a number of voluntary clinics continued to function – and prosper – into the 1950s, years after child guidance was embedded in the welfare state.

In chapter 4, Alexandra Wright provides an account of the development of children's welfare services in Scotland between the Beveridge Report and the passage of the Children (Scotland) Act in 1995 and traces the ways in which voluntary agencies have shaped and been shaped by changing attitudes to need and the policies to which these have given birth. The period from the 1940s to the 1970s, she argues, witnessed a significant expansion of services in response to the broader concept of need which provided the rationale for the replacement of the Poor Law with the Welfare State. This also involved a greatly enhanced role for the state as a means of meeting need and the development of social work as a profession. The high-water mark of these new approaches to welfare provision was the establishment in 1968 of local authority Social Work Departments (equivalent to Social Services Departments in England and Wales) which unified hitherto separate functions in a new generic structure with the ambitious aim of meeting universal needs.

The rapid expansion of welfare provision during the 1970s was accompanied by growing public criticism of its cost (at a time of economic downturn); the quality and quantity of the services delivered; and the bureaucratic structures through which they were provided. These led to a questioning of the role of the state in planning and providing services to meet social needs which paved the way for the major shift in policy that took place in the 1980 and 90s. Wright provides examples of the ways in which voluntary organizations contributed to the critique of the performance and appropriateness of state-run welfare bureaucracies.

In the 1980s and 1990s, she suggests, disillusion with the welfare system led to a major change in the way services were delivered and a new approach to the definition of need. On the one hand, there was a growing consensus that the state's responsibility for welfare should be shared with the market and with voluntary action. And, on the other, the concept of need was increasingly based on law rather than welfare culminating in the legislation of 1995 which introduced the notion of "children in need" which can be employed as a means of restricting access to services.

For Alison Penn, in chapter 2, the welfare reforms of the Liberal administration of 1906–11 represent a watershed in the relationship between the state and voluntary action. They brought with them a significant expansion of the institutional base of the state and the development of increasingly bureaucratic organizational forms as well as a major change of role from enabler and regulator to funder and provider. This had, she suggests, two important impacts on the activities of voluntary organizations. In the first place, a series of national organizations were set up to meet the new need to develop effective mechanisms for influencing government legislation and the development of social policy. And, in the second place, while the expansion of state activity impinged on areas which had been the preserve of voluntary action, it also offered new opportunities for voluntary agencies. In essence the state's reach exceeded its grasp: government at national and local level lacked the capacity to deliver the services for which it had assumed responsibility and had to rely on voluntary organizations to act on its behalf in many areas of work.

By 1945, she argues, the expanding role of voluntary organizations as agents of the state had formed "a relationship of interdependence underpinned by statutory funding". For some, this marked a stage in the process by which their work would be replaced by statutory forms of provision but, for others, their role as agents of the state and the support from public funds which this entailed proved to be a key to their survival; they carved out a specific role within the broad sweep of public provision and supplemented their income from other sources. Their ability to shape their future in this way, Penn suggests, was not solely dependent on the kinds of services they provided but was also related to their organizational characteristics: the older mutual aid organizations found themselves displaced as a distinctive organizational form whilst those from the philanthropic tradition were "better able to metamorphose and in so doing to evolve a form of partnership with the state".

As well as selecting partners which were most likely to succumb to isomorphism, governments have, according to Penn, sought more direct ways to influence and control voluntary organizations since before the Second World War. These have included attaching conditions to funding which involve close scrutiny of their actions and seeking representation on their governing bodies. And government agencies have also promoted co-ordination and amalgamation among voluntary organizations in order to make it easier for them to deal with the diversity of the sector. Overall, she says, these pressures have led to "the metamorphosis of philanthropy and the displacement of mutual aid".

The "springs" of voluntary action

Alison Penn's chapter also provides a useful starting point for a discussion of the rationale for voluntary action and the reasons why people establish voluntary organizations and give their time and money to supporting their activities. She reminds us of Bourdillon's view that "a voluntary organisation, properly speaking, is an organisation which, whether its workers are paid or unpaid, is initiated and governed by its own members without external control".[10] And she takes as the cornerstones for her account, the basic building blocks of philanthropy and mutual aid which had been identified by Beveridge as the twin components of voluntary action.

Two of the chapters in this book throw light on the interplay between the two elements of voluntary action – the "impulse from above" – as philanthropy has been defined – and the "impulse from below" which characterizes mutual aid. In chapter 5, Bridget Yates presents a case study of the establishment and maintenance of a local volunteer-run museum in Yorkshire and explores the interaction between the values and approaches of two different classes among its supporters. On the one hand she describes the contribution of the traditional leaders of rural society, the landlord and the parson, who are concerned about the education and improvement of the working classes and the professionalization of museum management. Ranged against these "top-down" forces, on the other hand are the "bottom-up" pressures of social change and the involvement of working-class people in the work of the museum as users, supporters and committee members.

A similar conflict between different approaches to voluntary action based in class differences is the subject of chapter 6. Here, Steven Thompson discusses the conflicting views of the provision of welfare and medical services in the South Wales Coalfield in the period from the late nineteenth until the middle of the twentieth century. This was a clash between the views of the coal owners and other industrialists as well as middle class professionals on the one hand and working-class actors – led by the South Wales Miners' Federation – on the other. The former emphasized the importance of individual responsibility and played down the role of the state (and elite philanthropy) while the latter stressed the need for collective action by the working classes and increasingly looked to the state to ensure that there was a minimum level of provision for all.

In a different vein, John Stewart's account of the development of the child guidance movement (in chapter 3) also explores the relationship between two forms of philanthropy. The movement largely owed its initial existence and impetus to the support of an extremely large and influential foundation – the Commonwealth Fund of New York – which had been established in 1918 by a bequest of ten million dollars from a Mrs Stephen Harkness. The Fund paid for the training – in the US – of the first generation of British psychiatric social workers and social work teachers; bankrolled a training course at the London School of Economics (LSE); and supported the work of the Child Guidance Council which, among other activities, "loaned out" staff to new clinics. But the continued existence of local clinics was dependent on contributions from local philanthropic sources until public funds were made available (and in some cases beyond that point). It was often the case that psychiatrists (and, more rarely, psychologists) made a donation of their time but clinics still needed to meet running costs and, in time, needed to find salaries to meet the increasing demand for services. The funds came from a variety of sources which included institutions such as the local Catholic Church and a Council for Social Service as well as wealthy – and sometimes anonymous – individuals.

The role of individual philanthropists is explored in chapters 7 and 8 of the book. Brenda Weeden looks at the life and philanthropic career of Quintin Hogg and his founding role in the polytechnic movement. She finds that Hogg's charity work – which he combined with paid employment in business throughout his life at the expense of his family and social life – was driven by his strong Christian faith. But, while his primary motive was to save souls, he was also aware of the need to help the ragged children who attended the school he founded to escape poverty by finding employment. He was an early manifestation or prototype of the social entrepreneur, harnessing his business skills to the development of the Shoeblack Society which provided paid work for boys and then devoting much of his life to the development of education and training which enabled young adolescents to improve their skills and better themselves. This culminated in the establishment of a new form of educational provision at the Polytechnic in Regent Street. Weeden concludes that the success of this great "social experiment" was due to Hogg's untiring energy and his long-term financial support – he had, he said, "given up my country house and my carriage to carry on this work".

Shurlee Swain's chapter examines the work of four pioneers of child rescue work and looks at the central role of religion in their thought and practice. Like Hogg, they were motivated by their Christian faith: indeed Swain argues that "at least in the time of the founders [of the child rescue movement], evangelism was their central purpose and child rescue is best understood as an epiphemenon". The argument thus takes us beyond today's interest in "faith-based organizations" as well as throwing new light on the history of child rescue: "to the founders . . . all charity was religious and religion properly understood embraced the whole field of charity". Swain's account discusses the way in which street children were perceived by these four philanthropists; their invocation of biblical texts; the way they thought that Christ might respond to the poverty of their day; and their belief that religion and charity offered alternatives to revolution. And she concludes that, while the impact of the child rescuers could be seen as benign, the theology on which it was based often led to the disempowerment of the "rescued" children: "the focus of the rescuers on eternal salvation too often left the supposedly rescued in a vulnerable situation".

Another factor in the mobilization of voluntary action, mentioned in other parts of the book, the key role played by women excluded from the labour market, is explored in chapter 9. In it, Anne Logan discusses the role of women in the criminal justice system in the early and middle years of the twentieth century. She describes how women magistrates drew on the tradition of charitable casework on the one hand and networks linked to the women's suffrage movement and other progressive causes on the other to play a significant and creative role in the development of policy and the management of prisons and prisoners' aftercare. Logan suggests that, despite the hard work of feminist organizations to promote women's employment, opportunities remained limited and "many well educated women ... put their energy into voluntary work such as in the magistracy" and began to bring professional approaches to roles such as that of Justice of the Peace. And she concludes that "they no doubt gained a great deal of personal fulfilment and satisfaction as well as performing valuable roles both in the criminal justice system and in the pressure groups that developed around it".

Organizational challenges

As we have already begun to discuss above, Alison Penn's chapter raises some of the key organizational issues and challenges that voluntary agencies still face today. The pressure of isomorphism that accompanied the new relationship as a junior partner and agent of government meant that voluntary organizations – like the new state agencies of the early years of the twentieth century – began to adopt the kinds of centralized bureaucratic forms that were found in corporate enterprises. Some kinds of organization were able to adapt themselves easily but those which were constituted as a federation of local bodies – like many of the friendly societies – found it more difficult to balance the demands for more centralized decision-making and the creation of larger scale units in the name of greater efficiency against the historical reality of largely autonomous local groups which were seen to encourage participation and democratic decision-making. Penn suggests that their history had an important impact on the outcome of the conflict between the two organizational imperatives; where local branches or units had existed before national or central bodies they were more likely to retain their autonomy than those which had been created by a national body.

Two further chapters in the book focus on organizational challenges which remain issues for today's voluntary sector managers. In the first of these (chapter 10), Jenny Cronin examines in depth the history of two Scottish convalescent homes founded around 1860 by committed individual philanthropists but also draws on the experience of other – similar – organizations. One of the two case study homes flourished briefly but struggled after the death of its two founders and closed around 1911, a time when other homes were enjoying the peak of their popularity. The other case study organization grew rapidly and continued to flourish until after the Second World War. Cronin looks at a range of factors that might help to explain the contrasting trajectory of the two organizations including the role of key individuals; their management styles; their relationship with other organizations; and the scale of their operation. Her conclusion is that the key difference lies in the number of people involved in the governance of the homes and their employment of paid staff rather than relying on volunteers. While the comparatively short-lived organization was managed almost single-handed by one of the founders with the help of a small group of trustees, its more successful counterpart had created a board of sixteen influential people with strong links with other institutions such as the university and the infirmary. The successful home also employed staff in three key roles – as medical director; to provide trained nursing care; and to collect the subscriptions which underpinned their finances.

Pat Starkey's chapter is also concerned with organizational change. It focuses on the attempts by the House of Charity in Soho – which had been founded in 1849 to provide temporary accommodation for "suitably recommended people" – to adjust to changing social circumstances. From the very beginning the organization had struggled to meet the challenge of keeping its accommodation full – and thus ensuring an adequate income flow – while admitting only the people who met the requirements of the founding mission that they should be respectable members of the deserving poor who were temporarily in need of short-term assistance. Starkey discusses the ways in which the House of St Barnabas – as it was renamed in 1951 "after nearly half a century of discussion" – responded to the recognition "that the characteristics of social need are not constant" and continued to exist into the twenty-first century.

Continuity and change

The book concludes with two chapters which address some of the issues of continuity and change: to what extent can we recognize in the history of voluntary action features, characteristics and challenges that remain current? Jonathan Fowler (in chapter 12) locates the roots of "scientific philanthropy" around the end of the eighteenth century and decades before the foundation of the Charity Organization Society. The pioneers were the members of the Society for Bettering the Condition and Increasing the Comforts of the Poor whose commitment to philanthropy as a science was expressed through the publication of a series of influential reports on projects and schemes from across the country and the forging of close working relationships with those providing charitable services, notably vaccinations and fever hospitals. Fowler argues that the SBCP thus became the central focus for the work of similar societies across Britain and overseas.

Our final chapter – by Beth Breeze – questions the growing consensus that there is something distinctively "new" about philanthropy in the early years of the twenty-first century. She argues that the three main features of the contemporary view of philanthropy can only be seen as new by those who know nothing of its history. As we have seen in the preceding chapter, there is nothing new about a concern on the part of donors to ensure that their money is well spent; attempts to make philanthropy rational and scientific have a long history. Secondly, she suggests that the characteristics of the "new donors" of the twenty-first century – young self-made entrepreneurs – could equally well be applied to earlier philanthropists like Andrew Carnegie. And, thirdly, she argues that the "new causes" of today are no newer than those of the past were in their time. She concludes that the popularity of the notion of "new philanthropy" can be explained by three factors: "a loss of historical memory"; a "preference for novelty"; and an attempt to put some distance between current activity and the negative image of philanthropy.

Some Concluding Reflections

While these two final chapters explicitly address issues of change and continuity, we would suggest that the themes that run through the whole of the collection provide us with a better vantage point from which to join in the contemporary debate about the role, contribution and defining features of voluntary organizations. Furthermore, they help us to understand that, while, as Breeze argues, voluntary action is constantly being re-invented to reflect current needs and values and the wider social context, there are enduring features and continuing issues and challenges for those who manage and lead voluntary organizations.

This book provides a rich vein of evidence of the ways in which voluntary action has changed and yet has remained recognisably the same over the past 200 or so years. It throws light on the "moving frontier" of state-voluntary sector relationships and suggests that there is more than one model for the distribution of roles and authority between them. And it puts into historical perspective New Labour's investment in "rationalising" the sector to make it more fit to play the role which government has allocated to it. The material offers new insights into both philanthropy – the impulse from above – and mutual aid – the impulse from below – by exploring ways in which, far from acting as completely separate streams, the two impulses have met and interacted. And it provides some new perspectives on some of the key organizational issues still confronting voluntary sector organizations today – notably the tension between bureaucratic managerialism and participatory democracy, often manifested in contested ground between central organizations and their local units or branches, and the conflict between the adherence to the founding mission and the need to adapt as needs change and in order to secure continuing sources of revenue. Overall, it offers an antidote to the ahistorical approach taken not only by commentators, as Beth Breeze suggests, but also by the politicians, the policy-makers and those who speak for the voluntary sector who are the main contributors to the current debate.

Notes

1 David Billis, *Welfare Bureaucracies: their design and change in response to social problems* (London: Heinemann, 1984).
2 Lord Wolfenden, *The Future of Voluntary Organisations: Report of the Wolfenden Committee on Voluntary Organisations* (London: Croom Helm, 1978), p. 29.

3 Caroline Glendenning, Martin Powell and Kirstein Rummery, *Partnerships, New Labour and the Governance of Welfare* (Bristol: The Policy Press, 2002).

4 David Billis, *Hybrid Organizations and the Third Sector: Challenges for Practice, Theory and Policy* (Basingstoke: Palgrave Macmillan, 2010), p. 11.

5 Margaret Harris, "Voluntary Organisations in a Changing Social Policy Environment" in Margaret Harris and Colin Rochester (eds), *Voluntary Organisations and Social Policy in Britain: perspectives on change and choice* (Basingstoke: Palgrave, 2001), pp. 219–20.

6 Steven Bubb, *Transforming our Public Services through the Third Sector* (London: Association of Chief Executives in Voluntary Organisations, 2007), p. 16.

7 Stuart Etherington, *Keynote Speech to the 2004 Annual Conference of NCVO* at http://www.ncvo-vol.org.uk/press/speeches/?id=246 accessed September, 2009.

8 Karl Marx, "The Eighteenth Brumaire of Louis Napoleon", *Die Revolution* (New York: 1952).

9 www.historyandpolicy.org (accessed November 2009).

10 A. F. C. Bourdillon, *Voluntary Social Services: Their Place in the Modern State* (London: Methuen, 1949), p. 3.

PART I

The Moving Frontier
between the State
and Voluntary Action

Social History and Organizational Development: Revisiting Beveridge's *Voluntary Action*

ALISON PENN

William Beveridge's 1948 report on *Voluntary Action*[1] is rightly seen as a landmark in the history of the voluntary sector. It was written at a time when the state, both at the central and local level, had moved centre stage as a provider and funder of welfare as part of the post-war welfare settlement of which Beveridge himself is widely seen as an architect.[2] It provides us with an important link between the development of voluntary action before and after the Second World War. The report was originally commissioned by the National Deposit Friendly Society, whose role had been eclipsed in the post-war settlement, but Beveridge widened its scope to include the philanthropic as well as the mutual traditions of voluntary action and made the case for ensuring that it remained "vigorous and abundant" at a time of a greatly increased state presence.[3]

This chapter revisits Beveridge's report to explore the ways in which it can help us to understand the organizational development of voluntary action. It begins by using his discussion of "motive" to examine the "springs" or origins of voluntary action and how they are linked to the associational nature of voluntary organizations – how they organize themselves to achieve their objectives. It suggests that, while organizations may change and move away from their founding mission, there can be remarkable continuities and newer manifestations of the original motives.

Beveridge's report also provides insights into some of the organizational challenges facing voluntary action, in particular how they combined local autonomy with central or national co-ordination. Such organizational issues do not take place in a vacuum and Beveridge's discussion of the impact on the Friendly Societies of the context of the emerging welfare state provides an illustration of the nature of the "moving frontier" between the state and voluntary action – a term which was deployed by Beveridge himself.[4] The chapter then goes on to suggest that the organizational consequences of this moving frontier were very different for bodies from the mutual and the philanthropic traditions: while the mutuals were displaced, philanthropic organizations underwent a process of metamorphosis.

The Springs of Voluntary Action: Mutual Aid and Philanthropy

In his preface to *Voluntary Action*, Beveridge refers to the work of the Nuffield College Social Reconstruction Survey whose findings were published as an edited book[5] and quoted the definition of voluntary action used by the book's editor, A.F.C. Bourdillon:

> The distinctively 'voluntary' character of [voluntary organisations] is the product, not of the kind of workers they employ [volunteers], but of their mode of birth and method of government. A voluntary organisation properly speaking is an organisation which, whether its workers are paid or unpaid, is initiated and governed by its own members without external control.[6]

This puts the emphasis on the nature of the activity – as autonomous, purposive action – and stresses the associational feature of voluntary action. This definition has the potential to widen the common focus on charitable social service provision to include a broader range of organizational forms: mutual aid, leisure groups, churches and even political parties. Beveridge's own overview does not go that far, focusing mainly on organizations concerned with welfare although, as the report looks forward, its scope widens to include organizations working in leisure and recreation.

This definition together with his discussion about "motive" also draws our attention to the importance of origins in understanding the development of voluntary action. Beveridge identifies two very different motives behind voluntary action to address the problem of poverty:

> The first motive has its origin in a sense of one's own need for security against misfortune, and the realization that, since one's fellows have the same need, by undertaking to help one another all may help themselves. The second motive springs from . . . social conscience, the feeling which makes men who are materially comfortable, mentally uncomfortable as long as their neighbours are materially uncomfortable.[7]

The organizational manifestation of these two motives broadly divides between mutual aid organizations, underpinned by the value of collective self-help, on the one hand and philanthropic bodies underpinned by the value of altruism or helping others, on the other. There are two important implications.

Firstly, these traditions have been characterized by a tension between contradictory and opposing impulses. The impulse present in philanthropic activity is based on an unequal relationship – "from above" – between helper and helped while mutual aid activity is a relationship amongst equals, essentially an "impulse from below". Secondly, these motives combined with the method of organizing (referred to above) saw the development of distinctive associational organizations.

An important feature of the mutual aid tradition was that it

> manifested itself in a number of democratic voluntary movements, started and run under working-class, or sometimes lower middle-class leadership and control.[8]

These organizations pioneered open membership and government of the association on the principle of one member, one vote with leaders elected from within the ranks, at a time when the majority of the working class was denied access to the democratic institutions of the wider society. In a radical sense, such organizations were "producing" their own democracy which they also "owned".

These mutual aid organizations also presented an alternative structure to that of the profit-making firm where ownership was vested in an individual, partnership or shareholders. For the Co-operative Movement, for example, ownership was based on one vote per member, no matter how much money was invested.[9] Furthermore, mutual aid organizations were not simply distinguishable on the basis of the way they provided goods or services; they also performed an important social function by providing an arena for bringing the membership together and involving them in the running of the society. This is well illustrated by Beveridge's description of the "club night" of the local branch of a friendly society:

> The club night may be monthly, fortnightly or weekly . . . If the meeting is that of the branch of an affiliated order, it is normally introduced by a ritual, designed to impress upon members the high aims of the society and the respect which should be accorded to these aims. There may be passwords and signs as a condition of admittance. The room will be brightened by insignia and adorned by photographs of past officers of the branch, and by other memorials testifying to the honourable antiquity and usefulness of the society. The business of every meeting . . . will include the administration of individual sick benefits, the branch receiving on that occasion the reports of the "sick visitors" . . . the individual members who have undertaken to call on sick brethren.[10]

Such a social function was not confined to mutual aid organisations and philanthropic bodies were about more than just the provision of a service, as Stephen Yeo's study of voluntary organisations in Reading from 1880–1914 showed:

> It was the sacred responsibility of different groups or classes to bear one another's burdens, often in a sacrificial manner. Different classes should act as if they were in a community, for that was what citizenship meant. If they did, something more nearly resembling a community than the existing social order, widely recognized as defective, could be brought into being. Participation in welfare-oriented organisations was essential. Such organisations had a life quite apart from their function as givers of first aid, and quite as important. They had to meet as well as to do.[11]

Philanthropic bodies also operated forms of democratic structure. The Reading Philanthropic Institution (which originated in the 1840s), for example, was also a participatory, membership-based, meeting-oriented society.[12]

However, a crucial difference lay in the issue of membership or ownership. In the case of the mutual aid organization, those being helped, through collective self-help, were both members and owners of the organization. In philanthropic bodies, membership, and thus ownership, was confined to the people providing the help rather than the beneficiaries. This difference is important to understanding the two contradictory impulses which have been, and continue to be, major features of voluntary action and an important factor in explaining why, historically, the two have been, as G.D.H. Cole put it, "bad mixers".[13]

The two traditions of mutual aid and philanthropy may appear to belong to the past but the impulses from below and above that each represent recur within the more recent histories of other voluntary organizations. One example can be found in the origins of the Community Association movement, where the traditions of community "for" clashed with the tradition of community "of". A similar clash occurred within the post-Second World War history of the National Council for Social Service, between community work as social work and community work as social or political action. It was also evident within the history of some of the newer voluntary organizations emerging during the 1960s and 1970s. In the field of homelessness, for example, the tension was evident in organizations like the Cyrenians in their attempts to develop more egalitarian ways of working within and around an unequal relationship between homeless people (the helped) and the Cyrenian projects (the helpers).[14]

Organizational Challenges: National–Local Relations

A second important piece of learning from *Voluntary Action* is that the tradition of organizing on a federative basis has been an important and longstanding feature of voluntary action. Beveridge argued that the tradition of independent organizations joining together in wider association was a practical solution to the problem of "combining the responsibility and personal contact of small units with the strength and capacity to weather storms that depend on size".[15] There are many examples of this organizational form in the mutual aid tradition – such as the affiliated order of the friendly society where the separate units formed a federation – as well as in the philanthropic world. The Charity Organisation Society (COS), for one, was organized as a federation of district committees which were represented on a General Council[16] while the auxiliaries or associated branches of the missionary and Bible societies were used as fund-raising mechanisms for these national bodies.[17] Thus an important feature of voluntary action from both traditions in the nineteenth century was the organizational practice of local groups and central (usually national) bodies bound together in an interdependent relationship with varying degrees of autonomy vis à vis one another. This organizational feature has also been a recurring theme in the subsequent development of voluntary organizations in the twentieth century.

Beveridge's report thus highlights the historical dimension to the national profile of voluntary action. The need for a national body or structure in voluntary organizations has evolved in association with the growing importance of the "national" in other areas of commercial and statutory activity. The benefits associated with a national structure – economies of scale in the provision of services and enhanced status, greater influence and a higher profile – have emerged and developed in the particular context of an increasing scale of organization in the commercial and statutory spheres. There have been organizational pressures on voluntary organizations to conform to such a pattern of development, to establish a national headquarters and to centralize and control decision-making processes. This pressure has been resisted with varying degrees of success. The relationship between national body and local group involves a contradictory element, or a tension with pulls in different and opposing directions. This tension has tended to be resolved to the advantage of the centre rather than the locality. Nevertheless this has not been a uniform or one-way process. Local activity has not only continued but has also maintained a tradition of autonomous organization. Such an issue cannot, however, be considered in isolation and this brings us to the third way in which Beveridge's report is useful, namely its emphasis on the importance of context for understanding voluntary organizational issues.

The Moving Frontier: The Importance of Context

The growth of commercial activity and the transformation to an industrial capitalist society in the eighteenth and nineteenth centuries resulted in both the expansion of the mutual benefit society and the diversification of charitable institutions. Furthermore, the increasing space taken up by commercial activity in the nineteenth and early twentieth centuries influenced not only the type, range and scale of voluntary activity but also the organizational forms through which such activities were carried out.

> Church and chapel, school and university, friendly society and social club, retail shop and public house, organised sport and entertainment, all were affected by the drive towards large-scale headquarters and branch, regionally or organised institutions.[18]

The drive to larger scale structures was accompanied by the increasing influence of approaches based on notions of efficiency and objective-oriented activity. Mutual aid organizations like the Friendly Societies found themselves under enormous pressure to "modernize" and move away from their social or non-market values in favour of commercial ones, and from direct, locally-oriented control of the organization, towards large, amalgamated and centrally directed forms of organization. Mutual aid organizations were, however, at a disadvantage compared to the profit-making firm. They had to reconcile apparently contradictory demands. On the one hand, they were driven in the direction of efficiency which involved concentrating and centralising decision-making while, on the other, they were expected to be democratic which meant facilitating the wide and active involvement of the membership in exercising control and making decisions. In order to survive, many mutual aid organizations were pulled towards efficiency and away from the demands of participatory democracy. Both Beveridge and G.D.H. Cole (writing at a similar time) discussed the impact on older mutual aid organizations. As the members of the Building Societies, for example, increasingly had less and less reason to interact with one another except for "business" purposes, they became bound by no more than a basic economic relationship, in effect that of a customer, and this was accompanied by a decline in direct participation.[19] Friendly Societies became Collecting Societies:

> which have no social activities to hold them together, and are in practice different from ordinary Insurance Companies only in that they are run rather for the benefit of their collecting agents than of a body of shareholders.[20]

Another important factor contributing to the increase in the scale of organizations was the trend towards statutory involvement in areas previously the domain of voluntary action. The struggle over the reform of the

Poor Law was an example of this process of change and was fought over the fundamental issue of whether or not the state should assume responsibility for the provision of key benefits such as sickness insurance and old age pensions. This has been frequently portrayed in terms of "statists" versus the "voluntaryists". The Webbs argued for a central role for the state, with voluntary organizations relegated to the role of junior partners[21] whereas the Charity Organisation Society in particular argued against the expansion of state activity and in favour of keeping the spheres of voluntary and statutory activity separate.[22] The outcome was a decisive switch away from voluntary activity in favour of expanded state provision and the reforms introduced by the Liberal administration of 1906–11 represent an important watershed, which altered "profoundly the frontiers between statutory and voluntary forms of social service."[23]

As the state moved from the role of enabler and regulator to that of funder and provider, it was seen at local and, increasingly, at national level as the arena through which to influence and to effect reform. Having a national organization to influence the state became seen as an essential mechanism for influencing government legislation and the development of social policy. The allotment movement provides an example of this process. Originally a mutual aid organization for rural labourers, the struggle to maintain their rights during the latter part of the nineteenth century required the organization of firstly local, and subsequently national, activity.[24] Similarly, in the field of mental health, the Mental Deficiency Act of 1913 was accompanied by the establishment of a national association, the Central Association for Care of Mental Defectives.[25]

As the expansion of state activity began to impinge increasingly on spheres of activity which had hitherto been the domain of voluntary action, the result was not only to place constraints on the nature and type of voluntary activity but also to offer new opportunities for its development. The reforms immediately prior to and during the First World War in effect marked an acceptance of the principle of the central role of the state in organising welfare provision. The reality was, however, that the state, either nationally or locally, simply could not assume complete responsibility for the provision of services and had to rely on using voluntary organizations as agents. These included mutual aid organizations such as the Friendly Societies and the Trades Unions involved in organising the administration of the National Insurance Scheme as well as organizations from the philanthropic tradition, for example, in the fields of infant welfare, mental health and blindness.[26]

The Displacement of Mutuality

Beveridge's report can help us to understand the importance of the changing environment within which voluntary organizations have operated and the way this influenced the choices and possibilities available to them. The pressures to amalgamate and to centralize were felt by voluntary organizations within the mutual aid tradition. This was not just the result of the expansion of state activity and its impact on such organizations, but also the result of competition from the commercially organized activity of the business firm. The example of the Friendly Societies is instructive, for these were subject to both types of pressure. Their experience shows the way this working-class strand of voluntaryism became increasingly residual. Beveridge's discussion, in *Voluntary Action*, of the involvement of the affiliated orders of the Friendly Societies, in the struggle over the introduction of a National Insurance scheme shows how private capital was able to influence the state to its own advantage, to the detriment of the mutual traditions of the friendly societies

The proposals for a National Insurance scheme would not have been possible without the work of the Trade Unions and Friendly Societies who knew how to organize the administration of benefit. The aim was to use the existing friendly societies as administrators – to be termed "Approved Societies". In the Bill introduced in 1911 the original proposals recommended that Approved Societies should not work for profit; should be democratically controlled by the insured members; and should not be societies that periodically divided their funds (that is, the deposit or dividing type friendly societies).[27] As a result of pressure from private business (what Beveridge refers to as politically powerful bodies), however, the scope of Approved Societies was widened, making it possible for societies or companies established for other purposes to set up separate sections as Approved Societies.[28]

This allowed the more business-oriented Friendly Societies such as the collecting societies and industrial assurance companies to register as Approved Societies. Private companies established a separate entity in order to fulfil the conditions. Yet such an arrangement did not change their essential character (profit-making) nor their internal workings (in the sense of promoting democratic participation and accountability). As Beveridge wryly noted, such companies had never undertaken the provision of sickness benefit prior to 1912 as it had been considered unprofitable. However, "the Industrial life offices . . . [saw] in this the opportunity to build up through State insurance connections for their own line of business."[29]

The option of establishing a National Insurance system on an alternative, mutual, local and self-governing basis was lost as the 1911 National Insurance Bill proceeded to statute. Furthermore, the new scheme severely restricted the autonomy of the Friendly Societies, which was noted by the Webbs, writing in 1911, on the form of the National Insurance scheme:

> And when we consider the question of self-government, we can hardly recognize as independence the condition of the 'Approved Friendly Societies' under the chancellor of the exchequer's scheme of 1911 – a condition in which the

hitherto autonomous society has to accept a government scheme of benefits in lieu of its own, performs none of the work of collection, exercises no control over the accumulating funds, has no responsibility for their investment, is compelled every three years to vary its benefits as it may, on valuation, peremptorily be required to do, and is even subject to governmental regulation and control in respect of the formation of branches, and the appointment and payment of the medical men on whose skill and honourable dealing the whole efficiency, and indeed, the actuarial solvency, of the organisation depends. In fact the 'Approved Friendly Societies' in this scheme become merely canvassing agents and benefit-paying cashiers to the great new government department which will control the taxation on employers and wage-earners.[30]

Furthermore, the effect on the internal workings of the Friendly Societies, and the affiliated orders in particular, was considerable. They became more official and less personal. There was pressure to concentrate in larger units, leading to the disappearance of a significant proportion of small societies. The activity of the small unitary accumulating societies, which prior to 1911 had featured local activity through informal meetings, diminished after 1911 and by 1939 such activity had disappeared altogether.[31] In addition, there was a stimulus to other types of friendly societies such as the Holloway societies, which had never had a strong component of local control.[32] The affiliated orders were further undermined by the way the system led to unequal benefits for equal compulsory contributions. Whereas the affiliated orders had organized the system of insurance so that there was an equalization of cost and risk, the new scheme effectively divided them up by ensuring that each branch of an affiliated order became a separate society and was valued separately. The benefits of belonging to a wider movement whilst retaining local autonomy were lost, whilst at the same time the new scheme encouraged a financial interest in economical administration, that is, profit-oriented activity. The new Approved Societies:

> had an interest in not admitting too many people of dangerous occupations or doubtful health or too many women. The societies which showed themselves most ready to be all-embracing were those whose sponsors had a financial interest outside insurance for sickness, that is to say, the industrial life offices.[33]

In the very different environment created by the National Insurance Act and under the pressure of competition from their commercial rivals, the mutual aid organizations opted for a model of efficiency based on concentrated and centralized decision-making at the expense of active involvement of the wider membership in governing and managing their affairs. And, at the same time, they became less "friendly". The example of the Friendly Societies explains how a particular strand of working-class mutual aid organization had become displaced by the time of the Second World War. It was not completely lost – it emerged in other forms, for example, in clubs of various kinds and in new forms of self-help and mutualism. So whilst the distinct organizational form became displaced, the "impulse from below" remained and manifested itself in new ways. However the displacement of the mutuals influenced the post Second World War discussions of voluntary action, leading to an emphasis on organizations from the philanthropic tradition.

The Metamorphosis of Philanthropy

In contrast to the working-class mutual aid organizations, those from the philanthropic tradition did not suffer from direct competition with business activity. Philanthropic activity, traditionally conceived of as the provision of social welfare for the poorest and most vulnerable sections of society and those who were least able to organize themselves mutually, was never in direct competition with business, which had never found such activity profitable. Philanthropic activity was affected by the expansion of state activity but was better able to metamorphose and in so doing to evolve a form of partnership with the state although this process was far from straightforward or uniform.

The Charity Organisation Society (COS) was less able to adjust to the new conditions than organizations in the mental health and infant welfare fields, largely as a result of its continued opposition to the expansion of the state. A dramatic loss of income immediately after the First World War resulted in continued friction between the districts and "Central"[34] and, as the COS ceased in practice to be a co-ordinating charity in its original sense, this was accompanied by the loss of its original purpose.[35] The COS did not address the issue of its own changing role until the advent of the Second World War when the further extension of state activity resulted in the recognition by the Society of the state as dominant provider. The COS welcomed Beveridge's *Report on Social Insurance and Allied Services*, published in 1942[36] and he, in turn, acknowledged the versatility of organizations from this tradition: "philanthropy has shown its strength of being able perpetually to take new forms". He cited the change of the Charity Organisation Society into the Family Welfare Association, and the emergence of newer organizations such as the National Council of Social Service (NCSS), the Citizens Advice Bureaux and the Women's Institutes.[37]

The new relationship between the state and voluntary organizations that developed after the 1914–18 war had important organizational implications. Using voluntary organizations as its agents presented the state with certain advantages, but their autonomy presented problems of how to influence and control their actions. One obvious way for the state to gain more control was through the conditions attached to funding which led to more emphasis on the scrutiny of voluntary organizations and standards and with it the need for training (to provide a specific service).[38] Indeed, one significant trend in the inter-war years was the emergence of the idea of a nucleus of trained, professional (statutory) workers being assisted by voluntary assistants (or volunteers).[39] Indeed voluntary workers often metamorphosed into caseworkers employed by the state. This in turn emphasized the distinction between paid, professional, trained social workers, and amateur volunteer social workers, with the latter subordinate to the former. Whilst there were signs of such an emerging distinction prior to the Second World War, for example within the COS,[40] this was greatly accelerated after the Second World War.

Another way the state shaped the parameters of voluntary action was by influencing voluntary organizations to join together, as the number and diversity of voluntary organizations was a "problem" for statutory bodies. The watchwords of "co-ordination" and particularly "amalgamation" were really about making it easier and more efficient for the state to deal with a diverse area of activity:

> From the point of view of the statutory authorities and the charitable trusts, amalgamation was to be welcomed as they sought for the most appropriate channel for the distribution of financial aid. Diversity had much in its favour, but it sometimes added to confusion.[41]

The pressures for some sort of centralization, either through the formal amalgamation of organizations or by grouping them under a single representative organization ("co-ordination") was an important feature of the inter-war years and continued through the Second World War. This served to strengthen the position of many national bodies vis à vis their branches or affiliates but also provided a mechanism though which voluntary organizations could attempt to influence the direction of statutory policy. In the mental health field, which had a tradition of close voluntary and statutory collaboration, there was relatively little resistance to such a process. The Board of Control in fact exerted a strong influence on the mental health societies to amalgamate[42] and the outbreak of the Second World War gave added impetus to this direction. A provisional National Council for Mental Health was formed in 1942, consisting of the Central Association for Mental Welfare, the Child Guidance Council, and the National Council for Mental Hygiene (this became the National Association for Mental Health in 1946).[43i]

The picture was rather different in the field of welfare for the blind, where the tradition of local autonomy was strong and the moves to join together met with resistance. Following the expansion of activity during the war, the National Institute for the Blind (NIB) was invited to join the central government's Advisory Committee on the Welfare of the Blind in 1917 and this presented the National Institute with the opportunity to become the medium through which to influence the development of state social policy. This depended, however, on the ability of the National Institute to co-ordinate its own activities. In this it encountered resentment and suspicion from both regional and local groups who were unwilling to surrender their financial autonomy[44].

Conclusion

Re-visiting Beveridge's *Voluntary Action* is useful to the historian in this field. It has its own context – written after the establishment of the welfare state settlement which emerged after the Second World War. It can be seen as an argument for the continuation of voluntary action at a time of vastly increased state provision and a useful overview of the field. More specifically it offers some important insights into the organizational development of voluntary action. Beveridge's report reminds of some of the essential features of voluntary action, in particular the importance of motives and values, self-government and autonomy and its associational nature. Voluntary action is more than simply the provision of a good or service: the way this is organized and the values attached are as important.

Beveridge's report also highlights the way that the tradition of organising on a federative basis, pioneered by, although not confined to, older mutual aid organizations, has been an important feature of voluntary action. This has involved independent locally-based organizations joining together in wider association, increasingly on a national basis. This national-local relationship has been a recurring theme within the history of the development of voluntary action, although the balance of influence or power between national body and local group has varied. The degree of autonomy and existence of centralising pressures has been influenced not only by the type of organizational structure, for example, federative (with autonomous local groups) as opposed to unitary or corporate (local branches owned by the national body) but also by the way the organization originated, that is, whether the national body came first or the local groups. The lesson of the historical development of voluntary action suggests that where local groups have existed separately and prior to a central or national body, the traditions of local autonomy and resistance to the national body have remained strong. In contrast, where the national body has existed prior to the subsequent development of local activity, the influence of the national organizations has tended to be more dominant. These differences have been important factors in the differing reactions of voluntary organizations to contextual pressures, for example the pressure for them to reorganize along similar lines to that of the expanding statutory sphere of activity.

Finally, Beveridge's report, and in particular his account of the changing relationship between the state and mutual voluntary action, reminds us of the importance of context. A particular reading of his discussion of the impact of the Liberal reforms shows how the Friendly Societies tried to resolve contradictory pressures within a particular context: maintaining a central identity as well as allowing local autonomy; continuing as effective organizations whilst operating a democratic structure; and maintaining their independence from the state. It shows how their struggle and decline was not simply a result of "apathy" or "inefficiency". They were operating in a period of rapid change where there were dominant directions of change providing structural constraints. Whilst mutuality tended to be displaced as an organizational form, philanthropic organizations were better able to adapt and change and to develop an agency relationship as junior partners to the expanding state institutions. These changes, combined with the continued emergence of new voluntary organizations, resulted in a relative blurring of the earlier and clearer distinctions between mutual aid and philanthropic activity. Despite these changes, certain continuities remained, for example, in the newer manifestations of the older impulses from "above" and "below".

A better understanding of these histories helps emphasize the importance of identifying major contextual influences on voluntary organisations and the structural constraints and opportunities with which they have been presented.

Notes

1 W. Beveridge, *Voluntary Action: A Report on Methods of Social Advance* (London: George and Allen Unwin, 1948); W. Beveridge and A. F. Wells (eds), *The Evidence for Voluntary Action* (London: George and Allen Unwin, 1949).

2 His 1942 report is often cited as a key part of that settlement. W. Beveridge, *Report on Social Insurance and Allied Services*, Cmd. 6404 (HMSO, 1942.

3 G. Finlayson, "A Moving Frontier: Voluntarism and the State in British Social Welfare 1911–1949", *Twentieth Century British History* 1, 2 (1990): p. 189.

4 Hansard, *Parliamentary Debates* (House of Lords), 5th series, vol. 163, col. 119 (23rd June 1949).

5 A. F. C. Bourdillon (ed.), *Voluntary Social Services: Their Place in the Modern State* (London: Methuen, 1948).

6 Bourdillon, *Voluntary Social Services*, p. 3.

7 Beveridge, *Voluntary Action*, p. 9.

8 G. D. H. Cole, "Mutual Aid Movements in their relation to Voluntary Social Service" in A. F. C. Bourdillon (ed.), *Voluntary Social Services: Their Place in the Modern State* (London: Methuen, 1948), p. 119.

9 G. N. Ostergaard and A. H. Halsey, *Power in Co-operatives: A Study of the Internal Politics of British Retail Societies* (Oxford: Basil Blackwell, 1965), p. 2.

10 Beveridge, *Voluntary Action*, p. 60.

11 S. Yeo, *Religion and Voluntary Organisations in Crisis* (London: Croom Helm, 1976), p. 220.

12 Yeo, *Religion and Voluntary Organisations*, p. 223.

13 Cole, "Mutual Aid Movements", p. 118.

14 For a fuller discussion see A. Penn, *The Management of Voluntary Organisations in the Post-War Period, with special reference to National–Local relations* (DPhil Thesis: University of Sussex, 1992).

15 Beveridge, *Voluntary Action*, p. 36.

16 M. Rooff, *A Hundred Years of Family Welfare: A study of The Family Welfare Association (formerly Charity Organisation Society) 1869–1969* (London: Michael Joseph, 1972).

17 F. Prochaska, *The Voluntary Impulse: Philanthropy in Modern Britain* (London: Faber and Faber, 1988), p. 62.

18 Prochaska, *The Voluntary Impulse*, p. 291.

19 Beveridge, *Voluntary Action*, pp. 32–52. G.D.H. Cole, "A Retrospect of the History of Voluntary Social Service" in Bourdillon, *Voluntary Social Services*, pp. 11–30.

20 Cole, "A Retrospect", p. 18.

21 Beveridge, *Voluntary Action*, pp. 306–7.

22 Beveridge, *Voluntary Action*, p. 147. Rooff, *A Hundred Years*, pp. 46–51. This was to be achieved by co-ordinating the work of charities and preventing them dispensing relief to those with a claim on the Poor Law.

23 Beveridge in Hansard, *Parliamentary Debates* (House of Lords), 5th ser, vol. 163, col. 119 (23rd June 1949) quoted in Finlayson *A Moving Frontier*, p. 189; Cole, *A Retrospect*, p. 22.

24 Newlin Russell Smith, *Land for the Small Man* (New York: King's Crown Press,1946), quoted in D. Crouch and C. Ward, *The Allotment: Its Landscape and Culture* (London: Faber and Faber, 1988), p. 113.

25 Rooff, *Voluntary Societies and Social Policy*, p. 105. This became the Central Association for Mental Welfare in 1921, and in fact was directly encouraged by the Board of Control.

26 Finlayson, *A Moving Frontier*, p. 194

27 Beveridge, *Voluntary Action*, p. 74.

28 Beveridge, *Voluntary Action*, p. 75.

29 *Ibid.*, p. 76.

30 B. and S. Webb, *The Prevention of Destitution* (London: Longmans, 1911), pp. 169–70, S. Yeo, "Working-class association, private capital, welfare and the state in the late nineteenth and twentieth centuries", in N. Parry, M. Rustin and C. Satyamrti (eds), *Social Work, Welfare and the State* (London: Edward Arnold, 1979), pp. 60–1.

31 Beveridge, *Voluntary Action*, p. 79.

32 *Ibid.*

33 Beveridge, *Voluntary Action*, p. 78. See also J. Davis Smith "The Voluntary Tradition: Philanthropy and self-help in Britain 1500–1945" in J. Davis Smith, C. Rochester and R. Hedley (eds), *An Introduction to the Voluntary Sector* (London: Routledge, 1995).

34 Beveridge, *Voluntary Action*, p. 136 and pp. 220–3.

35 *Ibid.*, p. 158.

36 W. Beveridge, *Report on Social Insurance and Allied Services*, Cmd. 6404 (HMSO, 1942).

37 Beveridge, *Voluntary Action*, p. 301.

38 Rooff, *A Hundred Years of Welfare*, p. 51 and p. 211.

39 *Ibid.*, p. 117.

40 *Ibid.*, p. 137. The increased use of paid workers had been one response by the districts to the lack of volunteers in the period immediately after the First World War.

41 Rooff, *A Hundred Years of Welfare*, p. 268.

42 *Ibid.*, p. 146.

43 *Ibid.*, p. 149. The Mental After-Care Association, based in London and supported by the London County Council, was, however, strongly resistant to the move to amalgamate.

44 Roof, *Voluntary Societies and Social Policy*, pp. 226–9.

Child Guidance in Britain, 1926–1955: From Voluntarism to the Welfare State?

JOHN STEWART

This chapter examines the development of child guidance in Britain from its origins in the 1920s to the mid-1950s, by which time it was embedded in the post-war welfare state. After an analysis of what child guidance was and what it sought to achieve, the role of voluntarism in both providing and supporting this form of preventive mental health care for young people is examined as is the motivation behind philanthropic and voluntary activity. It is then suggested that by the 1930s, thanks to growing local authority interest, a "mixed economy" had emerged. Local authority involvement can be construed as evidence both of the success of the child guidance message as promoted by voluntary bodies and the limitations of the latter in actually providing adequate coverage. The trend towards greater state intervention was accelerated by the Second World War. Legislation empowered local authorities to provide free child guidance services and for the first time acknowledged the state's obligation to the "maladjusted" child. The role of the voluntary sector was thereby significantly reduced although not entirely eradicated. As in other fields of modern welfare provision, therefore, a "moving frontier" of shifting, and sometimes porous, boundaries between state and voluntary action can be identified.

What Was Child Guidance?

In the 1930s, the London Child Guidance Clinic issued a publicity flyer, part of which read as follows:

Learning to Drive is child's play, compared with – Learning to Live! Learning to Drive is hard – sometimes courage fails and there's a crash, or a break-down. It's a nervous time anyway, especially for pedestrians. Learning to Live is harder – if courage fails, fears, anxiety, shyness and failure take its place: a crash may mean stealing, violence, rudeness or truancy, and a breakdown is tragic. It's a nervous time, anyway, especially for parents.

This leaflet tells us something about key child guidance concerns. Of equal significance for this chapter, the leaflet's aim in describing and promoting child guidance was to solicit donations to ensure that the clinic was able to continue its work.[1] Before turning to the question of funding, though, it is necessary to describe briefly what child guidance sought to do.

Child guidance was a form of psychiatric medicine and, in the inter-war era, part of a wider, international, movement – mental hygiene. Mental hygiene saw itself as a form of preventive medicine, seeking to head off mental health problems just as the nineteenth-century public health move-ment sought to eliminate water-borne disease.[2] Given the importance ascribed to early psychological and emotional development, this was an area in which children were a particular target for medical and psychiatric intervention. Child guidance emerged in the United States in the imme-diate aftermath of the First World War, spreading thereafter to Europe and parts of the British Empire. While it had deep historical roots it derived a large part of its inspiration from the so-called "new psychology". This emphasized the unconscious workings of the human mind and thereby the latter's potential for "irrational" behaviour.[3] The underlying premise of child guidance was thus that any child might, at some point in his or her emotional or psychological development, become "maladjusted". Such "maladjustment" might manifest itself in a range of ways, from bed-wetting to mild forms of delinquency. Child guidance did not seek to deal with, in the language of the times, the mentally defective nor with the severely delinquent. Rather, its target was the otherwise "normal" child who nonetheless, for reasons usually to do with family circumstances, might experience mental disturbance.[4] Not to address such maladjustment could lead to much more severe problems in adult life to the detriment of the sufferer, his or her family, and society as a whole. Hence child guid-ance's self-ascribed preventive medicine role and the medical language which permeates its discourse – the maladjusted child is a "patient" with "symptoms" whose "aetiology" it is necessary to uncover before "treat-ment" can be offered and "cure" effected.

Indeed the locus of child guidance practice was the dedicated clinic.[5] Here the child patient would encounter members of three professions – the medically-trained psychiatrist; the psychologist who administered various forms of mental test; and the psychiatric social worker, a new sub-profession whose development was intimately linked with that of child guidance. While the rhetoric of child guidance emphasized "teamwork", in most English clinics it was the psychiatrist who took the leading role.[6]

The Commonwealth Fund of New York

As noted, child guidance originated in the United States and here the role of philanthropy was crucial. American child guidance could not have taken off without the initiative and support of the Commonwealth Fund of New York, set up in 1918 by Mrs Stephen Harkness with a broad remit to "do something for the welfare of mankind". To give some sense of its size and the scale of its activities, the initial bequest to the Fund was $10 millions and by the early 1950s it had assets of over $90 millions, making it in these terms the seventh largest of the American philanthropic bodies. Among its principal concerns were child health and mental welfare.[7] The Fund was one of a number of large US foundations which had a significant impact on the development of American social policy.[8] In the aftermath of the First World War, moreover, the religious impulses which had initially inspired American philanthropy were replaced by an emphasis on, as David Hammack puts it, "scientific and medical research and . . . efforts to place the health-care, education, and social-service professions on a scientific non-sectarian basis". These were, for the major foundations, issues and approaches not just for the US, but also for what another historian characterizes as "Missions to the World".[9]

In line with this internationalist approach, it was the Commonwealth Fund which financially supported British child guidance, at least in the first instance. It did so under the Presidency of Edward S. Harkness, a convinced Anglophile and supporter of child health and welfare programmes.[10] And, bearing out another, earlier, point, it did so as the principal component of its English (sic) Mental Hygiene Program. This funding arrangement was initially prompted by a visit to the US in the summer of 1926 to examine child guidance practices by a delegation from the Child Guidance Council, an offshoot of two voluntary bodies – the Central Association for Mental Welfare and the National Council for Mental Hygiene. The delegation included prominent individuals in the field of psychology (Charles Spearman), psychiatry (Bernard Hart), and social work (Miss St Clair Townsend).[11] This was followed up shortly afterwards by an investigative trip to Britain by a leading Commonwealth Fund official, Mildred Scoville. On her return, Scoville told her immediate superior that the United States was some way ahead of Britain in its work with mentally disturbed children and that in her view "this is the psychological time to lay the foundations of child guidance work in England".[12]

Child Guidance Council members were drawn from a range of professions and bodies, voluntary and statutory. They included the psychologist Sir Cyril Burt; representatives from the Home Office, the Board of

Control, and the Board of Education; and delegates from non-statutory bodies such as the British Social Hygiene Council and the Catholic Women's League.[13] This voluntary input to the movement, by way of the Child Guidance Council, was to remain important into the post-war period by which time the Council had, as a result of the Feversham Report, been merged with various other bodies to form The National Association for Mental Health (NAMH – later MIND).[14] The role of voluntary bodies at local level is discussed below, but for the moment the focus is on the Commonwealth Fund's aims and strategy.

The Fund financially supported British child guidance in the following ways. First, it paid the costs of visitors to the United States. These included the delegation encountered earlier and the first generation of British psychiatric social workers. The latter were trained in American child guidance clinics and social work schools. Somewhat later, British social work teachers were brought to the US to study educational techniques. Fellowships were also available to psychiatrists interested in child guidance work, for instance Douglas MacCalman, a leading figure in the British movement. The second means of financial support was through the allocation of money to the Child Guidance Council and, through it, the London Child Guidance Clinic. While much of this was taken up with administrative costs, the Council also carried out educational work and public lectures and funded fellowships in psychiatry and psychology. So, for example, the 1939 accounts show that of a total expenditure of £4,738, over a quarter went on such fellowships.[15] The Council was thus both recipient and disburser of philanthropic funding.

Third, the Commonwealth Fund effectively bankrolled the Diploma in Mental Health, set up at the London School of Economics (LSE) in 1929. Students were trained on this course as psychiatric social workers.[16] Fourth, the Child Guidance Council operated a "loan system" of psychiatric social workers. Under this scheme new child guidance clinics were offered the services of a psychiatric social worker at no cost. Since it was often the case that psychiatric social workers were the only salaried members of staff at clinics, this was effectively a financial subsidy underwritten by the Commonwealth Fund. To give a sense of the Fund's commitment to its English Mental Hygiene Program, some $61,000 was appropriated in 1931/32. This rose to a peak of $86,600 in 1933/34; remained in the range $52,000 to $68,000 for the rest of the 1930s; and then declined rapidly during the Second World War.[17]

The Commonwealth Fund's role in developing British child guidance was recognized at the time and subsequently. Elizabeth Macadam noted it in her famous book of the mid-1930s on the "new philanthropy".[18] In the early 1950s, meanwhile, an official enquiry into psychiatric social work remarked that British child guidance "drew its inspiration from the pioneer work of the Commonwealth Fund" and that it was difficult to see how either child guidance or psychiatric social work could have developed when they did without the Fund's support.[19] The Fund's role has at least two implications. First, and unsurprisingly, in Britain it promoted the form of child guidance it had been instrumental in advancing in the United States, with the dominant professional being the medically-trained psychiatrist. There were, however, other models, and particularly that which gave the central role to the educational psychologist. The latter was strong in Scotland where considerable resistance was shown to the importation of what were seen as American – and misguided – ideas.[20] For the rest of Great Britain the medical model prevailed, at least down until the 1940s when it also came to be challenged here. It was thus highly significant that child guidance came to be embedded in the welfare state by way of educational legislation which allowed for educational psychology to claim in other parts of Great Britain the role it had already claimed in Scotland. This in turn raises complex questions about the extent to which American philanthropy influenced and shaped British practice in the long term.[21]

Second, the rapid decline of Commonwealth Fund support from the late 1930s was coincident with the Second World War but not caused by it. Rather, it was part of a more general strategy. For the Fund, as for most major American philanthropic bodies, its aim was to fund start up projects and then, gradually, withdraw as local sources of financial support emerged. This was precisely what was intended in the case of child guidance. In fact, funding continued for rather longer than was originally planned not least because of the politics and brinkmanship employed by some of those associated with British child guidance. Scoville, commenting on the LSE course's budgetary situation, told her immediate superior that the approach of the School's officials and management, not least Sir William Beveridge, was incomprehensible, uncooperative, and arrogant. LSE leaders were, she concluded, "a dangerous and unscrupulous gang".[22]

Other Forms of Philanthropic Support

Nonetheless funding was eventually withdrawn. In the early 1940s, and very much part of the wartime environment in which child guidance found itself, the Child Guidance Council was receiving financial support from the Board of Education.[23] And in 1944 the Council appealed to the Nuffield Foundation for support for organization and training purposes, the latter once again for child psychiatrists and psychologists. This met with a rather mixed response.[24] The Nuffield Foundation did grant £4,500 to the Council, but as the former noted this was interim funding which was to be used primarily for training.[25] However a much larger bid by the Council, for an annual grant of £12,000 and again for support for training, was rejected by the Nuffield a couple of years later.[26] By the early 1950s the NAMH was, in consequence, lamenting the "slow progress" being made in child guidance and the problems of securing sufficient adequately trained staff.[27] The financial problems of voluntary bodies are starkly illustrated by such episodes, not least as the Child Guidance Council was making its appeal to another voluntary body at precisely the time at which child guidance was being embedded in the post-war welfare state.

But of course the Council was a national body primarily concerned with promoting and co-ordinating the child guidance movement. Important as this undoubtedly was, to gain a full picture of the development of the movement attention has to be paid to the local as well as the national picture. Clearly, Commonwealth Fund monies were highly significant. However, with the exception of the loan system for psychiatric social workers, not much of this directly supported individual clinics. Although psychiatrists and sometimes psychologists generally gave their time for free, nonetheless there were maintenance and administrative expenses and, when any loan had expired, the salary of the psychiatric social worker.

How, then, did local clinics cope? In Birmingham a clinic was set up in 1931 as a result of, as the historian of the City Corporation put it, "the generosity of an anonymous donor and (the) assistance offered by the Commonwealth Fund". The anonymous donor was almost certainly a member of the Cadbury family and the Fund's contribution that of a loaned psychiatric social worker.[28] This allowed, it was further remarked, the establishment of "a clinic without cost to the ratepayers, for an experimental period of three years".[29] What happened after those three years is an important part of child guidance history and will be returned to below.

Elsewhere, other forms of charitable or voluntary support can be found. One of the most famous British institutions was the Notre Dame Child Guidance Clinic in Glasgow which gained considerable support – financial and practical – from the Scottish Catholic Church. So, for example, a report from the early 1930s noted a donation of £500 from an individual priest and a "generous annual subscription" from the Mother Superior of the Notre Dame Training College from which the clinic had emerged. The motivation behind this support was greatly influenced by Catholic concerns over what was seen as inappropriate advice – for example, on birth control – being given to parents.[30] In Liverpool, meanwhile, the City's Child Guidance Council report for 1933 noted that funding came from a variety of sources including the Liverpool Council of Social Service; individual subscriptions and donations; and a large "special donation" from an unspecified donor. Although the Liverpool Medical Officer of Health sat on the Council, overall it appears at this stage to have been dominated by the university and the voluntary sector in the shape of, for example, the social reformer Eleanor Rathbone, Professor A.M. Carr-Saunders, social workers from various voluntary agencies, and the Anglican Bishop and Roman Catholic Archbishop of Liverpool.[31]

But if such clinics appeared reasonably stable, others clearly struggled, especially as the numbers of children referred grew over the course of the 1930s. The Edinburgh Catholic Child Guidance Clinic was a much smaller, and more insecure, institution than its Glasgow counterpart. In the mid-1930s it noted that it received a small annual grant from the Educational Institute of Scotland – the Scottish teachers' union – and that certain overheads were met by the local Catholic hierarchy. No other sources of income are mentioned, suggesting none were presently available. Funds were, therefore, "urgently needed to meet the increased expenditure attendant on the expansion of the work. Materials for play and handiwork groups need constant renewal, and there are many other incidental expenses". Subscriptions and donations were thus sought.[32] In fact, the situation in Edinburgh was even worse than this suggested. In the course of the same year the clinic's leading figure, Lady Margaret Kerr, was told by the Child Guidance Council that she would not be granted a full-time psychiatric social worker under the loan system. In her response, Kerr remarked that "I think you know we are entirely penniless up here and get grants from nowhere for this work".[33] All this jeopardized the availability of psychiatric social work at this clinic.

Nor was the Edinburgh situation unique. A representative of the Cheltenham and County Child Guidance Clinic wrote to the psychiatrist Noel Gordon Addis in 1938 that a new psychiatric social worker was required but that the clinic had been "unable to make an earlier arrangement . . . because we were not sure whether our Clinic would be able to continue". It is clear from the context that it was financial difficulties which had given rise to this situation. But, in a passage which brings us to the next section of this chapter, the correspondent then noted that the future of the Cheltenham clinic was "now under consideration by the three Education Authorities in this district".[34]

Local Authorities and Child Guidance

Certain local authorities had, from the outset, monitored the development of child guidance. The London County Council, for example, discussed the matter as early as 1928 and a number of its staff were involved in visits to the US.[35] Legally, however, local authorities were not allowed to make any direct grants to child guidance clinics. This situation began to change in the first half of the 1930s. In 1933 members of the Child Guidance Council visited the Board of Education. They pointed out that the Council was in receipt of Commonwealth Fund support, but that this would diminish over time. The rather convoluted argument was then made that:

> the fact that the work of the Clinics depended on voluntary contributions strengthened the suspicion which still existed in many minds that they were in some way related to 'psycho-analysis'. It was desirable, therefore, that some official form of encouragement should be given to their work, and that the State should formally recognise its importance.

The civil servant involved expressed sympathy, although nothing was to happen immediately.[36]

However in 1935 a marked shift in policy occurred. Expenditure by local authorities was now, under certain strict conditions, permissible and Birmingham had been the first authority to be so recognized. The referral of a pupil to a child guidance clinic was acknowledged as counting towards school attendance and local authorities could also contribute to voluntary clinics to which their pupils were referred.[37] Both these rather abstruse points were important for funding reasons. Commenting on the new situation, the Chief Medical Officer of the Board of Education remarked that the Board's action was "in line with the general principles of English educational administration". These involved establishing any new development's worth under voluntary management and the demand for its services; and then permitting "extensions by Local Authorities in suitable cases which are kept under review".[38]

Like London, Birmingham Corporation had long taken an interest in child guidance and it too had the advantage of a voluntary-funded clinic on its doorstep. The decision to take over the clinic was taken in late 1934 by the Education Committee. This noted the role played by the voluntary funding up until this point, including the receipt of a Commonwealth Fund fellowship by the clinic Director, C.L.C. Burns. The experimental phase had been, in the Committee's opinion, a success and a recommendation should thus be forwarded to the City Council "for the continuance of this work and for the provision of public funds in support thereof".[39] Other local authorities followed Birmingham's example. So, for instance, in Manchester the Education Committee noted in 1937 that arrangements had been completed "for the taking over of the Child Guidance Clinic, and the appointment of the necessary staff".[40] In Oxford, meanwhile, it was claimed that at its "educational clinic" any "problem children" were "examined by experts"; and that this clinic was "the first of its kind to be provided by a Local Education Authority in England".[41] On one level what this quote illustrates is the difficulty of defining a child guidance clinic and in fact the Board of Education did not see the Oxford experiment as setting a precedent for more general local authority support of child guidance. But it had nonetheless sanctioned expenditure and the central point about local authority participation is clear enough.[42]

The Mixed Economy of Child Guidance

What began to emerge in the mid-1930s was, therefore, a mixed economy of child guidance with some clinics funded by local authorities, some still voluntary, and others a mixture of public and voluntary funding. Of this last category, a representative example was Liverpool which, as noted earlier, was initially supported primarily by the voluntary sector. In 1939, its clinic was still receiving support from the Liverpool Council of Social Services and among its other donors were the Notre Dame Convent, soon to set up its own clinic based on the Glasgow model. But Liverpool was also receiving monies from the city's Education Committee, its Hospitals and Port Health Committee and from local authorities across the region.[43] Such shifts in emphasis won government approval. In a speech in 1937 the Parliamentary Secretary to the Board of Education told a child guidance conference that the Commonwealth Fund had "done much to assist in putting child guidance on a satisfactory footing in this country". However, he continued, "its extension must now be a matter for private munificence and public grant".[44] From a different perspective, the Commonwealth Fund noted in 1938 that rapid growth in British child guidance over the preceding two years was due at least in part to Board of Education policy.[45]

Of course, this shift towards more public sector engagement was not uniform. There were local authorities, particularly in rural areas, which displayed little interest in child psychological services. Others wished to utilize any available services at as little cost as possible. In 1936, for example, representatives from a voluntary clinic located in the London suburbs visited the Board of Education seeking financial assistance and advice. The problem lay in the way in which children were referred to them and the apparent reluctance of the local education authorities, and especially Middlesex, to acknowledge responsibility for the payment of such referrals. The Board was able to offer little in the way of practical help.[46]

War and the Welfare State

However child guidance was to receive a significant boost as a result of the Second World War and one obvious manifestation of this was in the actual number of clinics. Definitional problems notwithstanding, in the late 1920s there were two clinics describing themselves as engaging in child guidance. By the late 1930s this had risen to around 60, albeit spread unevenly throughout Britain. This of itself attested to the growth of interest in child guidance and of those clinics whose records remain all note an increase in demand over the 1930s. By the end of World War II, the number of clinics had further risen to around 100. This can be attributed to, first, the ongoing interest in child guidance among voluntary workers, local authorities, and the planners of post-war reconstruction. And, second, it can be seen as a consequence of the more immediate impact of evacuation which had, inter alia, raised considerable concerns about the psychological and emotional effect on children of separation from their parents.[47] When the Underwood Committee reported on the "Maladjusted Child" in the mid-1950s, it noted that there were some 300 clinics throughout the country. The majority of these were run by Local Education Authorities although the Committee also noted the existence of some, albeit "a very few", still run by voluntary bodies.[48]

For many wartime reformers seeking expanded and more systematic child guidance services, this was something which would primarily come about through the state. In 1941 the psychiatrist and longstanding proponent of child guidance, Emanuel Miller, told a child guidance conference that money would no doubt be scarce in the post-war world. Nonetheless, and in a passage which illustrates the way in which child guidance saw itself, it was necessary to:

> convince local authorities and the central educational and health authorities that the care of the minds of the children is the best insurance against future wars, and the best safeguard against any form of social decay or upheaval.[49]

This was especially revealing in that Miller had been instrumental in founding the Jewish East London Child Guidance Clinic, a voluntary institution, in the late 1920s.

As the war came to an end, a group of child guidance professionals surveyed the history of their movement. Such movements, they suggested, often originate in the "goodwill, interest, and enterprize and sense of social responsibility of the few" before being adopted "by the cautious, slow-moving body of public opinion". In the particular case of child guidance its acceptance by statutory authorities marked "a great step forward", not least because this meant that "mental health has become a part of public health, and the satisfactory emotional development of children has become as much part of the accepted programme of the education authority as is their physical and intellectual development".[50]

Wartime demands for improved and expanded services also came from those not directly involved in child guidance provision. Thomas Johnston, Secretary of State for Scotland, told the Commons that under new education legislation local education authorities would be empowered to provide "a child guidance service for the study of handicapped, difficult or backward children". Experience had shown that this was a "service of primary importance".[51] A few years earlier, the Standing Joint Committee of Working Women's Organizations urged on the Board of Education "the need for the provision by local authorities of Child Guidance Clinics".[52]

In terms of post-war planning, civil servants, building on their pre-war engagement with both child guidance advocates and practitioners and with local authorities, began to push for more systematic provision. A 1941 Scottish Education Department memorandum on educational reconstruction argued that "Education Authorities should be encouraged to set up Child Guidance Clinics".[53] Around the same time, the Board of Education noted that the provision of medical care for schoolchildren, including child guidance, varied according to locality but also through lack of clear definition of what actually constituted medical care. Persuasion by the Board usually did not work and so it was concluded that legislation was necessary.[54] In 1942, meanwhile, the psychiatrist R.G. Gordon wrote to the President of the Board of Education, R.A. Butler, with concerns over the lack of public discussion of children's mental health in the debates over educational reconstruction. Butler reassured Gordon that the "development of child guidance work through clinics and in other ways will be fully considered as part of the plans for post-war educational reform". In conciliatory mode, Butler concluded by taking "this opportunity of saying how much my department value the work done by the Child Guidance Council to promote and preserve the mental health of children".[55] In 1944, shortly after the passage of the Education Act which allowed English local authorities to provide free child guidance services, correspondence took place between the Board of Education and the Board of Control over which central and local bodies held responsibility. The Board of Education's view, which prevailed, was that the service should at local level be the responsibility of the Local Education Authority and their School Medical Officers. As well as being a further indicator of the central planning undertaken with regard to child guidance this document is also notable for its lack of any mention of voluntary provision.[56]

Conclusion: From Voluntarism to the Welfare State?

On one level, the trajectory of British child guidance appears to conform to a once standard version of welfare history – the inevitable move from voluntary to state provision. But more nuanced analysis reveals a more complex picture. As Geoffrey Finlayson famously argued, there was a "moving frontier" between voluntary and state action in welfare and one way in which this manifested itself was through cooperation, not rivalry, between the two sectors, albeit a form of cooperation where voluntary agencies increasingly tended to act as agents of the state.[57] And the history of child guidance appears to bear this out, not least in the 1930s when a mixed economy of child guidance increasingly became the norm. Seeking to refine Finlayson's model, Julie Grier argues that certain constituents of child welfare can be seen as representing "the voluntary-state boundary at its most plastic", thereby allowing a particular form of autonomy, activism, and even influence on public policy.[58]

In the history of child guidance it is possible to find evidence to substantiate this argument. It has been noted, for instance, that the Child Guidance Council continued, after merger with other bodies, into the post-war era in the form of the NAMH. Individual voluntary clinics continued to operate although, as we have seen, by the mid-1950s they represented a small proportion of the total number. Even so, the Chief Medical Officer for the Board of Education observed that between 1945 and 1946 the number of clinics in England and Wales stood at 66 provided by local authorities, with a further 49 authorities "using clinics provided by voluntary bodies or other local education authorities".[59]

A notable example of a voluntary institution which continued to function, and even prosper, is the Notre Dame Clinic in Glasgow. In the mid-1940s the clinic acknowledged that it certainly received, as it had done for a number of years, grants from official bodies such as Glasgow Corporation and the National Committee for the Training of Teachers. Nonetheless, it also, so it was claimed, could not have survived without "many charitable friends and institutions", for instance the St Vincent de Paul Society. Notre Dame also benefitted from its location in a Catholic teacher training college in that the latter provided voluntary labour for a range of tasks.[60] In 1956, the clinic celebrated its silver jubilee. Commenting on this, it was noted that the clinic had been recognized "as a practice ground for students from the Social Science Department of Glasgow University, from the College of Speech Therapy, from the London School of Economics and from various English and European Universities". Moreover, the service of Visiting Psychiatrists – that is, those who gave their time freely – continued, at this particular point including R.D. Laing.[61] Notre Dame also bears out Grier's point about voluntary bodies having the potential for influence on public policy. The long-serving Medical Officer of Health for Glasgow, Sir Alexander Macgregor, recalled how the decision to set up a local authority service was influenced by council officials' "growing admiration" for "the excellent record of the Notre Dame Child Guidance Clinic since it was created in 1931".[62]

In summary, what points should be highlighted from the origins and early history of British child guidance, especially for historians of voluntarism and welfare? First, the movement originated in voluntary action and at least in its early years could not have survived without it. In the first instance child guidance was financially supported by two rather different forms of philanthropy and voluntarism – on the one hand, the monies (and power) of the Commonwealth Fund; and, on the other, indigenous, local, and small-scale resourcing. The motivations behind these engagements varied, from a desire to promote "mental hygiene" and a more "scientific" approach to child welfare through to religious concerns about what actually went on in child guidance practice. In addition, although extremely difficult to quantify, voluntary labour was also important. This ranged from the time given by Catholic social activists such as Lady Margaret Kerr through to the services given freely by psychiatrists.

Second, voluntary financial support proved inadequate for the longer-term development of child guidance, particularly as demand for its services increased. In the particular case of the Commonwealth Fund this was due to its overall strategy of providing support for relatively short periods. Third, some more "progressive" local authorities promoted child guidance as part of their school medical service, and this was recognized by the Board of Education in the mid-1930s – enter the state sector and thereby the "mixed economy". Fourth, the Second World War both exacerbated these trends and introduced new factors in support of more comprehensive child guidance arrangements. The experience of evacuation was especially important here, providing as it did a "laboratory" for the study of children separated from their parents. Child guidance was thus embedded in the post-war welfare state, part of the broader process of state-sponsored "reconstruction". Finally, however, it is also possible to see, not least in particular institutions such as the Notre Dame Clinic and in bodies concerned with child mental health such as the NAMH, the persistence of voluntarism. Child guidance from its origins to the early years of the welfare state thus illustrates and further illuminates some of the key trends and issues identified by historians of voluntarism and welfare and the shifting and fluid relationship between the voluntary and state sectors.

Notes

The author would like to acknowledge the support of the Wellcome Trust for his research on child guidance. For the historiography see John Stewart, "The Scientific Claims of British Child Guidance, 1918–45", *British Journal for the History of Science*, 42, 3 (2009): 407–32.

1 Wellcome Trust Library for the History and Understanding of Medicine (hereafter, Wellcome Library), John Bowlby Papers, PP/BOW/C.3/1, undated flyer (but 1930s), London Child Guidance Clinic.

2 Mathew Thomson, "Mental Hygiene as an International Movement", in Paul Weindling (ed.), *International Health Organisations and Movements* (Cambridge: Cambridge University Press, 1995), pp. 283–304.

3 Mathew Thomson, *Psychological Subjects: Identity, Culture and Health in Twentieth Century Britain* (Oxford: Oxford University Press, 2006).

4 On child guidance and the "normal" child see John Stewart, "'The Dangerous Age of Childhood': Child Guidance and the 'Normal' Child in Great Britain, 1920–1950", *Paedagogica Historica*, forthcoming 2011.

5 In practice much child guidance work was carried out by the psychiatric social worker in the child's home: John Stewart, "'I Thought You Would Want to Come and See His Home': Child Guidance and Psychiatric Social Work in Inter-War Britain", in (Mark Jackson (ed.), *Health and the Modern Home* (London: Routledge, 2007), pp. 111–27.

6 The Scottish situation was complicated by the strength of educational psychology. See John Stewart, "Child Guidance in Inter-War Scotland: International Influences and Domestic Concerns", *Bulletin of the History of Medicine*, 80, 3 (2006): 513–39.

7 See A. McGehee Harvey and Susan L. Abrams, *"For the Welfare of Mankind": The Commonwealth Fund and American Medicine* (Baltimore: Johns Hopkins University Press, 1986); and the earlier The Commonwealth Fund, *Historical Sketch, 1918–1962* (New York: The Commonwealth Fund, 1963), which includes details of income and expenditure. On the Fund's role in American child guidance, Kathleen W. Jones, *Taming the Troublesome Child: American*

Families, Child Guidance, and the Limits of Psychiatric Authority (Cambridge, Mass.: Harvard University Press, 1999).

8 See Judith Sealander, *Private Wealth and Public Life: Foundation Philanthropy and the Reshaping of American Social Policy from the Progressive Era to the New Deal* (Baltimore: Johns Hopkins University Press, 1997).

9 David C. Hammack, "Failure and Resilience: Pushing the Limits in Depression and Wartime" in Lawrence J. Friedman and Mark D. McGarvie (eds), *Charity, Philanthropy, and Civility in American History* (Cambridge: Cambridge University Press, 2003), pp. 263–80, at p. 274; and see also, in the same volume, Emily S. Rosenberg, "Missions to the World: American Philanthropy Abroad", pp. 247–57.

10 James W. Wooster Jr., *Edward Stephen Harkness, 1874–1940* (New York City, Privately Published, 1949), pp. 45–6.

11 For an account of the visit see University of Liverpool, Archives and Special Collections, Papers of Sir Cyril Burt (hereafter, Burt Papers), D.191/20/1/7, "Report Presented to the Child Guidance Council by the Signatories, Who Visited the United States to Enquire into the Working of Child Guidance Clinics", undated, but late 1920s.

12 Rockefeller Archive Center, New York, Commonwealth Fund Archives, Series 16 English Mental Hygiene Program (hereafter, CF), Box 10, Folder 107, memorandum, 27 July 1926, Mildred Scoville to Barry Smith.

13 Burt Papers, D.191/20/1/1, The Child Guidance Council, *The Child Guidance Council* (London: The Child Guidance Council, undated, but 1929), p. 2.

14 For a brief account, see National Association for Mental Health, *First Report: 1946–7* (London: National Association for Mental Health, 1947), pp. 5–6.

15 CF, Box 4, Folder 43, Analysis of Expenditure for Child Guidance Council, year ending 31 March 1939.

16 The complex negotiations around this course can be followed, from an LSE viewpoint, in Archives of the London School of Economics and Political Science, British Library of Political and Economic Science, Central Filing Registry/514/1/A-E.

17 Rockefeller Archive Center, New York, Commonwealth Fund Archives, Series 7, Box 7, Folders 51–3, data extracted from Reports of the Board of Directors for relevant years.

18 Elizabeth Macadam, *The New Philanthropy: A Study in the Relations between the Statutory and Voluntary Social Services* (London: George Allen and Unwin, 1934), p. 124.

19 Ministry of Health, *Report of the Committee on Social Workers in the Mental Health Services: Cmd. 8260* (London: HMSO, 1951), p. 11.

20 Stewart, "Child Guidance in Inter-war Scotland".

21 See John Stewart, "Child Guidance in Scotland 1918–1955: Psychiatry versus Psychology?", *History and Philosophy of Psychology*, forthcoming 2011.

22 CF, Box 5, Folder 49, memorandum, 9 March 1932, Mildred Scoville to Barry Smith.

23 The National Archives (hereafter, TNA), ED 50/274, Letter, 10 April 1941, Ministry of Health to Board of Education.

24 Wellcome Library, Dame Janet Vaughan Papers, GC 186/5, correspondence of early 1944 and especially letter and memorandum, 1 February 1944, Child Guidance Council to Nuffield Foundation.

25 The Nuffield Foundation, *Report on Grants Made During the Ten Years April 1943 to March 1953* (Oxford: Oxford University Press, 1954), p. 16.

26 National Association for Mental Health, *First Report: 1946–7*, pp. 19–20.

27 National Association for Mental Health, *Annual Report, 1949–1950* (London: National Association for Mental Health, 1950), p. 6.

28 There is no direct extant evidence regarding the anonymous donor. However, various Cadbury family members sat on, inter alia, the Corporation's Hygiene Sub-Committee and a Sub-Committee appointed to oversee the work of the clinic and funded, inter alia, the juvenile court and a boys' remand home. It is thus reasonable to suggest that the Cadbury family was involved with the child guidance clinic. I am grateful to Sian Roberts, Head of Collections Development, Birmingham Archives and Heritage, for this information.

29 Joseph Trevor Jones, *History of the Corporation of Birmingham, Vol. V, Part I* (Birmingham: General Purposes Committee, Birmingham Corporation, 1940), p. 235.

30 University of Glasgow Archives and Business Records Centre, UGC 58/1/2/1, "Report on Session 1931–32". See also John Stewart, "An 'Enigma to Their Parents': The Founding and Aims of the Notre Dame Child Guidance Clinic, Glasgow", *The Innes Review*, 57, 1 (2006): 54–76.

31 University of Liverpool Archives and Special Collections (hereafter, UoL), EX 65:33, The Liverpool Child Guidance Council, *Report for the Year 1933* (Liverpool: The Liverpool Child Guidance Council, undated, but 1934), pp. 9, 3.

32 Scottish Catholic Archives (hereafter, SCA), DE 125/3, "Edinburgh Catholic Child Guidance Clinic: Annual Report, April 1934 to April 1935", p. 9.

33 SCA, DE 125/17, correspondence between Child Guidance Council and Lady Margaret Kerr, 28 June and 30 June, 1934.

34 Wellcome Library, Noel Gordon Addis Papers, PP/NGH/43, letter, 30 September 1938, from Cheltenham and County Child Guidance Clinic.

35 London Metropolitan Archives, 22.06 LCC, Report of the Special Services Sub-Committee of the Education Committee, 7 May 1928; and Report of the Joint Sub-Committee of the Establishment, Education and Public Health Committees, 1 May 1929.

36 TNA, ED 50/102, Board of Education: Interview Memorandum, M406/651/2, 27 July 1933.

37 TNA, ED 50/273, letter, 13 November 1935, Board of Education to the Home Office.

38 *The Health of the School Child: Annual Report of the Chief Medical Officer of the Board of Education for the Year 1934* (London: HMSO, 1935), p. 118.

39 Birmingham City Archives, BCC/BH 1/1/1/32, Minutes of the Education Committee, 26 October 1934.

40 Central Library, Manchester: Local Studies and Archives, Minutes of the Education Committee, 18 October 1937.

41 A. C. Cameron, "Education in the City of Oxford", in A. C. Cameron (ed.), *Oxford 1935: A Souvenir of the World Educational Conferences* (Oxford: Oxford University Press, 1935), p. 252.

42 *The Health of the School Child*, p. 115.

43 UoL, EX 65:39, The Liverpool Child Guidance Council, *Report for the Year*

1939 (Liverpool: The Liverpool Child Guidance Council, undated, but 1940), p. 21.

44 TNA, ED 50/273, "Notes for a speech by Mr Shakespeare to the Child Guidance Inter-Clinic Biennial Conference, 29 to 30 January 1937".

45 The Commonwealth Fund, *The Commonwealth Fund: Nineteenth Annual Report* (New York: The Commonwealth Fund, 1938), pp. 31–2.

46 TNA ED 50/273, "Board of Education: Interview Memorandum, M406/112".

47 On evacuation, see John Welshman, "Evacuation and Social Policy During the Second World War: Myth and Reality", *Twentieth Century British History*, 9, 1 (1998): 28–53.

48 Ministry of Education, *Report of the Committee on Maladjusted Children* (London: HMSO, 1955), p. 13.

49 Child Guidance Council, *The Future of Child Guidance in Relation to War Experience* (London: The Child Guidance Council, 1941), p. 21.

50 W. Mary Burbury, Edna M. Balint, and Bridget J. Yapp, *An Introduction to Child Guidance* (London: Macmillan), 1945), p. 5.

51 Parliamentary Debates, 5th Series, vol. 410, 1944–45, col. 1269.

52 TNA, ED 50/274, Letter, 2 December 1941, Standing Joint Committee of Working Women's Organisations to the Board of Education.

53 National Archives of Scotland (hereafter, NAS), ED 7/1/47, memorandum, undated but 1941, "Proposals for the Development of the Educational System".

54 NAS, internal Board of Education discussion document *Education after the War*, 1941, p. 32.

55 TNA, ED 50/274, letter, 9 May 1942, R. G. Gordon, Child Guidance Council, to R. A. Butler, Board of Education; and letter, 13 May 1942, Butler to Gordon.

56 TNA, ED 50/274, letter, 26 April 1944, Board of Education to Board of Control.

57 Geoffrey Finlayson, "A Moving Frontier: Voluntarism and the State in British Social Welfare, 1941–1949", *Twentieth Century British History*, 1, 2 (1990): 183–206.

58 Julie Grier, "A Spirit of 'Friendly Rivalry'? Voluntary Societies and the Formation of Post-War Child Welfare Legislation in Britain", in Jon Lawrence and Pat Starkey (eds), *Child Welfare and Social Action* (Liverpool: Liverpool University Press, 2001), pp. 234–55, esp. pp. 234–5.

59 *The Health of the School Child: Report of the Chief Medical Officer of the Ministry of Education for the years 1939–1945* (London: HMSO, 1947), p. 66.

60 Sister Jude (Maureen McAleer), *Freedom to Grow: Sister Marie Hilda's Vision of Child Guidance* (Glasgow: John S. Burns and Co., 1981), pp. 45–6.

61 SCA, HC 44/8, Notre Dame Child Guidance Clinic *Notre Dame Child Guidance Clinic, 1931–1956: Report for the Period 1 April 1955–31st March 1956* (Glasgow: Notre Dame Child Guidance Clinic, 1956), pp. 5, 8.

62 Sir Alexander Macgregor, *Public Health in Glasgow, 1905–1946* (Edinburgh: E. & S. Livingstone, 1967), p. 133.

Responses to Children in Need in Scotland: Historical Challenges for Social Service Planning, Policy and Provision

ALEXANDRA WRIGHT

The concept of social need is inherent in the idea of social service. The history of the social services is the story of the recognition of social needs and the organisation of society to meet them.[1]

This chapter reviews society's main responses to the needs of children in Scotland (although at times it makes reference to Britain more broadly) from the Beveridge Report until the Children (Scotland) Act 1995. The review and analysis are aimed particularly at Scottish child welfare policy and services. The chapter is premised on the belief that need is a concept which is inherent in the ways in which society shapes its response to social issues and is fundamental in the determination of the eligibility criteria necessary to access societal resources. The discussion traces the development and changes to policy and services for children and their families and highlights the shifting roles and responsibilities between the state and voluntary organizations, reflecting the changing contexts within which policies are made and services provided.

Prior to the 1940s, need was considered to be an individual concern best met by a person's family, the community, and only in the last resort, the state. This residual approach to need ensured that charitable organizations and the market played key roles in responding to children's (and their families') needs in the late nineteenth and early twentieth centuries. More recently, however, the Poor Law System has been replaced by developments in welfare policy and services which have included the introduction of welfare pluralism in which need is addressed by a combination of the state, the voluntary sector and the market. During the period from the 1940s to the 1970s there was a dramatic increase in the range and scale of policies and services addressing need which was accompanied by a correspondingly increased role for state intervention and the establishment of the profession of social work. In the 1980s and 1990s, however, growing scepticism about the capacity of the state to meet social needs resulted in a restructuring of service planning and provision.

Four key issues are evident in society's responses to children in need. The first relates to the definition of need; who defines it and what kind of response does it call for? The answers to these questions have very serious implications for eligibility for and access to services. The second is connected to the administration of need: should this be the role of the state, voluntary organizations, or the market? The third key issue raises the question of who is responsible for funding in order to meet needs: the state, the community, or the individual? Finally, a fourth issue evident throughout the review relates to the concern of service effectiveness, in both quality and quantity. The historical review undertaken in this chapter review demonstrates that there has been continual friction between society's perceptions of the respective roles and responsibilities of the state, charitable organizations and the market. Throughout the period under review, there were tensions concerning the definition, administration, effectiveness and costs of meeting needs. But, before embarking on this historical survey, the chapter begins with an examination and definition of key terms.

The chapter's approach is based on a series of definitions. "Human needs" are defined as the resources required for people to live and function in society[2] and "unmet needs" refer to "needs currently unaddressed by existing programs".[3] "Need satisfaction" or "satisfiers" refers to all entities (goods, services, relations, self-expression) that are used to respond to human needs.[4] "Social needs" refer to human needs that are perceived to exist on a societal level, or to widely shared needs which are met by a collective response.[5] The chapter is premised on the belief that social service planning and provision, whether provided through the Kirk, charities or government, are fundamentally concerned with human need.[6]

The Poor Law System in Scotland:
A Residual Response to Human Needs

Until the early twentieth century, child welfare policy planning and provision was characterized by a gradual growth of state responsibility within a mixed model of welfare. in the 1400s poor relief was generally provided through membership to three prevailing forms of social organization: the noble class, the clan system and the feudal system.[7] There was neither a minimal quality of care provided by the state, nor a belief in state responsibility for those in need. Need was perceived as an individual problem whose cause was usually ascribed to moral weakness which evidenced itself as poverty.[8] Poverty, infanticide, disease, poor sanitation, physical cruelty, sexual abuse and child prostitution existed during this period but were not confronted by the government.[9]

Early poor relief legislation and government policy was mainly used to deter begging. In Scotland eligibility requirements for poor relief were strict. The Poor Law required that a man " . . . be disabled as well as destitute before he could be given relief":[10] the able-bodied poor were ineligible for relief. In order to respond to evident needs, people were categorized by those in charge of the Poor Law system: the deserving, undeserving, young, mentally or physically disabled, destitute, unemployed, vagabonds, beggars, women, the Irish.[11] Entitlement required evidence of moral standing and those deemed undeserving were condemned and treated harshly. Employment was considered the primary solution to poverty and any relief that was provided involved the stigmatization of the recipient. The Poor Law system was not a preventative model which sought to be proactive and to intervene in order to minimize the negative consequences of human needs, but was a reactive and residual model of welfare provision which responded to needs only in dire circumstances. Issues confronting poor relief were succinctly categorized by the Commissioners under the headings of entitlement, administration, funding, and service provision.[12]

The Poor Law system gradually developed into a kind of welfare pluralism in which the state, the Kirk, voluntary organizations, and the family shared responsibilities for the care of children. Local government reorganization[13] transferred duties for the protection of children from the Poor Law Boards to health, welfare and education departments, characterized by service fragmentation.[14] The latter half of the nineteenth and the early years of the twentieth century witnessed a growth in the number of charitable societies.[15] Early twentieth-century services for children in need included infant protection visitors, school meals, hospitals, homes for children with disabilities, playgrounds and crèches. There was, however a continuing variation and inconsistency in the application of poor relief from burgh to burgh and parish to parish.[16]

The 1940s to the 1970s:
A Broader Definition of Need
and an Expanding State Role

There are three main trends worth noting with respect to social service planning and provision for need between the 1940s and the 1970s. First, the concept of social need broadened; second, the role of the state in planning and providing for need grew and there was a corresponding decrease in the role of charitable organizations; and third, social work developed as a profession which resulted in social work organizations and social workers playing an increasingly important role in responding to need.

The Social Insurance and Allied Services Report (Beveridge Report)[17] of 1942 heralded a new approach to conquering need.[18] The report identified obstacles to social reconstruction in the form of 'five giants': Want, Disease, Ignorance, Squalor and Idleness.[19] Social programmes that were implemented based on the Report (for example the 1948 National Assistance Act) "officially concluded"[20] the Poor Law system; crucially, the Report did not target people specifically in the most need (such as the poorest citizens) but aimed to introduce social welfare planning and services for all and to promote cohesive citizenship.[21] The assessment of need and the corresponding benefits provided were based on professionally calculated requirements for basic nutritional needs and an acceptable standard of living, not on funding capacities or policy goals. As a consequence, the judgement of official experts determined what was necessary.[22] The state took on a paternalistic role in human needs policy planning, administration and the provision of services[23] and differentiated between the roles of women and men.[24]

Responsibility for Need:
The Emergence of the Social Work Profession

With the emergence of social work as a profession in the late 1960s and early 1970s, social work organizations began to play a key role in planning, assessment of needs, and responding to them.[25] Public services were "revolutionized"[26] and social policy focused on organizational restructuring in order to create more efficient ways of meeting human needs.[27]

The concept of need shifted to include not only physical needs (for example, food, clothing and shelter), but also psychological needs[28] and in the early 1970s became more "politicized".[29] At the same time there was a growing recognition of the benefits of a unified family welfare service and this was evident in the 1963 *Report of the Committee on the Prevention of Neglect of Children* (the McBoyle Report).[30] A similar approach to need played a dominant role in the thinking behind the Kilbrandon Committee's *Children and Young Persons Scotland Report* of 1964. In line with earlier legislation, the Report concluded that children in need of care and protection and those who had offended shared common needs. It proposed a system of juvenile panels with specific responsibility for care decisions which would operate separately from courts which dealt with issues pertaining to guilt or innocence.[31] In this system the " . . . needs of the individual child" were the criteria for intervention.[32]

Due to the perceived limitations of organizational structures on the ability of agencies to respond to children in need, the report also recommended the creation of a separate agency, the social education department.[33] This was a major step in the development of the social work profession as a key means of implementing the state's role in responding to need. The subsequent Government White Paper on Social Work and the Community issued in 1966[34] further inter-connected social work services and organizational structure to the planning and provision of human needs with the proposal for the creation of the social work department (SWD) (and corresponding Director of Social Work).[35] The state was clearly identified as primarily responsible for the provision and co-ordination of social services "thus shifting the balance of responsibility away from voluntary organisations".[36]

Influenced by the White Paper, the *Report of the Committee on Local Authority and Allied Personal Social Services* (the Seebohm Report) identified three limitations to the organizational structure which impeded meeting needs: lack of resources; inadequate knowledge about need; and divided responsibility in planning and meeting need.[37], it advocated a universal system of service provision, available and accessible to all families, and rejected the use of targeted categories of need. (Indeed, the Seebohm Report did not attempt to define need.)[38]

The Social Work (Scotland) Act 1968 integrated recommendations from the Kilbrandon Report (1964) and the 1966 White Paper, and unified social service provision by bringing together welfare services, mental health services, probation services and child care service in a single social work department (SWD), under local authority administration.[39] Need was a critical concept used within the newly created SWDs. The Act created a general duty to provide services to " . . . promote social welfare" and to provide assistance to children (Section 12). Section 12 of the Act allowed for an interventionist and preventive approach (with the potential to provide universal services) in response to need, and allowed local authorities and SWDs to respond at a community level rather than on an individual or familial basis.[40] The 1968 Act shifted social work services from a residual model to a supportive approach allowing for assistance to be "in kind" or financial support to avoid placements of children in care and prevent family breakdown. Section 12 of the 1968 legislation was, however, not without controversy; it was criticized for a lack of accountability over its application and for potentially high costs while there was a view that tackling poverty should be the responsibility of the social security system rather than social work agencies.[41]

The 1970s: Growing Tensions over Need

The 1970s witnessed a rapid expansion of social services and an increased demand for them[42] which corresponded to an economic downturn and high unemployment.[43] There was growing public criticism concerning the quality and quantity of services provided, the bureaucratic rigidity of service delivery structures[44] and the nature of the state's role in planning and providing services to meet social need.[45] Some critics argued for a decrease in professional authority and an overall restructuring of welfare provision.[46] Concerns were also raised that contemporary policies and programmes contributed to the oppression of the underprivileged[47] and that need had " . . . become a smoke-screen to hide the true intention of policy, to camouflage policies which in their intention and effect have the explicit purpose of increasing inequalities".[48] This criticism was echoed in the women's movement of the 1970s which advocated voluntary, mutual help services, and self-identification of needs.[49] Systemic sexism was identified within social policies and services (for example reducing social security benefits to women living with men).[50]

The concept of need played a major part in the restructuring and reform of local government in Scotland.[51] Proposals for reform were prompted by Government concerns over the costs of services, duplication of administration and services and a general lack of interest in local government affairs on the part of the electorate.[52] In 1969 there were more than 400 local authorities in Scotland, and no fewer than five different types of authority: "counties of cities, large burghs, small burghs, county councils and district councils".[53] A reorganization enacted in the Local Government (Scotland) Act in 1973 and 1975 saw the creation of three unitary authorities for the islands and a two-tier system for the mainland consisting of nine Regional and 53 District Councils.[54] Education and social work became a responsibility of the Regional Councils, while housing, leisure and recreation were administered by the District Councils.[55] This reorganization brought a drastic upheaval for Social Work Departments as their numbers were reduced from 50 to twelve and the size of the populations they served was significantly increased.[56]

There are thus three main trends worth noting with respect to social service planning and provision for need between the 1940s and the 1970s. These were: first, the broadening of the concept of social need to include physical needs and psychological needs; second, the growth of the role of the state in planning and providing for need; and third, the growth of social work as a profession which resulted in social work organizations and social workers playing an increasingly important role in responding to need.

The 1980s and the 1990s: Shifting Responses to Human Needs

In the 1980s, policy responses to social need underwent a clear shift as the result of concerns about the increasing costs of public service expenditure and growing disillusionment regarding its effectiveness. The Report of the Inquiry into Child Abuse in Cleveland 1987 chaired by Butler-Sloss[57] highlighted many of the concerns subsequently identified by the Report of the Inquiry into the Removal of Children from Orkney in February 1991(the "Clyde" Report), regarding the inadequacy of the quality of practice and the effects of under-resourced authorities as well as concern that children had been unnecessarily removed from their homes.[58] Both reports included in their recommendations the need for greater inter-agency coordination and collaboration in the planning and delivery of services.[59]

This period witnessed many changes in the area of social welfare including an increased role for market principles within the public sector in order to promote a mixed economy of welfare (for example in health services and in education management) and the privatization of the housing market.[60] This development took place alongside a continued focus on cost containment.[61] At the same time, there was criticism from both sides of the political spectrum prompted by frustration with the ongoing "persistence of inequality".[62] Despite the increase in public service provision since the end of the Second World War and the post-war promises of eliminating social need, poverty and inequality continued to exist and there was little evidence of a decrease in need.

The election of Conservative governments in 1979, 1983 and 1987 resulted in significant changes to the post-war welfare state, with a return to a more residual approach to welfare provision and planning under a "New Right" paradigm.[63] The new policies were based on the primacy of a free market system, minimal state intervention in social welfare, a greater role for voluntary organizations, privatization of services, means testing, choice, individualism, and reliance on the family.[64] Social need was considered an illusive concept, equated with "preferences" or wants which people were expected to fulfill through the market system.[65],[66] Need was viewed within the framework of absolute poverty for those in "absolute" need of food, clothing and shelter which could be best ser-viced by charitable organizations.[67]

Service Effectiveness and Choice

Throughout this period, continuing concerns were expressed about inef-ficient, costly, and wasteful bureaucratic organizations and their inability to provide effective services. To meet these concerns, the government put its trust in the idea of "new managerialism"[68] which was based on the management techniques of the private sector. These were applied to the social service sector with the introduction of competitive tendering, performance measures and quasi-markets.[69] Efficiency and effectiveness, cost-savings, targeted services, needs-led planning and consumer involve-ment were considered the ways through which services could be improved.[70] The new approach involved a needs-led approach in which the agency or the authority – rather than the individual – had the role of defining need[71] and a consumerist approach which offered the service user choice in determining need satisfaction. It also presumed that the service user had sufficient resources to engage in informed participation.[72]

Another means of improving service planning and provision advocated in the new climate was an approach to care management which focused on the individual's unique needs, maximized service user independence, and provided a choice of service options.[73] Under the care management system, the purchaser (care manager) and provider of service (care provider) have differentiated tasks and responsibilities: the care management component entails the assessment, arrangements and purchase of services to meet needs while the care provision aspect involves the direct delivery of services.[74] This approach led to local councils decreasing their direct provision of certain types of care – notably for care in the community – and increasingly purchasing services from a combination of state, voluntary and private agencies.[75]

Concerns have been expressed that a greater reliance on the voluntary sector to provide statutory services may threaten the "innovative and advocacy roles" [76] of voluntary agencies and that fundamental services are delegated to the voluntary sector which may lack the capacity to provide them.[77] Limitations on the ability of small local authorities to respond to need may result in gaps in services[78]. Rather than providing a means of responding to these gaps, contracting for services with private and voluntary organizations may in turn lead to variations in the services provided and additional gaps.[79]

In Scotland, local authority structures were blamed for the inability to meet needs and this, together with concerns about the bureaucratic nature of a two-tier system (as well as political interests aimed at dismantling the Labour stronghold of the Strathclyde region[80]), led to a further reorganization of local government.[81] The Local Government (Scotland) Act 1994 maintained the three island councils but created 29 unitary authorities of varying sizes, populations and urban/rural settings with statutory responsibility for social work, education, housing, leisure and recreation (health remains outwith the remit of local authorities).[82] SWDs and education departments were no longer legally required to appoint Directors.[83]

The 1990s: Responsibility Over Rights, Protection versus Prevention

The emergence of "New Labour" after 1994 (and its subsequent election successes in 1997 and 2001), led to a further shift in central government policy and corresponding changes in welfare provision as the emphasis was placed on social responsibility rather than rights.[84] Education and training for employment were identified as key factors to promote social cohesion and wealth creation and to respond to social need.[85] The 1990s also saw a move from the "medico-social" model of child abuse, in which prevention, diagnosis and treatment were the focus of social services provision, to a "social-legal" approach, in which the focus shifted to the criminal law and the gathering of evidence necessary for court proceedings together with the need to manage risk.[86] This increased emphasis on legal requirements raised concerns about the prioritization of protection over preventative approaches in child welfare.[87],[88]

The shift to a legal based model of childcare reflected the ongoing debate between a welfare approach to child care policies and services and a justice approach, particularly with regards to youth offenders.[89] A justice approach is concerned with the offences committed by a young person and seeks accountability through a court process. This is carried out with due process ensured for the alleged offender and results in punishment for those convicted. In contrast, a welfare perspective prioritizes the child's needs over the offence committed, is focused on rehabilitation, and treats offending and non-offending young people as having considered to have similar needs.[90] This perspective is deeply rooted in a Scottish tradition.[91]

Approaches to the welfare of children in Scotland were also informed by three key documents issued in the early 1990s. The first of these was the report of the "Review of Child Care Law in Scotland" (1991). This called for the positive promotion of children's welfare to ensure that their needs were met; argued that greater effort should be made to support children within their family and community; and recommended a considerable degree of "widening the eligibility criteria for assistance" under the "general welfare duty" set out in Section 12 of the Social Work (Scotland) Act 1968.[92] It also called for improvements in inter-agency co-operation. The second document was the government's 1993 White Paper, *Scotland's Children Proposals for Child Care Policy and Law* which contained three key recommendations aimed at making " . . . child care more sensitive to the needs of children" (Scottish Office, 1993:).[93] These were a revision of Section 12; a greater emphasis on management and service provider training; and a requirement on local authorities to publish plans in relation to childcare services including an assessment of future needs. The third document was the United Nations Convention on the Rights of the Child which was ratified by the U.K. in 1991. This Convention not only covers the protection of children, and the provision of services to meet their needs but also the participation of children in decisions affecting them. It emphasizes parental responsibilities to children and reflects the recognition of children's rights as separate from those of their parents.[94]

The 1980s and early 1990s witnessed a return to a residual approach to welfare provision and planning with a corresponding emphasis on social responsibility over rights. The effectiveness of services was questioned and concerns were voiced over the lack of funding to meet needs, with a growing reliance on the role of voluntary sector. Policy emphasized the importance of interagency coordination and collaboration in the planning and delivery of services while protection services were prioritized over preventative child welfare services. As in the pre-1940 period, education and employment training were considered key ways of meeting social need.

The Children (Scotland) Act 1995:
A New Category of the Deserving Poor?

The Children (Scotland) Act of 1995[95] essentially replaced the provisions of the Social Work Scotland Act 1968 for children's services. It emphasized the importance of the wishes of the child and the parents[96] and the view that children are people in their own right.[97] The Act attempted to locate a balance between meeting children's needs and protecting the family from state intervention. The new Children in Need (CIN) category replaced the Social Work (Scotland) Act 1968 "general welfare duty". This was a controversial classification and was opposed by Scottish children's agencies owing to concerns that it was a retrogressive move away from the positive welfare duty of Section 12[98] and was viewed as being imported from the 1989 Children Act for England and Wales.[99]

Section 22 of the Act gives local authorities the general duty to "safeguard and promote the welfare of children in their area who are in need" by the provision of a range and level of services to children under 18 years of age and families.[100] The Act provides four general categories on which to assess a child as being in need, which are: a poor standard of health or development; the likely or further impairment to the child's health or development; living with a disability; or being adversely affected by a disability of a person in the family.[101] In addition, the Act gives the local authority (L.A.) the responsibility of determining the comprehensiveness of services and how the services will be provided (although some services are required by the Act).[102] Help to children in need can be given to a particular child or to a family member and can also include financial support to encourage children to remain with their family. The Children (Scotland) Act 1995 Regulations and Guidance (Volume 1) provides an indicative (rather than exhaustive) list of 21 main "needs" of children. While the list is broad and encompassing it does not define nor prioritize needs of children.[103]

Section 19 of the Act requires local authorities to prepare, consult upon, publish and review plans for all "relevant" children's services. The Social Work Service Group guidance (1997) states that Children's Services Plans (CSP) should also identify needs not being met and gaps in services. In addition, the Act places local authorities under a duty to consult with health boards and trusts, some voluntary organizations, Reporters (to the Children's Panel), children's panel chairpersons, and housing agencies. When drawing up and reviewing CSP there is a duty to consult children and their families, however not necessarily directly (Section 19). The duty to safeguard and promote the welfare of CIN is a corporate duty and the responsibility of Social Work Services, Education, Housing, and "any other relevant services necessary".[104]

Research on CSP in Britain has found that local authorities take their responsibilities seriously.[105] However, limitations have been shown to exist in the consultation process (for example the limited role of service users and non-statutory service providers) and findings suggest that there are chronic problems associated with the definition, assessment and planning for CIN which raise concern about the relevance of the CIN category.[106] Other research examining the formulation of CIN policy in the United Kingdom found that there was a great variation and little agreement as to how a child "in need" ought to be defined.[107,108] Other findings include the difficulty experienced by those involved in the process of planning for CIN; the perception that eligibility criteria for CIN were a means to limit access to services as opposed to broadening service eligibility; that child protection and the needs of looked-after children were prioritized over other children in need; and finally that under-funding was a chronic problem which resulted in inadequate services.

Conclusion

This chapter has reviewed public policy responses to children's need in Scotland, from the early Poor Law system to the enactment of the Children (Scotland) Act 1995. It has shown that the expectations and demands on the state and the voluntary sector constantly shift and this in turn alters service eligibility and accessibility requirements, the responsibility for the administration of policies and service, and the quality and quantity of services provided. Historical trends reflect ongoing debates regarding the definition of need and those in need, the responsibility for administering and funding need, and the responsibility for service planning and provision.

The chapter provides evidence that the concept of need is a contested area. Widely diverging perspectives have equated need with individual moral failure at one end of the spectrum to the oppressive consequences of structural inequity in society at the other, reflecting or implying widely a differing understanding of, and associated responses to, human needs. Prior to the modern era, need was provided for on an individual basis, limited to absolute poverty under the Poor Law system, within a residual model of welfare. Although the emergence of the Poor Law system initiated welfare pluralism in which the market, the state and voluntary organizations shared responsibilities for social need, the chapter shows that, with the exception of the period from the end of the Second World War to the 1970s, need has been categorized and this has resulting in targeted approaches to service planning and provided a means of limiting provision. The concept of need broadened in the 1940s, 50s and 60s, and was accompanied by an enhanced role for the state which was evidenced by the expansion of the social work profession. The period after the 1970s and including the 1990s, however, was characterized by a narrowing of the definition of need, with an associated decreased role for the state and an enhanced contribution from the voluntary sector. Later, with the implementation of the Children (Scotland) Act 1995, new categories of need were created resulting in a further re-alignment of state-voluntary sector roles. The classification of Children in Need can be seen as a new state categorization of the deserving poor. Current responses to social need reflect these historical trends, particularly the challenges associated with the determination of authority and responsibility for fairness and effectiveness in service planning and delivery.

The role of the state and voluntary organizations within welfare pluralism remains changeable and contested. This chapter shows that voluntary agencies and social work organizations in particular have been shown to play a special role in responding to needs through the determination of eligibility as well as the quantity and quality of intervention. In more recent years social work has lost some of this prominence due partly to local authority restructuring and the greater role assigned to voluntary agencies since the 1990s. Tensions exist between who is responsible for planning and meeting need both within and outwith the local authority. This addresses issues of funding and service collaboration and co-ordination, issues that have been systematically raised since the inception of the Poor Law system, through local government reorganization, inquiries and legislation.

This lack of consensus regarding the definition of need raises further issues, issues identified under the Poor Law system that continue to remain relevant in the current context: about who is responsible for the administration of service planning and provision to meet need, the determination of eligibility for assistance; and the provision of services to children.

> "Need" is a concept that keeps appearing in social policy debates. There is a continuing debate for example, over the extent to which the state should be responsible for meeting human needs. Should the state assume responsibility for providing social welfare services to all people in all need areas?[109]

As a policy/planning issue, both the conceptualization of need and the methods of responding to it reflect the greater British social welfare transition from a crisis-response, residual model, to a state model of provision and reflects the 'moving frontier' between the state and voluntary organizations.

Notes

1   J. Bradshaw, "The concept of social need", *New Society* 19 (1972): pp. 640–3, esp. p. 640.

2 L. C. Johnson and C. L. Schwartz, *Social Welfare: A Response to Human Need* (Newton, Mass.: Allyn and Bacon, 1988).

3 B. L. Gates, *Social Program Administration: The Implementation of Social Policy* (Englewood Cliffs, NJ: Prentice-Hall, 1980), p. 136.

4 M. Kamenetzky, "The Economics of the Satisfaction of Needs", *Human Systems Management, 2* (1981): 101–11.

5 R. Mayer (1985). *Policy and Program Planning* (Englewood Cliffs, NJ, Prentice-Hall, 1985), p. 129.

6 J. Bradshaw, "The Conceptualization and Measurement of Need: A Social Policy Perspective", in *Researching the People's Health* (London: Routledge, 1994). Bradshaw, "The concept of social need". J. Cooper, *The Creation of British Social Services 1962–1974* (London: Heinemann Educational Books, 1983). L. Doyal and I. Gough, *A Theory of Human Need* (Hong Kong: Macmillan Education Ltd., 1991).

7 G. Nicholls, *A History of the Scotch Poor Law*, 2nd edition (London: John Murray, 1856/1967).

8 M. Langan, *Welfare: Needs, Rights and Risks* (London: Routledge/The Open University Press, 1998).

9 T. Ferguson, *The Dawn of Scottish Welfare* (Edinburgh: Thomas Nelson and Sons, 1948).

10 T. Ferguson, *Scottish Social Welfare: 1864–1914* (Edinburgh: E. and S. Livingstone 1958), p. 3.

11 Ferguson, *Scottish Social Welfare: 1864–1914*. J. Lindsay, *The Scottish Poor Law: Its Operation in the North-East from 1745–1845* (Devon: Arthur H. Stockwell, 1975).

12 Great Britain, *Report of the Commissioners' Inquiry* (London: HMSO, 1844).

13 Great Britain, *Royal Commission on the Poor Laws and Relief of Distress. Report on Scotland* (London: HMSO, 1909).

14 K. Murray and M. Hill (1991). "The Recent History of Scottish Child Welfare", *Children & Society*, 5 (1991): pp. 266–81, esp. p. 267.

15 Lindsay, *The Scottish Poor Law*.

16 Ferguson, *Scottish Social Welfare*.

17 W. Beveridge. *Social Insurance and Allied* Services (London: HMSO, 1942).

18 F. J. Wright, *British Social Services*, 2nd edition (Estover, Plymouth: MacDonald and Evans, 1976).

19 Beveridge, *Social Insurance and Allied* Services.

20 M. Lavalette and A. Pratt, *Social Policy: A Conceptual and Theoretical Introduction* (London: Sage, 1997), p. 5.

21 Langan, *Welfare: Needs, Rights and Risks*.

22 *Ibid.*

23 *Ibid.*

24 K. Woodward, "Feminist Critiques of Social Policy", in M. Lavalette and A. Pratt (eds), *Social Policy: A Conceptual and Theoretical Introduction* (London: Sage, 1997).

25 A. Alaszewski and M. Walsh, "Literature Review: Typologies of Welfare Organisations", *British Journal of Social Work*, 25 (1995): 805–15. Cooper, *The Creation of British Social Services 1962–1974*. Langan, *Welfare: Needs, Rights and Risks*.

26 E. K. M. Tisdall, *The Children (Scotland) Act 1995: Developing Policy and Law for Scotland's Children* (Edinburgh: The Stationary Office. 1997), p. 14.

27 G. Smith, *Social Need: Policy, Practice and Research* (London: Routledge & Kegan Paul, 1980).

28 M. Kellmer Pringle, *The Needs of Children* (London: Hutchinson, 1975).

29 Langan, *Welfare: Needs, Rights and Risks*, p. 13.

30 Great Britain (1963). *Report of the Committee on the Prevention of Neglect of Children* (Edinburgh: HMSO, 1963).

31 This was the origin of the Children's Hearings: Murray and Hill, "The recent history of Scottish child welfare".

32 Four categories of children and youth fell under the remit of the committee: 1) Juveniles alleged to have committed crimes or offences; 2) Children in need of care and protection; 3) Children who are refractory or beyond parental control; and 4) Children who are persistent truants (SHHD and SED, 1964, p. 9).

33 Scottish Home and Health Department and Scottish Education Department. (SHHD and SED). Great Britain. (1964). *Children and Young Persons Scotland. Report by the Committee Appointed by the Secretary of State for Scotland.* Edinburgh: HMSO, 1964), p. 91 – see following note.

34 Scottish Education Department and Scottish Home and Health Department (SED and SHHD). (1966). *Social work and the Community. Proposals for Reorganising Local Authority Services in Scotland.* Edinburgh: HMSO.

35 Smith, *Social Need. Policy, Practice and Research.*

36 M. Hill, K. Murray and K. Tisdall, "Children and their Families", in *Social Services in Scotland* (Edinburgh: Mercat Press, 1988), pp. 95–6.

37 Great Britain (1968). *Report of the Committee on Local Authority and Allied Personal Social Services.* London: HMSO. While the focus of the report was on England and Wales it is nevertheless relevant as it clearly linked organizational structure to the ability to plan and provide for human needs.

38 Bradshaw, "The Concept of Social Need"; Smith, *Social Need: Policy, Practice and Research.*

39 F. M. Martin, "Personal Social Services" in *Social Services in* Scotland (Edinburgh: Scottish Academic Press, 1979). University of Edinburgh. *Social work in Scotland. Report by a working party on the Social Work (Scotland) Act 1968.* (Edinburgh: Neill and Company, 1969).

40 Cooper, *The Creation of British Social Services 1962–1974* (London: Heinemann, 1983). C. Hallett, *The Personal Social Services in Local Government* (London: George Allen and Unwin, 1982). Murray and Hill, "The Recent History of Scottish Child Welfare".

41 Cooper, *The Creation of British Social Services 1962–1974.*

42 P. Hardiker, K. Exton and M. Barker, *Policies and Practices in Preventive Child Care* (Aldershot: Avebury/Gower, 1991); Martin, "Personal Social Services".

43 R. H. Kirk and D. Part, "The Impact of Changing Social Policies on Families" in M. Hill, R. H. Kirk and D. Part (eds), *Supporting Families* (Edinburgh: HMSO, 2001). Mary Langan, *Welfare Needs, Rights and Risks* (ed.), *Welfare: Needs, Rights and Risks, Routledge, London, 1998.*

44 Langan, *Welfare: Needs, Rights and Risks.*

45 Kearns, "Social Democratic Perspectives on the Welfare State" in: Lavalette, Michael and Pratt, Alan (eds) *Social Policy: A Conceptual and Theoretical*

Introduction (London: Sage, 1997). Kirk and Part, "The Impact of Changing Social Policies on Families". Langan, *Welfare: Needs, Rights and Risks.*

46 Langan, *Welfare: Needs, Rights and Risks.*

47 *Ibid.*

48 Bradshaw, "The Conceptualization and Measurement of Need: A Social Policy Perspective", p. 49.

49 Langan, *Welfare: Needs, Rights and Risks.*

50 Woodward, "Feminist Critiques of Social Policy".

51 Great Britain (1971) *Reform of Local Government in Scotland.* HMSO: Edinburgh. Great Britain, *Royal Commission on Local Government in Scotland 1966–1969* (Edinburgh: HMSO, 1969).

52 *Royal Commission on Local Government in Scotland 1966–1969.*

53 *Royal Commission on Local Government in Scotland 1966–1969*, p. 3.

54 J. English, "Central and Local Government", in *Social Services in Scotland* (Edinburgh: Mercat Press, 1998). *Royal Commission on Local Government in Scotland 1966–1969.*

55 J. G. Kellas, "Central and Local Government" in *Social Services in Scotland* (Edinburgh: Scottish Academic Press, 1979).

56 Martin, "Personal Social Services".

57 Great Britain, *Report into the Inquiry into Child Abuse in Cleveland* 1987 (London: HMSO, 1988).

58 Great Britain, *Report of the Inquiry into the Removal of Children from Orkney in February* 1991 (Edinburgh: HMSO, 1992).

59 Great Britain, *Report into the Inquiry into Child Abuse in Cleveland* 1987. Tisdall, *The Children (Scotland) Act 1995: Developing Policy and Law for Scotland's Children.*

60 Langan, *Welfare: Needs, Rights and Risks.*

61 A. Long, "Assessing Health and Social Outcomes", in *Researching the People's Health* (London: Routledge, 1994).

62 Langan, *Welfare: Needs, Rights and Risks*, p. 13.

63 Kearns, "Social Democratic Perspectives on the Welfare State".

64 M. Walsh, P. Stephens and S. Moore, *Social Policy and Welfare* (Cheltenham: Stanley Thornes, 2000), p. 22.

65 Doyal and Gough, *A Theory of Human Need.*

66 J. Percy-Smith, *Needs Assessments in Public* Policy (Buckingham: Open University Press, 1996), p. 6.

67 Bradshaw, "The Conceptualization and Measurement of Need: A Social Policy Perspective", p. 49. I. Illich, "Needs", in *The development dictionary: A guide to knowledge as power* (London: Zed Books, 1992).

68 J. Harris, "State Social Work and Social Citizenship in Britain: From Clientelism to Consumerism", *British Journal of Social Work* 29 (1999): 915–37.

69 T. Cutler and B. Waine, *Managing the Welfare State: The Politics of Public Sector Management* (Oxford: Berg, 1994).

70 M. Sheppard and G. Crocker, "Care management and Information Provision: Towards a Reasoned Method of Assessing the Range and Extent of Problems and Needs in Child-Care Social Work", *The British Journal of Social Work* 29 (1999): 69–95.

71 Langan, *Welfare: Needs, Rights and Risks.*

72 Harris, "State Social Work and Social Citizenship in Britain".

73 M. Sheppard, *Care Management and the New Social Work. A Critical Analysis* (London: Whiting and Birch, 1995).

74 Sheppard, *Care Management and the New Social Work*, p. 8.

75 M. McGrath and G. Grant, "Supporting Needs-led services: Implications for Planning and Management Systems (A Case Study in Mental Handicap Services)", *Journal of Social Policy*, 21 (1992): 71–97.

76 Hill, Murray and Tisdall, "Children and their Families", p. 94.

77 M. Hill and J. Aldgate, *Child Welfare Services Developments in Law, Policy, Practice and* Research (London: Jessica Kingsley Publishers, 1996).

78 P. Hudson, "Welfare Pluralism in the UK: Views from the Non-Profit Sector", *Critical Social Policy* 41 (1998): 1–16.

79 Hill, Murray and Tisdall, "Children and their Families".

80 English, "Central and Local Government".

81 Langan, *Welfare: Needs, Rights and Risks*.

82 English, "Central and Local Government".

83 Hill, Murray and Tisdall, "Children and their Families".

84 Walsh, Stephens and Moore, *Social Policy & Welfare*.

85 For example the "Report on Wealth Creation and Social Cohesion in a Free Society" (1995).

86 M. King, *A Better World for Children? Explorations in Morality and Authority* (London: Rutledge, 1997).

87 I. Freeman, "Social Work Intervention in Child Abuse – an Ever-Widening Net?", *Child Abuse Review* 5 (1996): 181–90.

88 J. Gibbons, S. Conroy and C. Bell, *Operating the Child Protection* System (London, HMSO, 1995).

89 Tisdall, *The Children (Scotland) Act 1995: Developing policy and law for Scotland's children*.

90 Hill, Murray and Tisdall, "Children and their Families".

91 Murray and Hill, "The Recent History of Scottish Child Welfare".

92 Scottish Office, *Review of Child Care Law in Scotland. Report of a Review Group Appointed by the Secretary of* State (Edinburgh: HMSO, 1991), p. 4.

93 Social Work Services Group, *Scotland's Children: Proposals for Child Care Policy and* Law (Edinburgh: HMSO, 1993), p. 47.

94 United Nations Convention on the Rights of the Child (1989).

95 Children (Scotland) Act 1995. London: HMSO.

96 Hill, Murray and Tisdall, "Children and their Families".

97 Tisdall, *The Children (Scotland) Act 1995: Developing Policy and Law for Scotland's Children*.

98 Hill, Murray and Tisdall, "Children and their Families".

99 Tisdall, *The Children (Scotland) Act 1995: Developing Policy and Law for Scotland's Children*.

100 Section 22 of the Children (Scotland) Act 1995, Section 17 of the Children Act 1989 in England and Wales, and Article 18 the Children (Northern Ireland) Order 1995 are virtually identical; except that the definition of children 'in need' in the Children Act 1989 in England and Wales, and the Children (Northern Ireland) Order 1995, does not include children affected by disability, only children who are disabled.

101 Section 93 (4)a of the Act.

102 Local authorities are to provide day care for pre-school children and out of school care for children at school who are "in need" (Section 27). An L.A. has a further duty to provide accommodation for children or young people under 18 if they have been abandoned.

103 Social Work Services Group, *The Children (Scotland) Act 1995 Regulations and Guidance Volume* I (Crown Copyright: The Scottish Office. The Stationery Office Limited, 1997).

104 Social Work Services Group, *The Children (Scotland) Act 1995 Regulations and Guidance Volume* I (Crown Copyright: The Scottish Office. The Stationery Office Limited, 1997), pp. 1–2.

105 B. Hearn and R. Sinclair, *Children's Services Plans. Analysing Need: Reallocating* Resources (London: National Children's Bureau: 1998).

106 S. Wheelaghan, M. Hill and K. Tisdall, *Children's Services Plans and the Voluntary Sector. Report of Stage 2 of a Two-year Research Study for the Baring Foundation* (1999).

107 J. Aldgate and J. Tunstil, *Making Sense of Section 17. A Study for the Department of Health. Implementing Services for Children in Need, Within the 1989 Children* Act (London: HMSO, 1995).

108 Audit Commission, *Seen but not Heard: Co-ordinating Community Child Heath and Social Services for Children in* Need (London: HMSO, 1994). M. Colton, C. Drury and M. Williams, *Children in Need. Family Support under the Children Act 1989* (Aldershot: Avebury, 1995). P. McCrystal, P. (2000). *Children in need: Implementing Article 18 of the Children (NI) Order 1995. The First Two* Years (The Centre for Child Care Research, The Queens University of Belfast: Belfast, 2000). L. Peyton, *Strategic Planning for Children in Need.* (Child Care in Practice: Special Children Order Edition, 1996). R. Sinclair and R. Carr-Hill, *The Categorisation of Children in Need* (London: National Children's Bureau, 1997). J. Tunstill and J. Aldgate, *Services for Children in Need from Policy to* Practice (London: The Stationery Office, 2000).

109 Walsh, Stephens and Moore, *Social Policy and Welfare*, p. 22.

PART II

The Impulse from Above
and the Impulse from Below

By the People Themselves? Social Class and a Volunteer-Led Museum, 1884–1915

BRIDGET YATES

The museum landscape in England today is a complex mix of institutions run by national and local government, universities, private and commercial bodies, and the charitable companies and trusts that now form the largest grouping in the sector. Over half of all museums in Britain were established after 1970, and this growth was particularly marked in the institutions that originated in voluntary action.[1] Although many of these museums now employ paid staff, there are approximately 200 museums, mainly in rural areas, that are entirely volunteer-led. Despite an increasing academic interest in the history of museums, and especially in the history of collections, there have been few, if any, studies of volunteer-led museums, and wider studies of museum and heritage volunteers have rarely distinguished between volunteer-involving organizations and the small museums that have no paid staff at all.

The purpose of this chapter is to show, through a case study of the oldest volunteer-led museum, the Victoria Jubilee Museum in Cawthorne, South Yorkshire, that such museums have a much longer and richer history than is commonly believed and that those museums which began before the "heritage boom" of the 1970s have much to tell about what makes village people become involved and stay involved in museums, how to create sustainable organizational frameworks for village museums and how village museums have adapted and changed over time and yet stayed true to their primary intentions of providing a resource and an amenity for their own communities.

Museum Expansion in the Nineteenth Century

In the second half of the nineteenth century there was a marked increase in the number of museums open to the public following a series of enabling acts of Parliament that began with the Museums Act 1845. This growth in museums was primarily an urban phenomenon, as funding from municipal rates was only permitted in towns with a population of 10,000 or more. This was part of a palliative response to the appalling conditions of many urban areas and provided "rational recreation" for working people in the form of public parks and gardens, libraries and swimming baths as well as museums.[2] Such museums were modelled, albeit on a reduced scale, on the national museums. Their subjects were geology, natural history, art and archaeology[3] – but not history, as a body of knowledge exemplified through material culture.[4] As Tony Bennett has said, "Nineteenth-century museums were thus intended *for* the people; they were certainly not *of* the people in the sense of displaying any interest in the lives, habits and customs of either the contemporary working classes or the labouring classes of pre-industrial societies".[5] What these museums and the people behind their establishment were interested in was the education and moral improvement of the working classes, nicely encapsulated by Thomas Greenwood, a follower of John Ruskin:

> The working man or agricultural labourer who spends his holiday in a walk through any well-arranged museum cannot fail to come away with a deeply-rooted and reverential sense of the extent of knowledge possessed by his fellow-men. It is not the objects themselves that he sees there, and wonders at, that cause this impression, so much as the order and evident science which he cannot but recognize in the manner in which they are grouped and arranged. He learns that there is a meaning and value in every object, however insignificant, and that there is a way of looking at things common and rare, distinct from regarding them as useless, useful or merely curious . . . . He has gained a new sense, a craving for natural knowledge, and such a craving may, possibly, in course of time quench another and lower craving which may at one time have held him in bondage – that for intoxicants or vicious excitement of one description or another.[6]

The Origins of the Victoria Jubilee Museum, Cawthorne

The Victoria Jubilee Museum was founded by two of the archetypal characters of country life, landlord and parson. However, it endured, as others did not, because landlord and parson shared the responsibility for setting its priorities and managing its activities with a wide variety of local people.

At the end of the nineteenth century the Spencer Stanhope family of

Cannon Hall was the largest landowner and the largest single employer in Cawthorne, a semi-industrial village near Barnsley in South Yorkshire.[7] The Spencer Stanhopes were paternalistic landlords and exercized their benevolence and control through the church, of which they held the living, and through the provision of and support for amenities that included schools for both boys and girls, a village library, a penny savings bank, a cottage institute with a nurse and, from 1884, a museum

John Roddom Spencer Stanhope was the younger son, a second generation Pre-Raphaelite artist and, like Greenwood, a follower of John Ruskin.[8] Although living mainly in Florence, he maintained a house in Cawthorne and stayed in close contact with its affairs. Rev. Charles Tiplady Pratt arrived in 1866 as curate-in-charge and succeeded to the living in 1874. He remained there until 1915, when ill health prompted his retirement to Cheltenham, where he died in 1921. He was an energetic and imposing man, described as "an autocrat who commanded respect . . . . He always wore a long, black frock coat and flat shovel-type hat, and carried a walking stick or crook."[9] From 1870 until 1915 he wrote, single-handedly, a monthly *Parish Magazine*, which frequently used the authorial "we", and which provides much of the information about the early history of the museum.[10]

Spencer Stanhope proposed establishing the museum in the expectation that its ownership would be invested in "the people themselves":

A Village Museum

A letter came to us from Mr Roddom Stanhope, now in Florence, very strongly advocating the establishment of a Village Museum 'to be managed, of course, by the people themselves'. It is not the first time that he has made a suggestion of this kind, and we strongly hope that the idea will be heartily taken up. 'A Natural History Collection' he says 'seems such an easy and inexpensive thing to start, and one in which so many might help. I hope the time is not far off when such a simple way of breaking the monotony of village life may be adopted, and, if it is started at Cawthorne, I shall be delighted to help both by subscribing and by sending anything that may appear to me to be of interest.' Some of our readers will have frequently heard us remark, that we believe that God would as surely have us study His works as His word; and that it is only through contemplation of God's marvellous creation,[11] that we can have any intelligent idea of His Almighty power, and His majesty, and His glory.

Pratt followed this invitation with a call to collective action:

All who are in the least interested in this Village Museum scheme will attend a public meeting, we hope, in the Boys' School on Monday 14th, at seven o'clock. The Meeting will be for a general discussion on the proposed Museum.[13]

A preliminary committee was formed, and after the first few meetings it appealed for contributions of objects worthy of display:

> It is only by a combination of many tastes and interests that our Museum can ever have a collection worthy of its name: and we allow that the attempt that is being made is a somewhat severe test of the education and intelligence of a Parish of this size. Still, there is no reason why it should not succeed, if even a very small proportion of our people show themselves in earnest.[13]

A start was made in April when "the first fruits of the museum were exhibited at the Boys' School.[14]

Later that month the preliminary committee sent round a circular appealing for local people to join the Cawthorne Museum Society, and in May the Society elected its first committee of eleven people, the majority of whom had some connection with the Cannon Hall Estate, including Pratt himself; the land agent and his son; Spencer Stanhope's private secretary; the Boys' School teacher; the head gardener and a colleague; the estate builder; and a wood agent. Spencer Stanhope was elected president; Pratt, chairman, a position he held until he left the village in 1915; the land agent, secretary; and the estate builder, treasurer.

Cawthorne was not the only community where a museum was set up by a paternalistic and philanthropic landowner. At St Michael's-on-Wyre in Lancashire a similar venture was started by a local landowner, but it was not supported by a museum society, and after several years of diminishing interest it finally closed after the death of its founder, despite the management having passed to a small number of trustees.[15] The museum at Cawthorne survived not because of its collections, its location or its endowments, but because it has been run by a museum society, "the people themselves", despite the apparent control and longevity of Pratt, its founding chairman. Throughout its history membership has been drawn from the village community, an organizational framework that is familiar and remains appropriate for many volunteer-led museums today.

The Cawthorne Museum Society

The Society took the institutional form of what R. J. Morris, in discussing the literary and philosophical societies of the early nineteenth century, has characterized as a "subscriber democracy".[16] In setting out General Rules in the *Parish Magazine* in June 1884, Pratt stressed that "it is the intention of the Committee that any Rules which may be made from time to time should be with the object of making the Museum as accessible and useful as possible to those who may be interested in it".[17] This openness included advertising the date of the general meeting each year, and, for a few years, publishing a summary of the Society's accounts – both practices which, to quote Morris again, "set out a claim for legitimacy".[18]

Membership provided benefits. For payment of a subscription of a shilling a year members received free admission to the museum, while non-members were expected to put "not less than a penny" in the box provided.[19] Members were also entitled to free admission to the lectures organized by Pratt and the committee during the winter months, many of them by curators from larger museums such as those at York and Leeds. Later members were able to borrow books from the museum's library and to use various items of equipment, such as the meteorological instruments acquired in 1889 and a telescope provided by Colonel Spencer Stanhope.

The Society was keen to attract working men and women, both members and visitors, and it set the times of opening accordingly as Monday evenings from 6.30 to 8.0 and Saturday and Sunday afternoons from 4.30 to 6.0 (with Sunday afternoons initially for members only). In addition it was open on public holidays such as Easter and Whitsun as well as on Cawthorne "Feast Days", when a considerable number of trippers visited. In this it was unlike the museum of the nearby Barnsley Naturalists and Scientific Society, which at this time was primarily for members' use only.[20]

Many of the Society's committee members had a very long association with the museum, and they were not drawn predominantly from Cawthorne's elite. For example, John Fretwell was a coal miner. Although illiterate, he had an extensive knowledge of natural history and was responsible for bringing together the collection of local butterflies and moths and, later, for leading natural history rambles from the museum.[21] Between 1884 and 1894 the results of the annual elections to the committee were reported in the *Parish Magazine*; after that date the committee seems to have been regularly re-elected *en bloc*. During this decade, twenty-nine people served on the committee, including two women. In addition to those working on the Cannon Hall Estate these included five employed in mining, four gardeners, a mason, a mason's labourer, a teamster, a post-master, a grocer, and a blacksmith.[22]

The working-class base of the committee appears to have been representative of the membership of the Society as a whole. On the basis of Census records for 1891 it has been possible to identify the occupations of 118 members listed in the *Museum Minute Book* between 1888 and 1900. Most were from the working and lower middle classes. The largest component, twenty-seven people, were those involved in coal mining – nineteen coal miners, three colliery labourers, two weighmen, an engine man, an engine stoker and a colliery cashier. There were also tradesmen – a blacksmith, boot and shoe makers, butchers, carpenters and a joiner, masons, two grocers, two linen weavers and an ironmonger; indoor and outdoor staff from the Estate; a police constable; and ten farmers, mainly with small farms. Only two members of the Society apart from the Spencer Stanhopes were described as "living on own means" and there was one "retired manufacturer". The Society began with eighty-four members in

1884 and had 152 in 1893. After that, despite the various strategies aimed at boosting membership such as family and household memberships and tickets for guests, there seems to have been a steady decline in numbers to a mere thirty in 1904, including members of Pratt's family.

Although caution is advisable in using contemporary models to describe earlier organizational forms, the Society seems to conform to Colin Rochester's "member activist" model of associations without paid staff:

> The members have come together to pursue a common interest or meet a shared need. Their goals are pursued and all of their operational and support activities are carried out by the members themselves and not delegated to a separate group of staff – paid or unpaid. The work is not shared equally, and clear distinctions can be made between passive and active members and between the majority of active members and a smaller inner group who undertake most of the work.[23]

In the case of Cawthorne, the Spencer Stanhope family and their friends who supported the museum through their subscriptions and other donations might be described as "passive members", since they took no other part in the activities of the museum; the members of the Society who visited the museum and attended its numerous activities, particularly its talks and lectures, demonstrations and lantern slide shows, to which members had free entry and non-members paid, could be described as "active members"; and the committee could be described as the "inner group". Certainly some of the committee showed remarkable longevity of involvement in the museum. Fretwell, mentioned earlier, was involved from 1884 until his death in 1933; Pratt was chairman and acted as curator from 1884 until 1915; and Douglas Charlesworth, a smallholder, joined the Society as a young man in 1894 and served as secretary and curator from 1918 until his death in 1940. In addition to contributing to and arranging the collections, committee members were also responsible for organising and in some cases for leading the events put on for the Society's members and others. For example, at a *conversazione* held in November 1892 "Miss Beatrice Pratt will play some violin solos. Mr Jas. Balme's party will sing some Songs and Glees, and some short Recitations from Tennyson will be given by the Rev C.T Pratt."[24] In March 1894 "Mr George Hindle and Mr John Fretwell will take charge of Field Classes of Members in Natural History as soon as the season is sufficiently advanced."[25]

A recent analysis of the governing bodies of voluntary and community museums concerned with the history of their own communities in small towns and villages in England has shown that the "museum society" model is still widely used. In addition to Cawthorne, there are thirty-one museums active today that are managed by museum societies. These range geographically from Honiton, Bruton, and Salcombe in the South West to Hedon and Pateley Bridge in Yorkshire and Millom in Cumbria.[26]

The Museum Collections

The collections in the museum testify to its original aims and how those aims reflected wider cultural concerns in late Victorian and Edwardian England. During the period of Pratt's curatorship the collections made by the museum were primarily of natural history and geological materials, particularly coal fossils found on the slag heaps in the neighbourhood. He made it clear that these were "not intended for mere natural curiosities only, but for everything illustrative of nature, science and art"[27] and that they were to be educational and instructive:

> Knowing what we do of Museums in other places and large Towns, we still feel it is a severe test to put the intelligence of Cawthorne to: for it is not intended only for a place of amusement: but for the encouragement of a taste for Natural Science, and that is a matter which requires a more active use of our brains than most people are prepared to make. The discipline and culture of our intellectual faculties does not come to us more naturally than the culture of our moral and spiritual powers. We are as responsible, however, for the use we make of our brains as of any other part of our nature.[28]

This emphasis was, as has been discussed earlier, entirely consistent with that of other museums at this period, and it is worth noting that enthusiasm for natural history was widespread across all social classes.[29] So although many of the collections came from Cawthorne and its surroundings, they were certainly not expressive of the history of Cawthorne or of the lives of its people. An entry in the *Museums Directory*, published by the Museums Association as a supplement to the *Museums Journal* in June 1903, described the exhibition space of the museum as:

> Minerals, 34 1/2 ft; coal fossils 7ft; birds nests 7 1/2ft; ancient pottery 6ft; coins 2 1/2ft; arts and manufactures 8ft; cases of birds are arranged against one wall for a space of 16ft by 8ft high; weapons and drawings shewing sections of neighbouring coal mines are hung from other portions of the walls, the moths and butterflies are in 20 small drawers, birds eggs in 5, shells in 14.[30]

However, not all of the collections came from the area. Pratt was active in soliciting gifts, mainly from his clerical colleagues and other acquaintances, and he also contacted John Ruskin:[31]

> It is a peculiar pleasure to us to make known that Mr John Ruskin has most kindly sent us some contributions for our Museum and promised us some more. 'I shall have great pleasure', he writes, 'in looking out some things for your Village Museum, and I have begun with a few minerals . . . . I will look out later on some Prints and such things as are likely to answer your purpose.' Those who know anything of Mr Ruskin will very greatly appreciate his kindly interest in our Museum.[32]

Ruskin was as good as his word:

Since we wrote in last month's MAGAZINE, a Box containing a most beautiful and interesting collection of Minerals has been received from Mr Ruskin, who has also sent a second Box within the last few days. It is intended that these should be exhibited by Easter in a case specially reserved for them, to contain all Mr Ruskin's most generous contributions.[33]

Pratt, of course, must have been well aware of the iconic nature of such gifts. G. W. Hudson Shaw's Oxford University Extension lectures on "English Social Reformers", who included Ruskin, drew an average attendance of 420 students at Huddersfield in 1887 and 400 students at Barnsley in 1888.[34] Pratt would certainly have seen these gifts as a significant additional attraction for visitors (note the Easter opening), as well as raising the status of the museum, and he noted Ruskin's death with proprietorial sadness:

The death of Mr Ruskin reminds us of the generous kindness with which he responded to our request that he would send some contribution to our little museum at Cawthorne, when it first begun, in order that it might have at least some slight connexion with his name.[35]

The Museum also exhibited materials given or loaned by members of the local elite, particularly the Spencer Stanhope family. These included "Arab shields, spears and knives, brought from the Field of Battle by W. Spencer-Stanhope, Lieut. 19th Hussars"[36]; Mr and Mrs Montague Stanhope's wedding presents, exhibited over three days in May 1890, which attracted over 1,000 visitors[37]; and in 1895 souvenirs from dresses worn by Queen Victoria:

Miss Cicely Stanhope has sent the Museum a large packet of pieces from morning and evening Dresses that have been worn by Her Majesty the Queen. Besides their natural 'curiosity', from their connection with our Sovereign, they illustrate very well the designs and fashions of royal dress some years ago. An arrangement will be made for temporarily exhibiting them, so that each pattern may be clearly seen, but probably not before the Summer season, when there are many visitors to our Museum who have a special interest in dress materials and designs.[38]

So it would seem that elite materials, and especially those that reinforced the social hierarchy and the imperial venture, had a place in the museum, although the "curiosities" of the people, the ordinary and everyday items that reflected the recent history of the village and the lives of its people, including Museum Society members, did not.

The Visitors to the Museum

It is unlikely that many people came to Cawthorne solely to visit the museum. Rather, given the increasing amount of leisure time available to working people in the nearby industrial towns and villages, visiting the museum was one of a number of agreeable activities open to them along with enjoying the park at Cannon Hall, the surrounding woodland and Tivy Dale. Visitors patronized the two pubs, the temperance inn and the small tea shops that catered for their needs at busy times. For many villagers, trippers' spending was a welcome addition to their income. Mrs Morley, widowed with six sons, at "Easter and Whitsuntide . . . catered for wagonette loads of visitors to the village or for cycling club outings, providing plain teas at 1s 6d or ham and egg teas at 3s".[39]

Remarkably, almost the entire run of visitors' books from 1889, the date when the museum moved into its present building, has survived. Entries in the Visitors Book for 1891 show from the order of the signatures and the places of residence that many visitors came together in informal groups, and it has been possible to identify some of their occupations from the 1891 Census. This analysis shows an overwhelmingly working-class audience. For example, a group of neighbours from Blackmoorfoot Road, near Huddersfield, included two stone quarrymen and five women – their wives, two woollen weavers and the wife of an ironmonger's assistant. The church outing led by Rev William Surtees of Hoyland Common included among its twenty-one holidaymakers three coal miners, a colliery labourer and a deputy, a butcher and a blacksmith and their families. A gaggle of young women from Clayton West included a dressmaker, a worsted spinner, a worsted weaver, a cashmere weaver and a manufacturer of boots and shoes. A group of eighteen young men, all members of the Skelmanthorpe Naturalists Society, included six coal miners, a banksman, a colliery trammer, five fancy weavers, a joiner's apprentice and a general labourer – and these were given permission to use the museum to arrange their specimens.

During 1891, 2,609 people signed the book, of whom 285 came from Huddersfield, fourteen miles away, and 193 from Barnsley, four miles away. Although there is a sprinkling of middle-class people in the book, including visitors brought by the Spencer Stanhopes, it is clear that the majority of the visitors, like the Society's members, were from what would now be described as social groups C2, D, and E – exactly the audience that Pratt and Roddom Spencer Stanhope (and indeed Ruskin) would have hoped would visit and benefit from the museum. Unfortunately it is not known how the visitors actually responded to what they saw, because no one asked for their comments, but throughout this period the number of visitors remained steady at between 2,000 and 3,000 people per year.

After Pratt: Collecting the Everyday

A recent museum leaflet describes the museum as a "typical Victorian hotch potch",[40] but, in fact, the nature of the collections has changed considerably over time. Today, although many of the original collections are still to be seen in the museum, the greater part of the exhibition space is devoted to items of local and social interest, such as agricultural and trade tools, local photographs, domestic items and memorabilia. Pratt was emulating the museums with which he was familiar when he turned away from "mere curiosities" and endeavoured to acquire mainly natural history specimens, geology and antiquities, and to order these collections systematically and clearly, sometimes with the help of professional curators. According to Gaynor Kavanagh, no museums before 1914 "considered popular or cultural history in ways which were already well-established in the folk museums of Sweden, Norway and Denmark".[41] After 1918, and particularly in the 1930s, a growing number of volunteer-led village museums were established to collect everyday material that reflected the history of their own communities. Ashwell Village Museum in Hertfordshire, for example, which opened in December 1930, mainly through the initiative of two schoolboys, was "as far as possible to be limited to things found in Ashwell and the immediate countryside, things illustrative of the past history of the life of people in Ashwell and the district from the time of the Norman occupation to present days".[42]

At Cawthorne the long tradition of collecting primarily natural history and geology specimens seems to have been so important to the Society and to its committee that change was slow in coming. Charlesworth, secretary from 1918 and later curator, was, like Pratt, an amateur naturalist with an enthusiasm for antiquities, especially coins.[43] However, Noel Moxon, who succeeded him as curator from 1943 until 1979, is known to have been a keen local historian.[44] In August 1951, the museum, as part of the Festival of Britain, decided to hold a local history exhibition in September. It made an appeal to local people which brought in a wealth of material, as described in the Secretary's Report for 1951–52:

> A long table was erected down the centre of the Museum, on which were placed a variety of objects made and used in Cawthorne during the past 100 years. The large cases were used to house old china & crockery, including Coronation mugs and cups. Over 200 photographs were displayed on boards the majority being the work of Mr R. Wilkinson. The annex was largely occupied by old Church and Parish Accounts, Coronation details, old sporting records and Flower Show data.[45]

The exhibition ran for nearly a month and was a great success. It raised enough money to enable the committee to commence the purchase of the museum building from the Cannon Hall Estate. The following year, the

Secretary's Report stated that "a display case containing local history exhibits has been placed in the bay window",[46] which suggests that such material, which now forms the majority of the exhibits, had become a regular feature.

Continuity and Change

There is continuity as well as change in the story of Cawthorne's museum and of the Society. The series of winter lectures instigated by Pratt is still organized each year. The museum continues to attract between 2,000 and 3,000 visitors in its season. The trustees, committee and volunteers, some of whom are related to original members, are drawn from the village community. A current leaflet from the museum states, "We receive tremendous support in our efforts, especially from the villagers."[47] That support stems partly from the changed nature of the collection: it is hard to see a collection focussed on natural history and fragments from imperial and elite cultures sustaining such interest in a village community today.

"Cawthorne", the leaflet states, "is very proud of its Museum". That pride is justified in terms of the longevity of this volunteer museum. But more than the continuous service of 126 years what should be celebrated is the organizational framework, the Society – "the people themselves". The Society survived the departure of its original driving force, the decline of the Spencer Stanhope family after the First World War[48] and the economic and social changes of the twentieth century. It was able to do this because the volunteer museum society was sufficiently flexible to enable it to adapt to the changing nature of village life and to the changing aspirations of village museums. Perhaps this is the most important lesson that this seemingly unique history of a village museum offers to other volunteer-led museums today.

Notes

I am extremely grateful to the Cawthorne Museum Society for its generosity in allowing me free rein of its archives – in particular, Barry Jackson, Hon. President; Mary Herbert, Hon. Secretary; Leslie Herbert, Trustee; and Alan Broadhead, volunteer, for sharing their knowledge and enthusiasm without stint and for making my visits to Cawthorne so enjoyable. I would also like to thank John Coldwell, Local Studies Librarian, Archives and Local Studies Department, Barnsley Metropolitan Borough Council, for drawing my attention to the visit of the Yorkshire Naturalists Union to Cawthorne; and my supervisors at the University of Gloucestershire, Andrew Charlesworth and James Derounian.

1 Adrian Babbidge, "Forty Years On", *Cultural Trends* 14, 1 (2005), pp. 3–66
   Victor T. C. Middleton, *New Visions for Museums in the 21st Century* (London: Association of Independent Museums, 1998).
2 Peter Bailey, *Leisure and Class in Victorian England: rational recreation and the*

contest for control 1830–1885 (London: Routledge and Kegan Paul, 1978); Tony Bennett, *The Birth of the Museum: History, theory, politics* (London: Routledge, 1995); and H. Cunningham, "Leisure and Culture", in F. M. L. Thompson (ed.), *The Cambridge Social History of England, vol. 2* (Cambridge: Cambridge University Press, 1990). The Museums Act 1845, Public Libraries and Museums Act 1850, Public Libraries (Amendment) Act 1866 and Public Libraries Act 1892 – all gave impetus to the movement and enabled municipal authorities to provide support to museums from the rates. None of the legislation required them to do so, and the provision of museums is not a "statutory" service in England. County Councils, established in 1888, were not empowered to support museums until 1919. As Cunningham notes, "The public parks, museums and libraries were supported precisely because they were public, open to scrutiny and controlled by bye-laws. They quite deliberately aimed to enforce a certain standard of behaviour" (p. 324).

3   Geoffrey D. Lewis, "Collections, Collectors and Museums in Britain to 1920", in John M. A. Thompson, Douglas A. Bassett, D. Gareth Davies, Anthony J. Duggan, Geoffrey D. Lewis, and David R. Prince (eds), *The Manual of Curatorship* (London: Butterworth, 1984).

4   Gaynor Kavanagh, "History in Museums in Britain", in David Fleming, Crispin Paine and John G. Rhodes (eds), *Social History in Museums: A Handbook for Professionals* (London: HMSO, 1993).

5   Tony Bennett, "Museums and 'the people'", in Robert Lumley (ed.), *The Museum Time Machine: Putting cultures on display* (London: Routledge, 1988), p. 63.

6   Thomas Greenwood, *Museums and Art Galleries* (London: Simpkin, Marshall and Co., 1888). Greenwood supported Sunday opening and the evening opening of museums for "cheerful and constructive conversatziones" and for lectures in which "the use of the lantern is most advisable", all of which were to take place at Cawthorne. A section of his book was devoted to a description of the St George's Guild Museum at Walkley, Sheffield, set up by Ruskin in 1875. This collection is now exhibited in the Millennium Galleries, Sheffield.

7   *Post Office Directory of the West Riding of Yorkshire* (London: Kelly and Co,1889); Barry Jackson, *Cawthorne 1790–1990 – a South Yorkshire village remembers its past* (Cawthorne: Cawthorne Victoria Jubilee Museum, 1991); Bryan E. Coates, "The Geography of the Industrialization and Urbanization of South Yorkshire, 18th Century to 20th Century", in Sydney Pollard and Colin Holmes (eds), *Essays in the Economic and Social History of South Yorkshire* (Sheffield: South Yorkshire Council, 1976).

8   Julian Treuherz, *Pre-Raphaelitism: the second generation* (Grove Art Online, Oxford University Press [accessed 22 November 2007 at http://www.groveart.com/shared/views/article.html?section=art.069496.2]); Julian Treuherz, *Stanhope (John) Roddam Spencer* (Grove Art Online, Oxford University Press [accessed 22 November 2007] at <http://www.groveart.com /shared/views/article.html?section=art.080974]); and John Christian, ed, *The Last Romantics: the romantic tradition in British Art Burne-Jones to Stanley Spencer* (London: Lund Humphries, Catalogue of an exhibition held at the Barbican Art Gallery, 1989). Roddom Spencer Stanhope would have known John Ruskin, if only through their mutual friendship with Edward Burne-Jones. He would certainly have been aware of Ruskin's views on museums and may

even have known of his articles in the *Art Journal* of June and August 1880, on "A Museum or Picture Gallery": "A Museum, primarily, is to be for *simple* persons. Children, that is to say, and peasants. For your student, your antiquary or your scientific gentleman, there must be separate accommodation, or they must be sent elsewhere. The Town Museum is to be for the Town's People, the Village Museum for the Villagers. . . . The Museum is to manifest to these simple persons the beauty and life of all things and creatures in their perfectness." E. T. Cook and John Wedderburn, eds, *The Works of John Ruskin*, vol. XXXIV (London: George Allen, 1907) pp. 251–2.

9 Jackson, p. 35.

10 Bound copies of the *Cawthorne Parish Magazine* are held in the archives at the Victoria Jubilee Museum. The title of the magazine was changed to *Cawthorne Monthly Magazine* in January 1891, but for clarity, the abbreviation *CPM* will be used throughout this chapter. No page numbers are given.

11 Pratt was a keen amateur geologist. In 1909 the Yorkshire Naturalists' Union held one of its periodic field outings to Cawthorne, later written up in its journal, *The Naturalist*: "Cawthorne, on the outskirts of Barnsley, with its pit shafts and waste heaps, was the rendez-vous of the members of the Yorkshire Naturalists Union on Saturday August 28th. Notwithstanding the artificial excrescences on the landscape, the district contains much that appeals to the naturalist. Under the guidance of the Rev. C. T. Pratt and Mr W. Hemingway, the geologists secured from the shale heaps, beautiful club mosses and ferns, so well-preserved, that even their most minute structures could be examined. Some new and undescribed forms were obtained." *The Naturalist*, 1909, p. 393.

12 *CPM*, January 1884.

13 *CPM*, March 1884.

14 *CPM*, April 1884.

15 S. H. Miers, *A Report on the Public Museums of the British Isles (other than the National Museums) to the Carnegie United Kingdom Trustees* (Edinburgh: Carnegie United Kingdom Trustees, 1928). Personal communication from Hugh Hornby.

16 R. J. Morris, "Clubs, societies and associations", in F. M. L. Thompson, ed., *Cambridge Social History of Britain 1750–1950, vol. 3* (Cambridge: Cambridge University Press, 1990), p. 412.

17 "1. That the Society be called 'The Cawthorne Museum Society'. 2. That the subscription of members, payable on admission, be one shilling each year ending with December. 3. That members be entitled to free admission to the museum at such times as the Committee may determine it shall be open, and also, on showing their tickets of membership, to any Lectures which may be given in connection with the Society. 4. That until further notice the Museum be open on Monday evenings between 6.30 and 8 and on Saturdays from 4.30 to 6. 5. That admission to the Museum may be obtained by non-members on any week-day between 10 a.m. and 7 p.m. on application to the care-taker, or in company with any member of the Committee at any hour. A box is to be placed in the Room, into which non-members are required to pay not less than a penny". *CPM*, June 1884.

18 R. J. Morris, "Urban Associations in England and Scotland, 1750–1914", in Graeme Morton, Boudien de Vries, and R. J. Morris (eds), *Civil Society,*

Associations, and Urban Places: class, nation and culture in nineteenth-century Europe (Aldershot: Ashgate, 2006), p. 156.

19 *CPM,* June 1884.

20 Peter Brears, and Stuart Davies, *Treasures for the People: The story of museums and galleries in Yorkshire and Humberside* (Yorkshire and Humberside Museums Council, 1989).

21 Fretwell would seem to be more representative of the "artisan naturalists" of the early nineteenth century than of the 1880s (see David Elliston Allen, *The Naturalist in Britain – A Social History* (Harmondsworth: Penguin,1978). Jackson quotes a letter written by Miss Winifred Pratt to a local newspaper following Fretwell's death in 1933: "Tales used to be told of his enthusiasm when he found a specimen he had not known before – how he flung his hat in the air in Sherwood Forest, shouting 'Isn't this worth more than three weeks at Blackpool.' His fellow miners told how every bird, insect or flower was noticed by him on the way to and from the pit where he had worked since early years, and in any natural history discussion, John Fretwell's intimate knowledge of birds and beasts was to be relied on to settle the disputed point. He was also full of the old knowledge of the uses of herbs", Jackson, p. 54.

22 Information on the occupations of the Society's members and committee members as well as information on the occupations of the visitors to the museum was obtained from Census records accessed data via www.ancestry.co.uk.

23 Colin Rochester, Angela Ellis Paine, Steven Howlett, with Meta Zimmeck, *Volunteering and Society in the 21st Century* (Basingstoke: Palgrave Macmillan, 2010), p. 35. See also Colin Rochester, "One size does not fit all: four models of involving volunteers in small voluntary organisations" in Justin Davis Smith and Michael Locke (eds), *Volunteering and the Test of Time: Essays for policy, organisation and research* (London: Institute for Volunteering Research, 2007).

24 *CPM,* November 1892. Both Beatrice Pratt and James Balme were members of the Committee at this date.

25 *CPM,* March 1894.

26 Bridget Yates, forthcoming.

27 *CPM,* June 1895.

28 *CPM,* May 1896.

29 See, for example, Allen, *The Naturalist in Britain*; and Lynn Barber, *The Heyday of Natural History* (London: Jonathan Cape,1980).

30 *Museums Journal,* Supplement to vol. 2 (1903).

31 Ruskin made a number of donations of minerals to museums, including the British Museum (Natural History), and also to schools and colleges (Michael Wheeler, *Ruskin's Museums and Galleries: the treasury, the storehouse, the school: A paper given at the National Gallery, London, 21st November 1994* (London: Pilkington Press). In 1884, he gave a collection of 200 familiar minerals to a new museum in Kirkcudbright with a catalogue (Cook and Wedderburn, vol. XXVI, p. 259). Unfortunately, Ruskin does not appear to have sent a catalogue or a list with his collection to Cawthorne, and it is now impossible to identify his gift of minerals. Ruskin's connection with the museum at Cawthorne appears to be previously unknown.

32 *CPM,* March 1886.

33 *CPM,* April 1886.

34 Lawrence Goldman, "Ruskin, Oxford and the British Labour Movement 1880–1914" in Dinah Birch (ed.), *Ruskin and the Dawn of the Modern* (Oxford: Clarendon Press, 1999).

35 *CPM,* February 1900.

36 *CPM,* June 1884.

37 *CPM,* June 1890.

38 *CPM,* February 1895.

39 Jackson, p. 77.

40 Anon, *Cawthorne Victoria Jubilee Museum – A Brief History of the Museum and the Society,* not dated, acquired 2007.

41 Gaynor Kavanagh, *Museums and the First World War* (London: Leicester University Press, 1994), p. 19.

42 Unattributed newspaper cutting dated 5 December 1930 held in Ashwell Village Museum archives (Yates, unpublished research).

43 Douglas Charlesworth, *Manuscript Diary of 1915 to 1918* (photocopy in the possession of the Victoria Jubilee Museum, Cawthorne).

44 Jackson.

45 Victoria Jubilee Museum, Minute Book 1924–1990.

46 Minute Book.

47 Anon, *Brief History.*

48 See Alun Howkins *The Death of Rural England: A social history of the countryside since 1900* (London: Routledge, 2003). Cannon Hall was severely affected by mining subsidence. It is now a museum managed by Barnsley Metropolitan Borough Council.

Varieties of Voluntarism in the South Wales Coalfield, c.1880–1948

STEVEN THOMPSON

The welfare state, established in Britain after 1945, was built on a foundation of pre-existing provision of welfare and medical care which was broadly based, complex and multi-sectoral. Voluntary provision, in particular, had a layered ecology of providers, services and recipients, and this varied across time, place and social class both internally and externally in relation to other (state and private) provision in the mixed economy of care. Voluntary provision had many sources – trade unions and friendly societies, paternalistic employers and middle-class and elite philanthropists. It had many faces – voluntary hospitals and convalescent homes, visiting nurses, ambulance services and club practice medical care. It had many recipients – working people in different occupations, including those in the lower reaches of the middle classes; widows and orphans; discharged soldiers and sailors; and the old and infirm.

In south Wales voluntary provision included a full range of providers and delivered a full range of services to a full range of recipients, and so it would be quite easy to examine provision in the region as just a case study of voluntarism. A study of voluntarism in the region, however, offers something more valuable, since, remarkably often, different and even contested conceptions of the role and significance of voluntarism were articulated by different sections of coalfield society, and bitter disagreements occurred about the extent of the freedom and independence of both providers and recipients. This freedom was absolutely crucial, since it was, and indeed remains, a fundamental element of voluntary provision.[1] Such disagreements give a fascinating insight into meanings and understandings of voluntarism in modern British society and, where the very basis of voluntarism came to be challenged, its flexibility and enduring force.

Historians have long recognized that voluntary provision varied in a number of different ways – over time; from one place to another; *between* different welfare services; and *within* those services.[2] To date, however, recognition of such variations has largely been concerned with variations over time and variations between states, and insufficient attention has been paid to variations that existed between different regions of the same country. Recent authors have begun the process of evaluating the impact of devolutionary tendencies on the provision of welfare and medical services in modern Britain, but, even here the focus is on the nation or nation-state as the unit of analysis.[3] A regional perspective on voluntary provision offers a number of new and interesting insights that can sharpen our understanding of voluntarism and can better situate the provision of welfare and medical care in particular contexts.

It is clear that the character of voluntary provision varied geographically across Britain. In large cities, with their accumulations of wealth, greater social diversity, and concepts of civic pride, it took place in structured and somewhat impersonal interactions and was delivered by sophisticated voluntary organisations with developed constitutions and bodies of rules. In rural areas it took place in face-to-face interactions and was delivered by the gentry and aristocracy, with their concept of *noblesse oblige* to tenants and the other inhabitants of agricultural communities. In many industrial towns and villages, which might be described as "company towns", it took place in workplace schemes that mixed benevolence with coercion and was delivered by paternalistic employers. In the South Wales Coalfield, as in other coalfields, it was delivered to a greater extent through self-help and mutualism, since uncaring or absent employers and a small middle class were overshadowed in importance by the organisations and societies established within the labour movement by workers and their families to look after their own welfare and that of their neighbours and work colleagues.

Many commentators throughout the second half of the nineteenth and first half of the twentieth centuries bemoaned the stunted development of voluntary provision of welfare and medical services in the South Wales Coalfield and attributed this chiefly to lack of action by the region's employers. In the early 1850s the *Morning Chronicle*'s correspondent noted, for example, that Merthyr Tydfil possessed no almshouses, endowed charities or hospitals, despite the large fortunes won in the town, and residents continued to note the absence of a hospital until late into the century.[4] Forty years later Thomas Bircham, Poor Law inspector for Wales, noted the undeveloped nature of philanthropic provision in the region and attributed it to absence of people other than those from the "labouring classes" in the valleys of south Wales.[5] In 1920 the Consultative Council on Medical and Allied Services in Wales found that the need to provide institutions and services in parts of Wales such as the coalfield was "exceedingly urgent", because of the failure of voluntary provision in the preceding decades.[6] In 1945 the survey of hospital provision in Britain found that south Wales was the least well-provided for region in terms of beds per head of population and the standard of the hospitals provided.[7] Therefore, a study of provision in south Wales confirms, if confirmation were needed, that there was considerable variation in the character and extent of voluntary provision across Britain during the nineteenth and twentieth centuries.[8]

South Wales: Economy, Community and Trade Unionism

The distinctive shape of voluntary provision in south Wales was due on the one hand to the particular characteristics of coalfield communities relative to other communities and on the other hand to the particular characteristics of south Wales relative to other coalfields.[9] South Wales developed early as an industrial region. From the second half of the eighteenth century the copper industry that was located in and around Swansea and, more importantly, the iron industry that stretched east and west from Merthyr Tydfil along the northern outcrop of the coalfield attracted people from surrounding rural areas and helped create new communities. The coal industry, which served these growing metal industries, was still of only very minor importance in the region in the late eighteenth and early nineteenth centuries and was certainly of less importance than the coal production of the Great Northern Coalfield of Durham and Northumberland.

But with technological developments and changes in its organization, the coal industry developed rapidly in the second half of the nineteenth century, as deeper pits were sunk in the central part of the coalfield. Coal was undoubtedly king. By 1913 the industry employed almost a quarter of a million men and boys, and production stood at 57 million tonnes a year.[10] Crowded, urban communities were formed in ribbon developments along the bottoms of the Rhondda, Cynon, Rhymney and other valleys in these latter decades of the century as thousands of people were attracted to the region from neighbouring Welsh and English counties. Despite the presence of certain metal industries in the region, these were largely mono-industrial communities, completely dependent on coal and possessing a very simple social structure dominated by miners and their families.[11]

Industrial relations in south Wales were relatively peaceful and conciliatory in the second half of the nineteenth century.[12] A Sliding Scale mechanism that pegged wages to the selling price of coal persuaded many of the identity of interest that existed between employers and workers, while the failure to establish a coalfield-wide trade union, as miners in other coalfields had done, undermined the ability of the south Wales miners to take concerted, effective industrial action.

However, this changed with the formation of the South Wales Miners' Federation in 1898 after a long industrial dispute. The "Fed", as it was known, grew very rapidly and soon won a reputation as one of the most militant of miners' trade unions – and indeed as one of the most militant of all trade unions in Britain. The Edwardian period was punctuated by a series of bitter, often violent, industrial disputes that were resumed after the hiatus of the First World War and culminated in 1926 in the dramatic lockout that followed the General Strike.

A cause, and indeed a consequence, of this industrial unrest was the increasing radicalization of certain sections of the labour movement in the region. Socialist missionaries toured the valleys in the latter years of the nineteenth century, but it was perhaps for its syndicalism, or, more accurately, industrial unionism, of the late Edwardian period that south Wales gained a reputation as a "cockpit for industrial conflict and class bitterness without parallel in the British Isles".[13] This reputation was heightened by the strength of support for the Communist Party in the coalfield in the interwar period, although it should be noted that the Labour Party was the main recipient of the political loyalties of the south Wales miners.

Employers, Voluntarism and Control

One of the most notable examples of voluntary provision of welfare and medical services in late nineteenth-century south Wales, and one that demonstrates the contested and controversial character of voluntarism, was the Monmouthshire and South Wales Miners' Permanent Provident Society, established in 1881. Similar to schemes established in other British coalfields, the Permanent Provident Fund was established to provide for men injured in colliery accidents and for the families of men killed in accidents.[14] Members of the Society paid a weekly sum from their wages, and their employers, if they chose to do so, paid a sum equal to one quarter of that sum into the Fund.

The main founder of the Society, and the first chairman of the Board of Management, was William Thomas Lewis (later Lord Merthyr of Senghenydd), one of the most prominent industrialists in south Wales in the decades before the First World War. Formerly agent of the Bute estate, Lewis built up his colliery holdings in the Rhondda, Cynon and Rhymney Valleys and owned much of Cardiff docks, in addition to numerous other enterprises. A Conservative and Anglican, he was an unbending and militantly anti-union employer, responsible for the creation of the Monmouthshire and South Wales Coalowners' Association. As Sidney Webb stated in the 1890s, Lewis was "the best-hated man" among the Welsh working class, while more recently the historian K. O. Morgan has likened him to a Texas "robber-baron".[15]

It seems, to some extent at least, therefore, that this instance of voluntary provision was an attempt on Lewis's part to undermine the appeal of trade unions, since unions often offered "friendly" benefits of the type provided by the Society. More importantly, perhaps, the creation of the Society can be viewed as an anti-statist measure designed to avoid statutory obligations under the new Employers' Liability Act 1880 and an attempt to discourage any further statutory interventions. Efforts were made by the employers in south Wales to establish a fund in 1878 to "contract out" any liabilities imposed by an Employers' Liability Bill that was then before Parliament. These efforts failed in the teeth of workers' opposition, but, when the Employers' Liability Act was passed in 1880, employers in south Wales forced the establishment of the Society and undertook to ensure that as many miners as possible agreed to forego their rights under the legislation and make "joint provision" with their employers by joining the Society. "Joint provision", voluntarily entered into by employers and workers, was infinitely preferable, according to supporters of the Fund, to a statutory legal framework to govern the relationship between the two parties.[16] Employers insisted that it would be cheaper for them to indemnify themselves against the costs of any industrial injuries but that they chose, voluntarily, to enter into this "mutual provident fund", because it promoted better industrial relations and co-operation.[17] The very existence of the Society, therefore, was an assertion of the importance and effectiveness of voluntary over statutory provision.

And yet this Society also demonstrates the beginnings of a critique of the voluntary provision of welfare and medical services by the labour movement in the region.[18] Doubts were raised about the voluntary character of the Society right from its inception, as complaints were voiced that workmen were coerced to contract out of their rights under the legislation and join the Society. David Morgan, miners' agent at Aberdare, insisted that the Society was in the control of the employers, despite claims to the contrary, and that colliery managers and officials placed undue pressure on their workmen to join the Society.[19] For their part, employers who supported the Society were repeatedly forced to deny any compulsion.[20]

This opposition to employers' voluntary arrangements grew in extent towards the end of the century, when Workmen's Compensation legislation drew even greater attention to industrial accidents and injuries. The Rhondda No.1 District of the Federation, for example, sought to persuade its members to leave the Fund and utilize the provisions of the 1897 Act and faced considerable difficulties in extricating workmen from the Fund as a result of employers' actions.[21] Therefore, this instance of voluntarism was, if critics are to be believed, coercive in character and intended to undermine the appeal of trade unions. It was also intended as an anti-statist measure to discourage state regulation of the relationship between workers and employers. The voluntarism advocated by industrialists, middle-class philanthropists and other elites of these valley communities thus had very definite political and industrial aims and was increasingly challenged and rejected, particularly in the first decade of the twentieth century, as the labour movement in south Wales became more class conscious and industrially militant.

The Society was, however, a less controversial area of voluntary provision in late nineteenth- and early twentieth-century south Wales than the control of "club practice" medical care. Many industrialists in the region employed doctors funded by deductions, often compulsory, from their workers' wages. Such doctors could not be dismissed by workmen and received the whole of the money that accrued from these weekly deductions. There was a trend at the end of the nineteenth century and in the first decade of the twentieth century for workmen to gain control of the money deducted from weekly wage packets, appoint doctors directly and pay them set salaries. This issue of control of club practices was a very bitter area of contention, and the voluntary nature of such arrangements was called into doubt. The older works' clubs, in which doctors received the total sum from the weekly deductions from workers' wages and were appointed by employers, were described as "exploitative", "tyrannical", "extortionate" and "oppressive" and the workers were said to exist in "bondage" and "slavery".[22] Those who opposed these arrangements and advocated reform of the system argued that they sought "justice", "liberty", "freedom", "emancipation", "salvation", "respect" and "equality".[23]

Such struggles had been evident in the very earliest part of the nineteenth century but were given greater impetus by the Employers' Liability and Workmen's Compensation legislation of the late nineteenth and early twentieth centuries that made the injuries of workmen a financial consideration for coal employers and control of the appointment of doctors a crucial issue in the context of compensation cases. Such battles again demonstrate that class analyses of voluntarism were particularly common in south Wales, since different areas of voluntary provision of welfare and medical services were the cause of disagreement and dispute, and indeed since the voluntary character of provision was called into question. They also demonstrate the fundamental importance of freedom as a constituent element of voluntary provision.

Mutualism, Socialism and Voluntarism

While the provision of medical attendance was the most controversial aspect of voluntarism in south Wales, the provision of that most emblematic aspect of British voluntarism – voluntary hospitals – was also controversial and became increasingly more so as the new class analysis gained popular support. Hospital provision in nineteenth-century south Wales was mainly confined to the coastal towns of Newport, Cardiff and Swansea, and only with the more rapid development of the coal industry in the latter decades of the nineteenth century were hospitals, albeit small, cottage hospitals, founded in the coalfield.[24]

In towns such as Pontypool, Maesteg and Abertillery discussions about the founding of small accident hospitals in the first decade of the twentieth century included suggestions from socialists and other members of the labour movement that hospitals be rate-aided rather than funded by voluntary contributions.[25] The most sustained calls for a rate-aided rather than voluntary institution came in Pontypridd in the winter of 1907–08, when different groups within the community differed in their evaluations of the fairness of voluntarism and their estimations of the relative merits of public and voluntary provision. Prominent individuals in the local labour movement, or "rate-aiders" as they were dubbed, argued that hospitals should not be left to the "vagaries of charity" or the generosity of private individuals, since this conferred privileges on donors and left without rights those individuals unable to make large contributions. They argued that "unless a man belonged to a certain clique or was a member of a certain political party, or denomination, they have to bow and scrape, cap in hand". A rate-aided hospital, on the other hand, would be democratically managed by the district council and would be supported by all members of the community equally through the rates.[26] Public provision was therefore far preferable to voluntary provision.

In contrast, some members of the middle class and local industrialists, or "voluntaryists" as they were described in the local newspaper coverage, argued that "poor ratepayers", including working-class families, would bear the burden of funding the hospital if it were built and maintained out of the rates through having to pay higher rents. They asserted that a rate-aided institution was inconsistent with freedom of action and that fund-raising would be more productive if contributors were asked rather than coerced to give.[27]

In the event, the power of the middle-class "voluntaryists" and their supporters among the local industrialists was too much for the "rate-aiders" to withstand, and a voluntary hospital was opened in the town in 1911. Significantly, even as the labour movement gained in power in south Wales in the following decades, the accident hospitals that were established were voluntary in character, which may be evidence of the power of voluntarism, but also, perhaps, of its flexibility in adapting to a range of different contexts.

This attack upon, and rejection of, philanthropic voluntarism grew in strength and extent as the twentieth century progressed and is most evident in south Wales in relation to the Federation. Its responses to voluntary provision and its own methods of medical and welfare provision tell us not only a great deal about the contested nature of these aspects of modern British culture but also about the enduring hold of voluntarism on the British welfare system.

The Federation made extensive social and welfare provision for its members, their families and the communities in which its lodges were situated.[28] It provided many services directly: "comforts funds" for artificial limbs, false teeth, trusses, and other surgical and medical appliances to injured workers; "Little" or "Special" funds for small cash sums to aid members and their families in times of difficulty; strike pay, victimisation pay and out-of-work payments for members in these particular circumstances; ambulance funds for transport to hospitals for miners who required medical treatment; and other funds for a whole range of additional causes and needs. In making such provision, the Federation clearly intended to better the lives of its members and their families, but it also intended to attract and retain members, to provide them with the means to challenge their employers and blacklegs more effectively, and to regulate the labour market to its advantage. Just like employers, therefore, trade unions were motivated by a whole range of different considerations and looked to do far more than merely improve people's lives through the voluntary provision of medical and welfare services.

The different forms of direct welfare provision made by the Federation demonstrate the mutualism that was at the heart of a great deal of voluntary provision in south Wales, especially that provision made by trade unions. While membership conferred rights of eligibility on members, and while appeals for assistance of different kinds were occasionally rejected, nevertheless this was not a form of welfare provision that was run on strict actuarial insurance principles, where members gained carefully-defined rights to services as a result of strictly-observed rules of eligibility. Rather, officials of the Federation, similar to those in other trade unions, endeavoured to be as generous as the funds of the union allowed and, crucially, on occasion, distributed assistance according to the needs of the members and families involved rather than according to strict rules of eligibility. They made a real effort to defend and support the most vulnerable members of the workforce and the community. This mutualism was reflected in the schemes set up for aged and infirm miners who found themselves without work in the first decade of the twentieth century because of the Workmen's Compensation legislation;[29] in the provision of out-of-work payments to boys aged under sixteen and men aged over sixty-five not eligible for unemployment benefit in the interwar period;[30] and in the donations and contributions to a whole range of charities and causes, whether local, regional or national.

This mutualism was perhaps most evident in south Wales in the club practices through which workers arranged for medical attendance for themselves and their families. In those instances where workmen had wrested control from their employers efforts were made to develop them into non-profit schemes that offered a comprehensive range of services to their members. Almost uniquely in Britain, the schemes in south Wales were funded on the "poundage" system whereby workers paid 2d. or 3d. in each pound of their wages. As was noted by a member of one of these schemes, "Now we can help the others, and hundreds and hundreds there are, who, if they did not club together in this kind of way, would never be able to get any doctor at all".[31] This was a very different voluntarism to that expressed through philanthropic action, never mind that which motivated employers' paternalism.

Not only did the Federation's provision of welfare to its members and their families indicate its belief in the rightness of collectivist and mutualist provision as opposed to individualistic and patronising philanthropy, but its critique of voluntarism also led to a focus on the state as the collectivist provider of welfare and medical services. At a local level this commitment was reflected in the close involvement of the Federation and the broader labour movement in valleys' communities and in district and county council politics. Local lodges of the Federation and coalitions within the trades and labour councils expended a great deal of time and effort in the support of the Labour Party's candidates in local elections who, once elected, were expected to advocate the extension of local authorities' welfare and medical provision.[32] In such activities can also be found another important link between voluntarism and the state.

In addition to this focus on local authorities as the communal providers of welfare services, the Federation gave attention to the role of the central state in provision for different groups of the population. It passed resolutions calling for state provision of universal, non-contributory pensions payable at sixty-five years of age in 1902[33]; state funding of hospital services in 1907[34]; state funding of institutes for the blind in 1919[35]; an "all-in" scheme of insurance that would cover health and unemployment insurance, national assistance, pensions, and industrial injuries compensation in 1927[36]; state payment of firemen and safety-men in 1929[37]; and state funding for pit-head baths in conjunction with the Miners' Welfare Fund in 1933.[38] Given the strength of feeling in favour of the nationalisation of the coal industry, it is not particularly surprising that the south Wales miners should view the state's provision of welfare and medical care so favourably.[39]

Other historians have demonstrated how trade unions and other organisations within the labour movement were suspicious and indeed resistant to provision of welfare and medical care by the state, but it is clear that the Federation was different in this regard and positively advocated state provision.[40] Perhaps it did so because it recognized that voluntary provision could not possibly bring about the socialist utopia it desired and that only the state had the power and the resources to re-make the world along more collectivist and mutualist lines. As such, it was forced into an uneasy reliance on voluntary provision that perhaps went against its more mutualist preferences. Indeed, it was required to arrange access to the more traditional and individualistic voluntary services for its members: it collected regular subscriptions from members and paid them to hospitals to gain rights to care; it occasionally imposed levies on members to pay the annual subscriptions to The Rest Convalescent Home, Porthcawl; and it also procured in similar fashion rights to the services provided by ambulance brigades and nursing associations. As far as hospitals and the local convalescent home were concerned, it collected payments and received tickets of admission and distributed these among members that needed their services. In so doing it served as a facilitator of members' access in much the same way as did prominent landowners and employers.

One of the avowed aims of the Federation, at least from 1917, was the "abolition of capital", but it is clear from this involvement in voluntary provision that the necessary corollaries of this policy were not easy to maintain in a capitalist economy.[41] The failure of the Federation fundamentally to transform voluntarism suggests how very deeply this ideology had penetrated British culture and the extent to which it dominated welfare provision even in an area such as south Wales where voluntarism was relatively weak. As such, it might be argued that the provision of welfare and medical services by trade unions such as the Federation set out to reform capitalism rather than overthrow it. Nevertheless, perhaps the Labour Party's welfare settlement after the Second World War constituted the triumph of the Federation's vision via the influence of two of its most prominent former members, James Griffiths and Aneurin Bevan who, as Ministers for National Insurance and Health respectively, were the two main architects of the British welfare state.[42] The careers of these two men, it might be argued, encapsulated the idea of a "moving frontier" between the voluntarism and the state.

Conclusion

A study of south Wales suggests that voluntarism varied from region to region and that its specific form was determined by the particular economic activities, social structures and political traditions of those regions. In south Wales, the social structures of coalmining communities, dominated by miners and their institutions and unleavened by a critical mass of middle-class philanthropists and interventionist industrialists and landowners, resulted in voluntarism shaped by the mutualism and self-help of organisations in the labour movement. The increasing militancy of the miners and their trade union in the twentieth century resulted in an attack on employers' voluntarism as coercive, unjust and ineffective and indeed prompted a critical reconsideration of the very nature of voluntarism. This debate fore-grounded freedom as an essential part of voluntarism and demonstrated that it was worth fighting for – and over. And, paradoxically, this fight for the soul of voluntarism led many, particularly the more ideologically-committed members of the labour movement, down the path towards state provision.

Notes

1 Geoffrey Finlayson, *Citizen, State, and Social Welfare in Britain, 1830–1990* (Oxford: Oxford University Press, 1994), p. 8.

2 Norman Johnson, *Mixed Economies of Welfare: A Comparative Perspective* (London: Prentice-Hall Europe, 1999), p. 23; Norman Johnson, "Problems for the Mixed Economy of Welfare", in Robert E. Goodin and Deborah Mitchell (eds), *The Foundations of the Welfare State*, vol. 1 (Cheltenham: Edward Elgar, 2000), pp. 361–2; Martin Powell, "The mixed economy of welfare and the social division of welfare", in Martin Powell (ed.), *Understanding the Mixed Economy of Welfare* (Bristol: Policy Press, 2007), p. 3.

3 Charles Webster, "Devolution and the Health Service in Wales, 1919–1969", in Pamela Michael and Charles Webster (eds), *Health and Society in Twentieth-Century Wales* (Cardiff: University of Wales Press, 2006), pp. 240–69; John Stewart, "The National Health Service in Scotland, 1947–74: Scottish or British?", *Historical Research* 76, 193 (2003): 389–410; Chris Nottingham (ed.), *The N.H.S. in Scotland: The Legacy of the Past and the Prospect of the Future* (Aldershot: Ashgate, 2000).

4 Jules Ginswick (ed.), *Labour and the Poor in England and Wales 1849–1851: The Letters to The Morning Chronicle. Vol. III: The Mining and Manufacturing Districts of South Wales and North Wales* (London: Cass, 1983), p. 74; *Western Mail*, 12 June 1883; *Merthyr Express*, 26 February 1881 and 24 July 1886. A General Hospital was founded in Merthyr Tydfil in 1888.

5 Local Government Board, *Twentieth Annual Report* [C.6460], 1890–91, xxxiii, p. 257.

6 Ministry of Health, *First Report of the Welsh Consultative Council on Medical and Allied Services in Wales* [Cmd.703], 1920, xvii, pp. 5–6.

7 Martin Powell, "How Adequate was Hospital Provision before the NHS? An examination of the 1945 South Wales Hospital Survey", *Local Population Studies* 48 (1992): 22–32.

8 Important in this regard is Julian Tudor Hart, "The Inverse Care Law", *The Lancet*, 27 February 1971: 405–12.

9 On coalfields and the particularities of south Wales, see Stefan Berger, Andy Croll and Norman LaPorte (eds), *Towards a Comparative History of Coalfield Societies* (Aldershot: Ashgate, 2005).

10 On the economic development of south Wales, see A. H. John, *The Industrial Development of South Wales 1750–1850: An essay* (Cardiff: University of Wales Press, 1950); John Davies, *A History of Wales* (London: Penguin, 1993); Gwyn A. Williams, *When Was Wales? A History of the Welsh* (London: Penguin, 1985).

11 Chris Williams, *Capitalism, Community and Conflict: The South Wales Coalfield, 1898–1947* (Cardiff: University of Wales Press, 1998).

12 On industrial relations in the coal industry see J. H. Morris and L. J. Williams, *The South Wales Coal Industry, 1841–1875* (Cardiff: University of Wales Press, 1958); and Hywel Francis and David Smith, *The Fed: A History of the South Wales Miners in the Twentieth Century* (London: Lawrence & Wishart, 1980).

13 K. O. Morgan, *Rebirth of a Nation: Wales 1880–1980* (Oxford: Oxford University Press, 1981), p. 74.

14 John Benson, "Coalminers, Coalowners and Collaboration: The Miners' Permanent Relief Fund Movement in England, 1860–1895", *Labour History Review* 68, 2 (2003): 181–94.

15 Neil Evans, "Cardiff's Labour Tradition", *Llafur* 4, 2 (1985): 78; Morgan, *Rebirth of a Nation*, p. 69.

16 For an example of this idea being voiced by Lewis, see Cymdeithas Ddarbodawl Barhaol Mwnwyr Swydd Fynwy a Deheudir Cymru, *Anerchiad gan Mr. W. Thomas Lewis* (Aberdare, 1881), p. 6.

17 *Western Mail*, 9 February 1881.

18 For an account that emphasizes the collaboration that sustained similar societies in other coalfields, see Benson, "Coalminers, Coalowners and Collaboration".

19 *Western Mail*, 9 February 1881.

20 See, for example, The Monmouthshire and South Wales Miners' Permanent Provident Society, *Report of the Proceedings at the Second Annual General Meeting, March 27th, 1883, and Statement of Accounts to December 31st, 1882* (Aberdare, 1883), pp. 12–13; and *The Provident* (March, 1881), p. 2 and (March, 1882), p. 122.

21 Monthly Reports of the Rhondda No.1 District of the Miners' Federation, 4 January 1904; 4 February 1904; 6 February 1905, 21 August 1905.

22 For examples of such language see *Merthyr Express*, 1 February 1902 and 29 October 1904; and *Rhondda Leader*, 23 September 1905.

23 For examples see *Merthyr Express*, 11 January 1902 and 25 January 1902; *Rhondda Leader*, 23 November 1907; *Aberdare Leader*, 29 March 1913 and 19 April 1913.

24 For more on this see Steven Thompson, "To relieve the sufferings of humanity, irrespective of party, politics or creed: Conflict, consensus and voluntary hospital provision in Edwardian south Wales", *Social History of Medicine* 16, 2 (2003): 247–62.

25 *Pontypool Free Press*, 22 November 1901; *Glamorgan Gazette*, 2 October 1908 and 9 October 1908; *South Wales Gazette*, 14 July 1922.

26 *Pontypridd Observer*, 18 January 1908 and 15 February 1908, Supplement; see also Pontypridd Trades and Labour Council, minutes of meetings, 1906–8. Keir Hardie articulated this criticism in very strong terms in 1901 when, in a letter to a local newspaper, he urged secretaries of charitable causes not to solicit funds from him. Apart from having no funds to donate, Hardie was opposed to charitable giving and viewed it as a form of corruption by which individuals bought a good reputation and appealed to voters in elections; *Merthyr Express*, 13 April 1901.

27 *Pontypridd Observer*, 18 January 1908 and 15 February 1908, Supplement.

28 For a more detailed treatment of the Federation's provision, see Steven Thompson, "'Brodyr trwyadl mewn tywydd garw': Welfare provision and the social centrality of the South Wales Miners' Federation", *Welsh History Review* 24, 4 (2009): 141–67.

29 Monthly Reports of the Rhondda No.1 District of the Miners' Federation, 1901–7, *passim*.

30 South Wales Miners' Federation, Minutes of Council Meetings, Annual and Special Conferences, 1920–39, *passim*.

31 *Merthyr Express*, 25 January 1902.

32 Chris Williams, "Labour and the challenge of local government, 1919–1939", in Duncan Tanner, Chris Williams and Deian Hopkin (eds), *The Labour Party in Wales, 1900–2000* (Cardiff: University of Wales Press, 2000), pp. 140–65.

33 Monthly Reports of the Rhondda No.1 District of the Miners' Federation, 3 February 1902; the Annual Conference made a similar call in 1907: South Wales Miners' Federation, Minutes of Annual Conference, 18–20 March 1907, p. 14.

34 Monthly Reports of the Rhondda No.1 District of the South Wales Miners' Federation, 30 November 1907; also, Caerau Lodge, Annual, General and Committee Meetings minutes, Committee meeting, 28 February 1918.

35 South Wales Miners' Federation, Minutes of Council Meetings, Annual and Special Conferences, 21 March 1919.

36 *Ibid.*, Annual Conference, 1 and 2 July 1927; see also South Wales Miners' Federation, Minutes of Council Meetings, Annual and Special Conferences, Annual Conference, 22–23 November 1932; and South Wales Miners' Federation, Minutes of Council Meetings, Annual and Special Conferences, 17 August 1934.

37 South Wales Miners' Federation, Minutes of Council Meetings, Annual and Special Conferences, Annual Conference, 21 and 22 June 1929.

38 *Ibid.*, Annual Conference 15–16 September 1933.

39 Bill Jones, Brian Roberts and Chris Williams, "'Going from darkness to the light': South Wales miners' attitudes towards nationalisation", *Llafur* 7, 1 (1996): 96–110.

40 Henry Pelling, "The Working Class and the Origins of the Welfare State", in *Popular Politics and Society in Late Victorian Britain* (London: Macmillan, 1979), pp. 1–18; José Harris, "Did British workers want the welfare state? G. D. H. Cole's Survey of 1942", in Jay Winter (ed.), *The Working Class in Modern British History* (Cambridge: Cambridge University Press, 1983), pp. 200–14; Pat Thane, "The Working Class and State 'Welfare' in Britain, 1880–1914", *Historical Journal* 27, 4 (1984): 877–900.

41 Francis and Smith, *The Fed*, pp. 24–5.

42 Both Bevan and Griffiths claimed that their experiences in the South Wales Miners' Federation inspired and influenced the choices and decisions they made in planning welfare reforms after the Second World War; see David Green, *Working-Class Patients and the Medical Establishment* (Aldershot: Gower, 1985), p. 175; James Griffiths, *Pages From Memory* (London: Dent, 1969), p. 82.

Quintin Hogg and the Original Polytechnic

BRENDA WEEDEN

The word "polytechnic" disappeared from the British education system in 1992 when the Higher and Further Education Act abolished all the remaining distinctions between polytechnics and universities. This brought to an end more than a hundred years of a distinctive approach to education which had its origins in the establishment by Quintin Hogg of the original Polytechnic in London's Regent Street. The author's interest in the Polytechnic stems from her appointment in 1994 to establish the archive at the University of Westminster – the successor to the Polytechnic which still has its headquarters building at 309 Regent Street. This led to an exploration of the development and particular characteristics of Hogg's philanthropy, and also (more tentatively) of what was lost and gained in its shift from a private organization to an institution which was part of the educational system administered by local government.

This chapter thus reviews the life and philanthropic career of Hogg leading to the foundation of his Polytechnic; discusses the unique character of this pioneering venture into education for young men and women of the "poorer classes"; and looks briefly at the development of the broader poly-technic movement. In the process it aims to throw light on the motivation of a leading philanthropist of the late Victorian age as well as offering some thoughts about the ways in which the original aims of the founders of voluntary agencies can be changed by circumstances. It is based to a large extent on primary sources – and has particularly drawn on the pages of the *Polytechnic Magazine* founded by Hogg in 1879. These provide a rather different perspective from that of more established accounts which describe the polytechnic movement either as an exercise in "enlightened self-interest"[1] or as a means of social control. What emerges instead is an emphasis on self-help and developing the individual. The overriding impression from the internal sources is of a strong sense of community, which played a very important part in the lives of many of those – members, students, staff or volunteers – who belonged to it.

Quintin Hogg

Quintin Hogg's background was one of privilege; he was born into a wealthy and influential family, and educated at Eton, where he excelled at football. When he left school to work in the City, he was given a business opportunity by a family connection that enabled him to build a lucrative career. At first glance Hogg appears to fit the stereotype of a Victorian "do-gooder", but the reality is both more complex and more elusive.

The main source for Hogg's life is the biography written by his youngest daughter, Ethel Hogg[2], which was first published in 1904, within two years of his death. There is no known reason why Ethel was chosen to write the book although it has been suggested that it was considered a suitable task for an unmarried daughter (Ethel was born in 1876 and did not marry until she was 30). She was able to draw on the memories of many who knew her father, as well as to borrow his letters back from their recipients. Since his personal papers have apparently not survived, this makes the book a unique source. It is also a frustrating one. Ethel was one of the few members of Hogg's immediate family who, in her youth, did not share his commitment to the Polytechnic. Her involvement did not begin until after 1945 but continued until she died on her 94th birthday in 1970. In later life she often spoke of how jealous she was of the Polytechnic as a young woman because her parents and beloved sister gave all their time to it. This may explain why her father remains a rather remote figure, especially in the second half of the book.

The driving force in Hogg's life was his Christian faith. His mother gave him a small Bible in May 1855, when he was ten. It was found open on his desk the day he died; the many annotations in tiny handwriting are testimony to its constant use.[3] His family was Anglican, but Hogg himself disliked religious ceremony and was not a regular churchgoer. At Eton he began a Sunday afternoon meeting for bible reading and prayer in his room. A number of boys joined him, and apparently it was only his prowess at football that saved him from general ridicule.[4]

Hogg left Eton at Christmas 1863. His journey to work from his parents' home in Carlton Gardens, St. James's, to his office in Mincing Lane in the City, was a short one, but it brought him into contact with the extremes of wealth and poverty which characterized Victorian London. Tom Pelham, a school friend who was to join Hogg in his early voluntary work, later remembered that the area near Hungerford Bridge, the Adelphi Arches and Temple Pier, was one where "many ragged boys found their playground by day and their dormitory (under arches or in boxes, etc) by night", and that passers-by were often accosted by shoeless children, begging or trying to sell papers or lights.[5]

The eighteen-year old Hogg was deeply affected by what he saw, most especially by the plight of the children, who lacked everything that he most valued in his own life. He was determined to help, although his first attempt met with failure. His version of the story is often retold in accounts of the Polytechnic's history:

> My first attempt was to get a couple of crossing-sweepers whom I picked up near Trafalgar Square, and offered to teach them how to read. In those days the Thames embankment did not exist, and the Adelphi Arches were open to both the tide and the street. With an empty beer bottle for a candle stick and a tallow candle for illumination, your humble servant as teacher, and a couple of Bibles as reading books, what grew into the Polytechnic was practically started.[6]

The lesson ended as a policeman approached; one boy shouted a code word to the other and both ran off, leaving Hogg to explain his presence. Hogg always told this story against himself, to show that his ignorance of the boys' language and way of life meant that in spite of his intentions he was ill-equipped to help them.

In order to address this lack of understanding of the boys' lives, Hogg purchased a second-hand shoeblack's uniform and kit, and for several winter months spent his time after work in the streets around the Strand, attempting to earn a few pence, and sleeping rough under tarpaulins on Thames barges or on a ledge in the Adelphi Arches, returning home to wash and breakfast before leaving for the City. At the same time he was taking advice on how best to direct his energies. He was also being drawn into the network of well-to-do evangelical families which frequently met in the home of Lord and Lady Kinnaird at 2 Pall Mall East, just around the corner from the Hogg family home in Carlton Gardens. Quintin's school-fellow Arthur, who later became the 11th Lord Kinnaird, was to be a life-long friend. Another close friend was Frank Bevan, son of R.C.L. Bevan of Barclays Bank; Frank was later to marry Hogg's sister Constance. Many of Hogg's future supporters can be traced back to this influential group.

Some of the particular characteristics of Hogg's philanthropy can be identified at an early stage of his work. The first is that, whatever new direction his work took, he remained essentially a missionary whose fundamental aim was to bring individuals to salvation in Christ. He continued to teach Bible classes and preach throughout his life. Hogg became close friends with the American evangelist Dwight L Moody. In spite of the social differences between the two men, they had much in common, combining strong religious conviction with much practical business sense-

and a schoolboy sense of humour. During Moody and Sankey's visit to London in 1875, Moody stayed with Hogg and Sankey with the Kinnaird family. Quintin Hogg and Arthur Kinnaird helped to organize the campaign. Hogg acquired brief notoriety in establishment circles when he arranged for Moody to visit Eton to preach to the boys. The proposed visit caused a storm of protest expressed in letters to *The Times* and questions in the House of Lords. E.H. Knatchbull-Hugesson (later Baron Brabourne) wrote:

> Such performances are excusable in the case of the large masses of people whom the agencies of Church and Dissent have failed to reach, but this cannot be applicable to Eton boys, while at their age spasmodic and sensational religion is likely to be productive of evil rather than good.[7]

In the event, the visit took place without incident outside the school grounds, but this episode does serve to illustrate both the strength of Hogg's convictions and his independence of mind.

Throughout his life, Hogg combined paid employment with personal involvement in philanthropic work. During the 1870s and 1880s he made a personal fortune from the import of sugar from estates in Guyana, becoming senior partner in the firm of Hogg, Curtis, Campbell and Co. Hogg was actively involved in managing and developing the business, making frequent trips to the West Indies. The sugar trade could be lucrative but it was also high risk. In 1878, when he was trying to persuade his eldest brother James to invest in further development, Hogg wrote:

> Don't show these figures or mention this to Frank Bevan – he would put it all over the City of London; he cannot understand properties making largely one year and losing the next.[8]

While still in his early thirties, then, Hogg was accustomed to making bold decisions, planning and risk taking on a large scale. This approach also became characteristic of his philanthropic work, which absorbed the major part of his fortune.

Hogg made time for his philanthropic work by working all hours at the expense of his personal and family life; nevertheless his marriage was a very happy one and his wife Alice shared in his work. An insomniac, he was notorious among his colleagues for starting meetings after the Polytechnic had closed its doors at ten o'clock at night. It is impossible to say how much money he devoted to the Polytechnic; he was constantly giving gifts to individuals as well as to the Institution. According to Henry Lunn, who worked as chaplain at the Polytechnic from 1890–1898, Hogg once casually remarked to him "I sometimes feel it has been a little hard on my family that I should have given up my country house and my carriage to carry on this work. It has cost me over £250,000."[9]

Hogg became well known for his philanthropy, but he was a somewhat reluctant public figure, rejecting many invitations to speak in favour of spending as many evenings as he could in the Polytechnic. He was no intellectual, and always a practical man of action rather than a theorist. When Sir Lyon Playfair came to speak at a Polytechnic prize-giving in 1888, he began his speech by saying that "while he had been talking for many years, how many he could hardly remember, about Technical Education, Mr. Hogg had been acting, and had done what they who had been trying to influence the public in certain directions had probably not the time, means or ability to carry into execution. Mr. Hogg has shown the way, and had been a pioneer in a great movement for Technical Education".

He also left a more personal legacy. Hogg's fervent evangelism and his paternalistic language can make him appear an unsympathetic character today, but there can be no doubt that he had a deep impact on the lives of thousands of young people. Henry Lunn describes making a visit to Harvard to lecture in 1895. At every stage of his trip, individuals in very different walks of life introduced themselves to him as former "Poly boys" and enquired affectionately after "Q.H." Lunn went on to say the same thing happened to Hogg wherever he went; "all over the British Empire today thousands of men are scattered who owe their start in life- in many cases their rescue from being part of the 'submerged tenth'- to the kindly words and warm handshake of Quintin Hogg".[10]

His Early Work

Hogg's first major initiative was the York Place Ragged School and Mission close to the Adelphi Arches which he opened in 1864. A woman teacher was employed to teach the children, and a mission worker to visit homes in the area, but volunteers, including Kinnaird and Hogg, took Sunday Schools, Bible classes and preached at evening services in York Place. The school grew steadily and in 1870 moved to larger premises in Castle Street (since renamed Shelton Street) in Covent Garden.

One characteristic of Hogg's philanthropy was its practicality. His concern for the ragged children's spiritual salvation was matched by his desire to help them escape from poverty by finding employment. In the 1860s he turned with characteristic enthusiasm to the Shoeblack Society, forming his own brigade – the Central Brigade, also called the 'Reds' after the colour of their uniform. Boys were provided with a uniform and a box of kit, and each was allocated a recognized "station" where they cleaned shoes for a penny. From their earnings, they were given sixpence as daily pocket money. Of the remainder, a third went to the boy, a third was banked on his behalf and a third went to the Society to cover expenses. Hogg told many stories of how he was pursued by angry parents eager to get their hands on their sons' earnings. In 1867 a dormitory, the first home for working boys, was attached to the ragged school, to provide an alternative to the notorious common lodging houses for homeless shoeblacks.[11] Some boys at least managed to save enough to secure an apprenticeship, the means to set up a small business or at least to buy decent clothes to improve their chances of finding more permanent employment.

Hogg had an undoubted rapport with young people. At first he did not intend to teach in the ragged school, but when the female teacher had problems controlling the older boys, Hogg found to his own surprise that he was able to command their attention and restore order, and he spent more and more time in their company, teaching classes in the evening, playing impromptu games of football, and taking the children for outings into the country. Boys accompanied him to his country house, to Guyana, on holiday – there were never any clear-cut boundaries between his personal and his public life. Other volunteers envied Hogg his natural authority. Tom Pelham, when he first joined Hogg in Castle Street, found preaching to the often rowdy Sunday evening classes of about 130 boys (Sunday School was compulsory for shoeblacks) an ordeal. Only once did he follow Hogg's example and deputize for the Home superintendent, spending a single sleepless night in the small room next to the dormitory:

> For the first two or three hours I was hunting for a flea. Soon after 3 a.m. a boy came hammering on the door and said that QH always gave him a penny for calling him at 5 o'clock.[12]

Hogg was convinced that emigration, especially to Canada and the United States, provided a great opportunity for young people to escape the evils of metropolitan life and during his lifetime he assisted between 1,000 and 1,500 of them to leave the country. The average cost at first was about £10 per person, and both R.C.L. Bevan and Hogg himself made donations specifically for this purpose. The *Polytechnic Magazine* published many letters from emigrants relating their experiences. Some flourished, while others were bitterly homesick and some even risked Hogg's wrath by returning home. Hogg himself travelled widely, for business and for pleasure, and often visited former members overseas.

The Youth's Christian Institute and Reading Rooms

In 1873 Hogg's work took what was to prove a significant new direction when he founded the Youth's Christian Institute and Reading Rooms. At first the Institute occupied rooms adjoining the school and home in Castle Street, but in 1878 it moved to separate premises at 48–49 Long Acre. The focus of Hogg's interest moved from providing for the basic needs of the poorest of young children (both girls and boys) to supporting adolescent working boys.

His biographer explains this major shift in terms of the lessening of the need for ragged schools following the 1870 Education Act, but a more convincing explanation seems to be that Hogg was responding to the demands of the boys themselves.

By the early 1870s there were some 70 or 80 young men in their mid to late teens, former pupils or residents of the home, no longer ragged and dirty, who kept returning to the Boys' Night School every night after work; nothing would persuade them to go elsewhere.[13] The Institute provided them with a place to meet, books, games and writing materials. Members paid a small subscription and elected a committee from among their number to manage their affairs. Charity, as well as thrift, was strongly encouraged. Members assisted in the care of the younger children and also with the mission work, while Hogg provided a savings bank and a sick fund on generous terms. Elementary educational classes in short-hand, grammar and technical drawing were available and more subjects were added in direct response to the requests of members. But the boys were not just interested in education, and in 1874 they proposed that an athletic club be formed within the Institute.

Since Hogg, Kinnaird and Pelham were archetypal 'muscular Christians' – Hogg and Kinnaird were footballers and Pelham a cricketer- this request was met with enthusiasm. Rowing, swimming, cricket and football were the first sports. Initially games were played in the public parks, and soon matches were arranged against other clubs. Frank Dawes, in his history of the Boys' Club Movement, identifies St Andrew's Home for Boys in Market Street, Soho, as probably the first club to put a soccer team of working lads into the field, for a match played on Primrose Hill on Boxing Day 1875. Their opponents that day were the Hanover Club – which was the name given to Hogg's Institute team.[14] The volunteers played alongside the members, and Hogg began to make the generous provision for sport which was to be such a feature of the later Polytechnic. The Long Acre Institute had its own gymnasium, and from 1879 its own playing field. The Institute held an increasing number of social events; it had a brass band and a drum and fife band which performed regularly at Saturday evening concerts, which also included singing and recitations by members. Members of the Athletic Club later recalled that when Hanover won "what was probably the first football competition in London" against Bloomsbury, the teams "marched off the battlefield to the accompaniment of the drum and fife band".[15]

When the Institute moved to Long Acre, Robert Mitchell, the secretary, left his job as a metal worker to become a full time paid employee. Mitchell had first joined the Institute when he was 17. The significance of Mitchell's contribution to the development of the Polytechnic was incalculable. Mitchell and Hogg worked so closely together that it is often impossible to say whether a particular initiative originated from one or the other. Mitchell was a constant presence while Hogg was away from London, but both men spent as many evenings as they could at the Institute, meeting and greeting members. Mitchell, as his friends and co-workers came to realize, turned out to have a genius for organization. The first outlet for his abilities was developing the educational activities of the small Covent Garden Institute into Regent Street Polytechnic with its thousands of students.

By 1880 the Long Acre Institute was offering 22 evening classes. Some of these were in general educational subjects which helped members to make up for the deficiencies of their schooling – including reading, arithmetic and writing skills, as well as elementary and advanced French. Increasingly, however, both Hogg and Mitchell were looking for ways to improve members' opportunities of progressing in the work-place. Hogg's experiences convinced him that the best chance of financial security for his members would result from improving their skills, whether as a tradesman or office worker, to enable them to take the next step up the ladder. Mitchell began to negotiate with the Science and Art Department in South Kensington about providing classes under their auspices, and by 1880 eight Science and Art classes, including geometry, building construction and mechanical, model and freehand drawing, were also on the timetable. Other subjects were added at the request of members. Elocution was included from the beginning, and Regent Street Polytechnic was to develop a pioneering School of Elocution.

With their deep personal knowledge of their members' circumstances, Hogg and Mitchell set fee rates for the classes which were affordable by those earning thirteen or fourteen shillings a week. They were also sensitive to the fact that the background and education of many of their members meant that it was easier for them to learn in a practical workshop environment than in the classroom. Practical trade classes, taught by experienced tradesmen, were to become the trademark of Regent Street Polytechnic. In fact they had been pioneered by another Covent Garden institute, the Artisans' Institute at 29 Castle Street, established by the Rev Henry Solly in 1874. Solly lacked financial support and his Institute proved short-lived. He later acknowledged that it is remembered principally for the influence that it had on Hogg and Mitchell.[16]

Regent Street

Soon after the move into Long Acre, Hogg was once again looking for new premises. He had already purchased a plot of building land in nearby St Martin's Lane when the building at 309 Regent Street, previously the home of the Royal Polytechnic Institution, a gallery of practical science which had recently become bankrupt, came onto the market, and Hogg decided to buy that instead. It was an enormous gamble, because fashionable Regent Street was an unlikely location for an Institute, and if it failed he would have been left with an expensive white elephant. Hogg wanted the building because its location matched the scale of his growing ambitions for the Institute; he knew that it would gain more public attention for his work. He felt the main risk to be that his members might be intimidated by the location and was at pains to assure them that they could certainly attend straight from work as usual; he was installing showers and hot-water basins so that they could wash away the grime of the work-place when they arrived. Although he took every opportunity to expand the membership, Hogg remained ambivalent about the growing numbers, concerned that the homely atmosphere and personal relationships which he had fostered so carefully would be lost.

The move was an overwhelming success. The Polytechnic building had been a well-known and much visited landmark since its foundation in 1838, and it was not long before the Young Men's Christian Institute became popularly known as the Polytechnic, or more simply the Poly. The new location led to a period of astonishing expansion. In Covent Garden, limitation of the size of the premises had meant that Institute membership had been held at 500. Hogg planned to expand to 2000 in Regent Street, but, in the event, 6000 enrolled when the building opened in September 1882, and by 1888 the number was over 10,000. In addition, there were some 800 young women (Hogg had founded a separate Young Women's Institute which opened in April 1888) and about 500 boys in the secondary day school, founded in 1885 to make better use of a building which was mainly occupied in the evenings.

The scale of this expansion shows that the Institute was genuinely popular with young working people. Characteristically, Hogg does not seem to have considered limiting membership as an option, but by the late 1880s the pressure on resources meant he was approaching crisis. The financial burden was enormous and growing, but Hogg, who suffered from bouts of poor health and had a strong sense of his mortality, was most concerned that the institution which was wholly dependent upon him should be placed on a more permanent basis. In 1888 the Polytechnic was desperately anxious to secure external funding and launched its first public appeal for funds accompanied by a carefully orchestrated publicity campaign.[17]

The evening trade classes in particular gained rapidly in popularity under Mitchell's direction. He promised to follow up all requests to introduce new subjects, providing that at least 15 members promised to attend, and some 100 new classes were added in the first twelve months.[18] Hogg and Mitchell devoted time and effort to establishing the credibility of these classes with labour organizations and employers. They were particularly concerned not to be accused of flooding the market with "amateurs"; for this reason entry to these early classes was restricted to those already employed in a particular trade, in spite of the fact that many members objected to this restriction, which also effectively excluded women. Where possible, students in trade classes were encouraged to take the new City and Guilds of London Institute examinations which were being developed in the same period. If a subject was not available from CGLI, the Polytechnic set its own exams. Trade bodies were consulted about the content of courses. There was great interest in the new classes and a stream of visitors came into Regent Street from home and abroad, including the Royal Commissioners on Technical Education.

For the remainder of Hogg's life-time (he died as a result of an accident in 1903), the creation of a Board of Governors and the assurance of a regular source of income did nothing to limit his involvement in the Polytechnic. Indeed, the late 1880s and early 1890s saw the flowering of a number of ambitious new schemes. Hogg had always provided cheap holidays for Polytechnic members, in the country or by the sea. It was Mitchell who pioneered the Polytechnic tours abroad which developed into the Polytechnic Touring Association – which was eventually sold off in the 1950s to become part of the tour operator Lunn Poly. Hogg provided the initial finance – for example to buy the chalets in Lucerne and the steam yacht which sailed the Norway fjords – and any profit went into the Polytechnic. Hogg also organized and sponsored the Polytechnic Saturday night concerts which filled the Queen's Hall, and he continued to pay for the *Polytechnic Magazine* which reported the activities of the growing number of sports and social clubs, as well as news of former members and students around the world.

The Polytechnic Movement

By 1888 the Polytechnic had not only "quietly won its way to a position of astonishing success through the devotion and boundless munificence of one man, Mr Quintin Hogg"[19] but had also rapidly become the model for the development of a dozen similar institutions in London. Polytechnics were a popular focus of philanthropy in the London of the 1880s, to the extent that *The Times* could begin a leader on 19 July 1888 by suggesting that: "[A] cynic might easily set down the present activity in founding what are called Polytechnics in London as the fashionable craze of the moment".[20]

On a more serious note, the article went on to analyze what lay behind the current activity and came to the conclusion that: "there is a definite work to be done, and there is a definite reason for doing it now". What was needed was technical education which the Times defined as "the training of the eye, the hand, the taste and the intelligence which makes a lad able to master his trade with ease and certainty". The British workman needed to improve his skills in order to fight off the threat of foreign competition. In rhetoric that had become increasingly familiar since the days of the Great Exhibition of 1851, it went on to argue that:

The days of rule of thumb are numbered. The nation which depends upon it, and which thinks it can fight with obsolete weapons, is doomed to commercial extinction. Already the better sort of men realise this, as do the commercial leaders; and we may be sure that it is a feeling of this kind, far more than a philanthropic sentiment, which is at the bottom of the efforts that many leading commercial men are making to set these Polytechnics on foot. They are, in fact, guided as much by a feeling of enlightened self-interest as by any other motive . . .

But the polytechnics were not just concerned with technical education; as the *Times* pointed out, they also provided the "best recreative clubs for young men and girls of the working and business classes" which allowed them to enjoy themselves "in a sensible way".[21]

Another influential advocate of the polytechnics was the Assistant Charity Commissioner, Henry Cunynghame, who had been entrusted by the Charity Commission with the task of exploring the need for technical education and the means by which it might be met. His enquiries led him to Bordeaux, Paris and Regent Street where, in 1887, he paid an unannounced and incognito visit to the Polytechnic and, according to Hogg's daughter, "was immensely struck with all he saw, brought other members of the Commission to investigate it also and reported very strongly on some of the money being spent in establishing or endowing similar conditions".[22]

Cunynghame's report on his researches was submitted to the Charity Commission in December 1987. He recommended what was in effect the Polytechnic model: "if it is decided to benefit the great mass of artisans and the poorer classes generally, the cheapest and most effectual plan would be to provide for institutions which should combine healthy recreation with instruction chiefly designed for evening work, but also having day sides to be assisted by scholarships of small value". Cunynghame's formal and informal lobbying of his colleagues at the Commission led to the creation, in 1891, of a dozen polytechnics in London to be partly funded by the newly established City Parochial Foundation with the balance to be provided by voluntary subscriptions.[23]

The Charity Commission defined the purpose of these new organizations as "the promotion of the industrial skill, general knowledge, health and well being of young men and women belonging to the poorer classes".[24] As providers of technical education, they were intended to make available to the working man the opportunity to improve his skills by attending evening classes, thereby improving the employment prospects of the "deserving poor" and ensuring an increased supply of skilled labour to meet growing business and commercial needs in the capital.

Different Perspectives

Two years after the creation of the new polytechnics in London – in 1893 – they received significant additional support in the form of funding from the Technical Education Board of the London County Council. This was the first manifestation of an interest on the part of the local authority which was to lead over time to increased control by local government. The chair of the Technical Education Board of the London County Council and later of its Higher Education Committee, Sidney Webb, was an admirer of Hogg's achievements, but there were significant differences between the two men's views of polytechnics.[25] The first of these was religion which had no place in Webb's approach. This was, as we have seen, the key driving force for all that Hogg did and he consistently said that he would have refused external money rather than give up his religious work, which continued at Regent Street during his lifetime and beyond. This was possible because no religious activity at the Polytechnic was compulsory.

Secondly, while Webb recognized the value of the polytechnics' recreational activities, these were not supported by local authority funding. The sporting and social tradition at Regent Street was so strong that it survived until after the end of the Second World War, but during that time the educational and the Institute sides (as they came to be called) drifted further apart. The other polytechnics tended to drop the social aspects of their work to concentrate on their educational provision much more quickly even though the Schemes of Administration under which they operated were modeled on the full range of activities in Regent Street.

This would have been anathema to Hogg. Whenever he was asked to explain the success of the Institute, he always identified the social side as the critical element, involving "more trouble and personal labour than all the portions of the Polytechnic work put together".[26] He did not want anyone to attend a class and then leave without having made friends or found an activity to interest him. "A successful and comprehensive Polytechnic must be something of a club and a home, not just an academy."[27] The experiences gained in serving on a club committee or speaking in the Polytechnic parliament were as much a part of education as learning technical skills, and it was in these areas that Hogg's family and friends continued to work as volunteers, mixing with the members on a daily basis.

In his writing about polytechnics, Sidney Webb emphasized the research work that was done in them, and the achievements of the few very able students who went on to obtain degrees. In *London Education,* published in 1904, he outlined a vision in which polytechnics became linked to the University of London. Hogg was quite determined that polytechnics and universities had very different purposes, and Regent Street was not among the first polytechnics to employ teachers recognized by the University of London, nor to enter students for external degrees. His polytechnic was for the working man, and he did not want it to be taken over by the middle classes.

Hogg always hoped that the work of clerks and mechanics would be regarded as of equal value, so that a young man could choose the path most suited to his particular aptitudes. This view ran counter to the highly stratified class distinctions in Victorian society, and the social superiority which clerks felt over tradesmen is a subtext which can be traced through the pages of the *Polytechnic Magazine*. It could be argued that in the long term, both the middle classes and the clerks have prevailed and that state provision has never provided a very satisfactory environment for technical education.

Conclusions

It is difficult to quarrel with the judgement of Victor Belcher, historian of the City Parochial Foundation, that "[T]he Polytechnic . . . was the remarkable achievement of a remarkable man".[28] Quintin Hogg brought to his philanthropic career a commitment born of his evangelical Christian faith and gave liberally of his time and his money to his causes. He took pains to understand the needs and way of life of those he sought to serve; his approach was practical; and his career in the City had given him experience of boldness in decision-making. All of these factors help to explain how he was able to create the Polytechnic, an institution which not only attracted large numbers of members, students and volunteers but also provided a name and a model for a host of similar initiatives. But the impact he had on so many thousands of young people and the warmth with which they remembered him suggests something more. This is evidence both of his ability to establish a rapport with young people and the success of the "holistic" approach which offered so much more than technical education. How might further education for the working classes have developed had those who came after him followed his vision of the polytechnic rather than the narrower approach offered by Webb and the LCC?

Notes

1 *The Times*, 19 July 1888, p. 9.
2 Ethel M. Hogg, *Quintin Hogg: A Biography* (London: Constable, 1904).
3 The Bible is held in University of Westminster Archives, ACC2005/37.
4 *Quintin Hogg*, p. 36.
5 The Hon. T. H. W. Pelham, *Recollections of the Pre-Historic Days at the Polytechnic* (Reprinted from the *Polytechnic Magazine*, London, 1914), p. 3.
6 *Quintin Hogg*, p. 50.
7 *The Times*, 21 June 1875, p. 9.

8　British Library, IOR MSS EUR E 342/43, QH to Sir James McGarel Hogg, 25 June 1878.

9　Sir Henry S. Lunn, *Chapters from my Life* (London: Cassel, 1918), p. 138.

10　*Chapters from my Life,* p. 139.

11　In 1873 the Castle Street Home became part of an organization called Homes for Working Boys, of which Pelham was secretary. Under the name of St Christopher's Fellowship, this body continues to provide housing and care for children, young people and vulnerable adults in London. http://www.stchris .org.uk/pages/who-we-are/our-history.html <accessed 29 June 2008>.

12　*Recollections,* p. 12.

13　University of Westminster Archive, P52d, *5th Annual Report,* pp. 7–8.

14　Frank Dawes, *A Cry from the Streets: the Boys' Club Movement in Britain from the 1850s to the Present Day* (Hove: Wayland, 1975), p. 33.

15　*Polytechnic Magazine,* March 1903, p. 7.

16　Henry Solly, '*These Eighty Years*' *of the Story of an Unfinished Life,* 2 vols (London: Simpkin and Marshall, 1893), p. 269.

17　See, for example, *The Times,* 23 April 1888, p. 14.

18　*Home Tidings,* March 1882, p. 41.

19　*The Times,* 19 July 1888, p. 9.

20　*Ibid.*

21　*Ibid.*

22　Belcher, *The City Parochial Foundation 1891–1991,* p. 59.

23　*Ibid.,* p. 61.

24　*Charity Commission: Scheme of Administration for Regent Street Polytechnic Institute, approved by the Queen in Council, 23 June 1891,* p. 8.

25　John Izbicki, "The London Polytechnics" and Brenda Weeden, "The London County Council and Higher Education" in Roderick Floud and Sean Glynn (eds), *London Higher: The Establishment of Higher Education in London* (London: Athlone, 1998).

26　Quintin Hogg, 'Polytechnics', *Journal of the Society of Arts,* 45 (1896–7): 859.

27　LSE Archives, Booth Papers, A56, p. 87.

28　Belcher, *The City Parochial Foundation 1891–1991,* p. 59.

Child Rescue as Mission in Britain, 1850–1915

SHURLEE SWAIN

To the founders of England's major child rescue organizations, all charity was religious and religion properly understood embraced the whole field of charity. Later scholarship, however, has been uncomfortable with this synergy, focusing on the religion to the exclusion of the charity, or, more usually, the charity shorn of its religion.[1] Drawing on an analysis of the publicity material produced by four prominent child rescuers, Thomas Barnardo (1854–1905),[2] Thomas Bowman Stephenson (1838–1912),[3] Edward de Montjoie Rudolf (1852–1933),[4] and Benjamin Waugh (1839–1908),[5] this chapter seeks to argue that evangelism was their central purpose and child rescue is best understood as an epiphenomenon.

The organizations which they founded, now known as Barnardos, Action for Children, the Children's Society and the National Society for the Prevention of Cruelty to Children (NSPCC), continue to play an important role in Britain's voluntary sector. This analysis of the role of religion in their histories contributes both to an understanding of their rapid growth in the nineteenth century and the impact their founders' theology had both on the way in which their services were constructed and the experiences of the children who were subject to rescue. In order to undertake this analysis, the chapter draws heavily on the writings of the founders and their supporters. In their introduction to this volume the editors point to the need to use history to gain an understanding of the springs of voluntary action. This chapter argues that, at least for these child rescue organizations and their descendents, an analysis of their theological underpinnings is essential if the origins and development of voluntary action over time is to be understood.

Origins

Directly or indirectly the English child rescuers drew their inspiration from the German Inner Mission established by Johann Wichern in the wake of the 1848 revolutions. Wichern's "Inner Mission" was philanthropy with a wider purpose:

> its object is to do within the sphere of Christendom what the church is endeavouring to accomplish in heathen lands . . . It aims at a relief of all kinds of spiritual and temporal misery by works of faith and charity; at a revival of nominal Christendom, and a general reform of society on the basis of the Gospel and the creed of the Reformation.[6]

Stephenson, a Wesleyan minister posted to Lambeth in 1868, embraced the idea of the Inner Mission as a way of meeting both the physical and spiritual needs of his neighbours. The Inner Mission, he argued, dissolved any imagined distinction between charity and religion, claiming the relief of all "who need a brother's help" as the highest form of Christian service, the "noblest sphere in life".[7]

Although Barnardo rarely acknowledged the key influences on his charitable activities, the language of the Inner Mission is reflected in published justifications of his work.

> Our work for Christ among the neglected *children* of our large towns . . . is *mission* work . . . the very title, mission work, reminds us both of the *need* for such work and the *character* of it: the need for it, for the word brings to mind the idea of the *heathen*; the character of it, because it reminds us . . . that to be successful with this class, or any other class of the poor and sorrowful, we must bring them in contact with the blessed Lord Himself.[8]

Barnardo had come to London in 1866 as a candidate for the China Inland Mission, but he found his vocation in evangelical activities in the East End. His increasing focus on the work amongst children did not detract from his effectiveness as an evangelist. To Barnardo, rescue was a means to salvation rather than an end in itself.

Benjamin Waugh, a Congregational minister, had also had experience in inner city evangelical work before moving to the NSPCC.[9] Although his close collaboration with Cardinal Manning in the early years of the NSPCC acted against the more overt expressions of Evangelicalism common amongst his fellow child rescuers, he freely invoked religious language in attracting support to the cause. His theology, it was reported, was simple. "Earth's greatest blessing and heaven's nearest likeness is a child."[10] However, it was touched, as well, with a sense of millenarian urgency, warning:

> The time is coming when every place of worship worthy of the name of the House of God will feel that Divine service is only a blasphemous species of spiritual self-indulgence, unless means are taken to secure the discovery of every hidden, starving, and tortured little one in its neighbourhood, and to secure its protection from . . . ill-treatment.[11]

Although the Anglican Rudolf was less identified in his later life with the evangelical movement, his initial involvement with child rescue work also came through inner-city mission work. He, too, cited as his motivation an urgency that children should be brought to Christ, but he saw the Church as providing the essential pathway.[12]

Located within a Christian meta-narrative which constantly looked forward to the end times, these child rescuers understood themselves as doing God's work. Like Wichern's Inner Mission, their target was not the foreign heathen, but the local unchurched population who had an entitlement to salvation. London, Stephenson argued, should not be thought of as "'outcast', but rather as 'sought out'", a mission field in which "Christian men, imbued with the Master's spirit, are bravely endeavouring to lessen the evils which infest the lives of thousands in this great centre of English activity".[13] "If the Church of Christ would but cast the arms of her faith and love round about the Children of Darkest England, before the devil raises his standard in the neglected and unhappy child-heart", wrote Barnardo, "the greatest increase the Church has ever known since apostolic days would be made in her ranks".[14]

Reconstituting the Threatening Child

The clue to the success of these pioneer child rescuers lay in their ability to reconstitute the everyday phenomenon of the street child as an object of pity and a victim of vice and neglect. Central to this transformation was the much repeated notion that the child was created in the image of God.[15]

> 'Mother' for you has no meaning,
> The name of all most mild:
> Yet each has a yearning Saviour,
> Himself a mother's child;
>
> And each has a loving Father,
> In the high and holy place;
> And each an angel, pleading
> With eyes on the Father's face.[16]

"Under the rags and under the dirt of our poor children", argued Archdeacon Farrer, "we ought to see them as their angels see them."[17]

"Beneath the dirt and rags, in spite of the unmannerly laugh, the cadging or the tricky ways, we must still trace the Christ likeness"[18] for, with "the foulness of the past . . . cleansed . . . 'these little ones' show that they still bear the image of the Divine Father".[19]

> Soiled as they are, and His image almost effaced,
> The Spirit of God still broods o'er the face of the deep;
> And if in that depth no ray illumine our vision,
> Let us look up to the faces of Angels that weep.[20]

Not only the angels, but Christ himself is understood as constantly watching over the fate of his children, with workers told: "Hear Him saying to you: 'These are Mine; they and I are one; between Me and them there is no break; they are the children of My Father which is in heaven.'"[21]

> Do not let us shirk our responsibilities: we may not be able to do much, but that is no reason why we should do nothing. Let us not rest content till one child at least is rescued from a life of sin, and brought back to God.[22]

Invoking the Biblical Text

Lydia Murdoch has argued that the invocation of the symbolic and allegorical power of the pauper child allowed the "intervening philanthropists" to cast themselves as "heroic, even Christ-like".[23] But the use of religious discourse in child rescue literature played more than a symbolic role; it provided a vocabulary and a shared sense of meaning through which the process could be understood. In the construction of this shared sense of meaning the Bible proved to be the most fruitful source. In his use of scripture Wichern had observed a strict demarcation. When he was describing the caring work of the Inner Mission he drew exclusively on the New Testament, but turned to the Old when he wanted to impress on his audience God's ways of blessing the obedient and punishing those who rejected his ways.[24] The English child rescuers had a wider and more flexible repertoire. Addressing a Biblically-literate audience they were able to use examples drawn from both Testaments to convey their message quickly. By substituting the name "Ishmael" for the more commonly used, but racially-loaded, "Arab", for example, they were able to reconstitute the despised street urchin as part of God's plan, rejected yet capable of being saved.[25] The infant Moses could be invoked to stand for all abandoned infants,[26] and the Exodus used to demonstrate that the children of the streets had yet to reach their promised land.[27]

New Testament texts proved capable of an almost infinite variation. The most popular by far was Matthew 25:40 "Inasmuch as ye have done it unto one of the least of these my brethren, ye have done it unto me", a text so redolent of meaning that it could be summed up in the single word "Inasmuch".[28] It appears in its whole or in its constituent parts in poetry and prose, as an invocation and a justification, an encouragement and a warning, across time and place, simultaneously reminding the reader that the child stands in the place of Christ, and that in helping the child they provide direct service to the Saviour.[29]

> The archway their only shelter,
> The pavement their nightly bed:–
> Thou too, when on earth, dear Saviour,
> Hadst nowhere to lay Thy head.
>
> So we know Thou art new, dear Master,
> Thy form we can almost see;
> Do we hear Thy sad voice saying-
> 'Ye did it not to me'?[30]

Charity, Rudolf reminded supporters, was not a claim of the poor upon the rich, but a service owed by man to God.[31]

The image of Christ as the Good Shepherd was also open to multiple uses with the suffering children equated with the lambs to be fed,[32] or the lost sheep which needed to be found.[33] Without a shepherd the children were left at the mercy of the cold, and at risk from wild beasts, which often functioned as a metaphor for temptation.[34] "Will ye fold your arms, and lie/Down to sleep", supporters were asked:

> Though the Lord, who came to die,
> Bids you listen to their cry-
> His lost sheep?[35]

The parable of the lost sheep was invoked to remind readers of the work Christians should be doing in the cities. For those who chose to ignore such encouragement, the story of Dives and Lazarus was used as a potent reminder that wealth could not ensure eternal life, with a miser shown in a dream the consequences of his actions:

> The ragged child he drove away,
> 'Mid snow and piercing wind,
> Is now a blessed saint of God,
> While he is left behind.[36]

The childhood of Christ as detailed in the Gospels, and the special attention he paid to children during his ministry, also provided valuable material. Born in a stable because there was no room at the inn, Christ was imagined as having a particular empathy with children, displayed throughout his life.[37]

> And truly He looks down and loves them
> As much as He did long ago;
> And sees when His little ones suffer,
> And feels for their pain and their woe.[38]

His more positive experiences of family life could also be invoked. Christ the "mother's child" could empathize with the motherless.[39] His childhood in Nazareth within "the pattern home of the world" gave him an understanding of the best that a family could be, and hence he would be anxious that all children should enjoy its benefits.[40]

The most powerful text in this context was Matthew 19:14: "Suffer little children, and forbid them not, to come unto Me", used both in its literal meaning to illustrate Christ's inclusive attitude towards children, but also to imply that children should not be suffering. Christianity was credited with revolutionizing attitudes towards children. "Love of, and reverence for, the child are among the most beneficent of the *Gesta Christi*. The new conception He has given us of childhood has created a new civilization and a new world."[41] In his ministry Jesus took children into his arms and blessed them, putting them forward as models of the humility needed to enter the Kingdom of Heaven.[42] Hence Christian nations stood to be judged by the way in which they treated their children.

> If in the midst of this great and rich city, there is one child motherless, home-less, hungry, wailing in the night, and there are no hands to minister to that child, there are no feet to run and rescue it, there are no tender hearts to care for it, that single, forgotten, despised child, might in the judgment of God outweigh your wealth and commerce, and bring London, with all its greatness, to what Nineveh is.[43]

"Suffer the little children" thus became an order to latter-day disciples to seek the suffering and bring them into his care.

If Christ Came to London

The gospels were used more generally to argue that child rescuers were both following Christ's example and obeying his explicit instruction to bring children back to God. If Christ came to London, readers were reminded, he would be found "not feasting at the rich tables of the West End, but lamenting the wretchedness and weeping over the miseries of the helpless little children of the East End slums and alleys".[44] Such behaviour provided the standard against which his followers would be judged. Child rescue work was depicted not as a penance to be borne but as a privilege undeserved. "To lead the wandering feet of these poor outcasts to Jesus Christ were indeed a task worthy of angels' toil; but God in His sovereign grace has delegated it to none others than saved sinners", wrote Barnardo.[45] Opportunities to serve had to be grasped, rather than delayed.[46] Christ himself was calling, "asking help for little ones He made",[47] and supporters were constantly asked whether they would be seen to have done enough.[48]

> And will He not angry be,
> If we let them go in the storm so rough,
> To perish with want, while more than enough
> For them and us we have?[49]

Preventing Revolution

The theology underlying such Biblical interpretation was essentially conservative. The religious mission central to the child rescue movement ensured that concern for the soul over-rode concern for the body, with the gospel invoked to justify submission rather than liberation. Death haunts the promotional literature, but not with any sense of regret for the injustice of a young life lost. Rather poor children were constructed as looking to a good Christian death to release them from the suffering they faced on earth.[50] Dying children were depicted as welcoming Christ and his angels who had come to take them and, through their testimony, bringing friends, relatives and neighbours to salvation. Last words, carefully reported, were designed to spread this impact beyond the immediate witnesses. Readers were encouraged to emulate the ragged school scholar who, on the point of death, exclaimed: "I'm going to Jesus! I'm going home! I'm going to that happy land!"[51]

But what impact did such a conservative reading of theology have on the children who did not die? Like Wichern, child rescuers saw religion as a remedy to revolution. In pre-1848 Germany, Wichern observed, "an immense gulf has arisen between the rich and the poor. The poor are filled with envy, the rich with greed". But the gap was to be bridged not by economic redistribution but by the gift of love.[52] Child rescuers promised a similar transformation amongst the children that came under their care, rather than being "steeped in the disaffection, vice and lawlessness" of their old neighbourhoods, where "Nihilists, Socialists, Communists or Anarchists" abound, they were "boys and girls who have had a good, healthy, sensible, English training, who have been taught to have the fear of God before their eyes, and to do their duty in that state of life to which it shall please God to call them".[53]

The influence of millenarianism predisposed its followers to see the existing social distress as part of God's plan. Because this plan could not be changed, in their analysis of poverty they emphasized the moral rather than the social or structural issues:

> the only way of permanently elevating our degraded population is through the instrumentality of the word of God. The disease under which they are labouring is a moral disease, their other evils being simply the effects. The remedy is the Bible applied to the heart by the Holy Spirit.[54]

"If the lodging-houses and the street may be called *colleges of crime*", wrote Barnardo, "surely our Homes may with equal if not greater accuracy be designated NURSERIES FOR HEAVEN."[55] The recipe for success was simple: "Religion, as the very mainspring of the whole life; Industry in various forms, meeting the physical and mental requirements of the children; and Home-life, with its individual treatment, its thorough yet easy supervision, and its play of the kindly emotions".[56] Through such means both the individual and the nation could be saved.

In her discussion of the anti-slavery movement Catherine Hall notes the "paradoxical conviction that slaves were brothers and sisters, all God's children, but younger brothers and sisters who must be educated and led by their older white siblings".[57] Neglected and abused children occupied a similar position in relation to their rescuers and social betters. The family was seen as the location of change but the child rescuers' definition of family did not include those from which the children had come. If we understand the child rescue message in terms of a conversion narrative its fundamental message was "that salvation required pauper children's permanent separation from their dysfunctional families and past lives".[58] Most parents were constructed as a threat to their children's salvation, but even the poor but worthy were encouraged to accept the necessity for separation. What the children were offered as an alternative was an artificially constructed family, located well away from their homes and often segregated by gender and age, designed to break their links with the past in order that they could be transformed into "useful citizens while on earth, and, some day, as heavenly citizens in God's eternal kingdom".[59] Central to such usefulness was subservience:

> St. Paul used to say to people who were in the most embarrassing situations – slaves and women married to heathen husbands – stay where you are, but have God abiding with you . . . There is no legitimate trade or calling in which a man or woman may not find that which will nourish their conscience, their reason, their faith in God, their general spiritual forces.[60]

Songs for shoe-blacks and servants urged the young workers to see God in their menial labour and work to earn his approval.[61] Theology also underwrote the other great tool in the child rescue repertoire: child emigration. Just as Elisha cleansed the spring at Jericho, modern day Christians could purge their own nation by supporting child rescue. Emigration would help not only to cleanse the nation but would also help fulfil God's plan to purify the earth through Anglo-Saxon colonization.[62] "God wants us to impress our stamp upon that large portion of the world He has committed to us, and it is of supreme importance that our Colonists should maintain the traditions of the British race."[63]

Conclusion

The rapidity with which each of these organizations grew in the last quarter of the nineteenth century is testament to the appeal of such a conservative theology to the Evangelical Christians who were the movement's core constituency. However the way in which it distorted both the diagnosis of the problem of child neglect and the treatment it offered in response is also instructive for those with an interest in the origins and impact of voluntary action. The founders of the British child rescue movement have been widely praised for the contribution they made in establishing citizenship rights for children, freeing them from their prior legal status as paternal property.[64] Through the propaganda they produced, they created an environment in which parliaments were prepared to legislate to establish and enforce children's rights to food, clothing, education and medical care. Yet the movement has also been condemned because of the negative impact which removal often had, leaving children unprotected in environments which could and did become abusive.

This analysis of the theology of the child rescue movement, offers a clue to explaining how an overtly humanitarian movement could also produce such negative results. The insistent reminder that neglected children, despite their rough and dirty exterior, were made in the image of God positioned them at the centre of any evaluation of Britain's claim to be a Christian nation, but it did not empower them to take action on their own behalf. It was the failings of their parents or other caregivers, often articulated in terms of the old evangelical discourses of morality and sin, rather than an unjust economic system, that was at the root of their distress. The remedy lay in removal from, rather than the strengthening of, their families, and the attainment of individual salvation through conversion and hard work.[65] There were many children, undoubtedly, for whom this formula worked, but those for whom it did not were particularly disempowered. The focus of their rescuers and their supporters on eternal salvation, too often left children vulnerable while still on earth.

Notes

1 For the history of the child rescue movement see: A. Allen and A. Morton, *This Is Your Child: The Story of the National Society for the Prevention of Cruelty to*

Children (London: Routledge and Kegan Paul, 1961); George K. Behlmer, *Child Abuse and Moral Reform in England, 1870–1908* (Stanford: Stanford University Press, 1982); Hugh Cunningham, *The Children of the Poor: Representations of Childhood since the Seventeenth Century* (Oxford: Blackwell, 1991); Harry Hendrick, *Child Welfare: England, 1872–1989* (London: Routledge, 1994); Lydia Murdoch, *Imagined Orphans: Poor Families, Child Welfare and Contested Citizenship in London* (New Brunswick: Rutgers University Press, 2006); June Rose, *For the Sake of the Children: Inside Dr. Barnardo's, 120 Years of Caring for Children* (London: Hodder and Stoughton, 1987).

2 Dr Barnardo's Homes (1868).

3 National Children's Homes (1869).

4 Church of England Waifs and Strays Society (1881).

5 National Society for the Prevention of Cruelty to Children (NSPCC) (1889).

6 John F. Hurst, *History of Rationalism* (London: Trubner and Co., 1867), p. 264.

7 T. Bowman Stephenson, "The English Inner Mission", *The Children's Advocate and Christian at Work*, January 1873, pp. 1–2.

8 T. J. Barnardo, "Little Emigrants", *Night and Day* VIII, 87 & 88 (1884): p. 101.

9 George Behlmer, "Waugh, Benjamin (1839–1908)", *Oxford Dictionary of National Biography* (2004), http://www.oxforddnb.com/view/article/36787.

10 "The Angel of the Little Ones, or the National Society for the Prevention of Cruelty to Children", *Review of Reviews* 4 (1891): p. 524.

11 *Ibid.*, pp. 526–7.

12 Brother Bill, "An Interview with Uncle Edward", *Brothers and Sisters*, 142 (1905): p. 6.

13 "The Postman's Missionary", *Highways and Hedges* III, 28 (1890): p. 92.

14 T. J. Barnardo, "The Economics of Child Rescue", *Night and Day* XIX, 182 (1895): p. 3.

15 See for example: R. J. T., "The S. Nicholas Home", *Brothers and Sisters*, 36 (1896); Maria Osborn, "The Little Street Girl", *The Children's Advocate*, May 1872, p. 6; Poet laureate, "Untitled", *Night and Day* XXXII, 249 (1909): p. 21; T. Bowman Stephenson, "Reject? ", *Highways and Hedges* IX, 97 (1896): p. 13.

16 W. St. Hill Bourne, "Waifs and Strays", *Our Waifs and Strays* I, 103 (1892): p. 7.

17 Archdeacon Farrar, "The Church's Duty and the Children's Cry", *Night and Day* XV, 153 (1891): p. 70.

18 A. L. L. and J. W. H., "No Room for the Child?", *Our Waifs and Strays* I, 21 (1886): p. 2.

19 "Raw Material", *Highways and Hedges* XII, 139 (1899): p. 145.

20 F. J., "De Profundis", *Our Waifs and Strays* I, 17 (1885): p. 5.

21 Rev. Canon Barker, "A Plea for the Homes", *National Waifs' Magazine* XXV, 217 (1902): p. 73.

22 "Whose Is This Image and Superscription? ", *Our Waifs and Strays* V, 147 (1896): p. 314.

23 Murdoch, *Imagined Orphans*, p. 32.

24 Hartmut Lehmann, "Pietism and Nationalism: The Relationship between

Protestant Revivalism and National Renewal in Nineteenth-Century Germany", *Church History* 51, 1 (1982): p. 50.

25 See for example: A. W. Mager, "Lights and Shadows of Child-Life: The Modern Tantalus", *The Children's Advocate* VIII, 85 (1887): p. 10; Rev. C. F. Tonks, "A Great Nation", *Our Waifs and Strays* XIV, 334 (1913): pp. 82–3.

26 Rev. C. F. Tonks, "The Waif of the Waters", *Our Waifs and Strays* XIV, 331 (1913): pp. 7–8.

27 "Child, Trade and Nation", *The Child's Guardian* XVII, 6 (1903): p. 66.

28 All Biblical quotations are from the King James Bible.

29 See for example: A. A. M, "A Christmas Appeal", *Night and Day* XXII, 207 (1898): p. 88; Rev. L. L. Barclay, "Do Help the Little Ones", *Our Waifs and Strays* IV, 108 (1893): p. 54; Archdeacon Farrar, "Archdeacon Farrar on the Children's Home", *Highways and Hedges* VI, 66 (1893): p. 114.

30 "Where Do the Children Sleep? A Plea for the Emigration of Hundreds of Homeless Children Now Starving in London", *Night and Day* VII, 79–80 (1883): p. 139.

31 "Principle in Charity", *Our Waifs and Strays* I, 19 (1885): p. 2.

32 John 21: 15.See for example: Elliot, "Haunted", *The Children's Advocate and Christian at Work*, May 1873, p. 66; Mrs Merrill E. Gates, "Feed My Sheep!", *Night and Day* XXXIV, 257 (1911): p. 39, J. W. Horsley, "Cui Bono? ", *Our Waifs and Strays* XIV, 335 (1913): p. 109.

33 Luke 15: 6. See for example: Marian Isabel Hurrell, "Young Tent-Dwellers", *Young Helpers' League Magazine* (1900): p. 193; G. B. H. B., "Lovest Thou Me? Feed My Lambs", *Our Waifs and Strays* I, 37 (1887): p. 7; J. C. W., "Gather Them In!", *Night and Day* XI, 119 (1887): p. 46.

34 T. J. Barnardo, "From the Shadows of the Back Courts", *Night and Day* XVII, 170 (1893): p. 14.

35 "Lines Written on the Narrative Entitled 'Found Dead'", *Night and Day* II, 8 (1878): p. 108.

36 "The Miser's Dream", *Our Waifs and Strays* I, 15 (1885): p. 4. The reference is to Luke 16: 19–31.

37 K. L. S., "The Christmas Sermon", *Our Waifs and Strays* V, 141 (1896): p. 209; Esther Wigglesworth, "Christmas Day", *Our Waifs and Strays* I, 21 (1886): p. 7.

38 Fides, "A Christmas Word for Waifs and Strays", *Our Waifs and Strays* I, 21 (1887): p. 6.

39 St. Hill Bourne, "Waifs and Strays", p. 7.

40 Rev. E. Whitmore Isaac, "Words to Children No 4.", *Brothers and Sisters* 1, 4 (1890): p. 59; Cardinal Henry Edward Manning and Benjamin Waugh, "The Child of the English Savage", *Contemporary Review* 49 (1886): p. 687; Edward de M. Rudolf, "A New Year's Message", *Brothers and Sisters*, 166 (1907): p. 3.

41 Rev. James Wells, "The Child under Paganism", *Night and Day* XXXII, 248 (1909): p. 19; Manning and Waugh, "The Child of the English Savage", p. 687; A. W. Mager, "Neglected Children", *Highways and Hedges* II, 23 (1889): p. 209.

42 Farrar, "Archdeacon Farrar on the Children's Home", p. 114.

43 Rev Dr Fitchett, "Children's Home Conference Meeting", *Highways and Hedges* XII, 141 (1899): p. 206.

44 "Give the Lad a Chance", *Our Waifs and Strays* XI, 277 (1907): p. 157. See

also Rev. F. B. Meyer, "An Appreciation", *National Waifs' Magazine* XXV, 221 (1902): p. 157.

45 T. J. Barnardo, "Deep Sea Fishing", *Night and Day* II, 2 (1878): p. 33.

46 "Teach The 'Little Ragged Heathen'", *Ragged School Union Magazine* 10, 109 (1858): p. 17.

47 H. M., "A Plea for the Waifs and Strays", *Our Waifs and Strays* I, 25 (1886): p. 6.

48 "Some Thoughts for the Dying Year; or, the Master's Questions", *Night and Day* VIII, 92 (1884): p. 164.

49 "The Litter Beggars", *Ragged School Union Magazine* 5, 49 (1853): p. 17.

50 See for example: "Annie's Ticket", *Night and Day* III, 12 (1879), "Honora's Effort", *Our Waifs and Strays* I, 10 (1885): p. 5; John S. Adams, "Out in the Cold", *The Children's Advocate* VIII, 95 (1887): pp. 262–3.

51 "Hope in Death", *Ragged School Union Magazine* 2, 13 (1850): p. 17.

52 Johann Wichern, "Germany", in *The Religious Condition of Christendom*, ed. Rev. Edward Steane (London: James Nisbet and Co., 1852), p. 486.

53 Anon., "Personal Notes", *Ups and Downs* IV, 1 (1898): p. 4.

54 "The Boys' Refuge, Whitechapel", *Ragged School Union Magazine* 8, 91 (1856): p. 127.

55 T. J. Barnardo, "The Drunkard's Child", *Night and Day* I, 12 (1877): p. 162.

56 "Child Rescue Work", *The Spectator and Methodist Chronicle*, 15 January 1892, p. 61.

57 Catherine Hall, *White, Male and Middle-Class: Explorations in Feminism and History* (Cambridge: Polity, 1992), p. 208.

58 Murdoch, *Imagined Orphans*, p. 32.

59 "The Bishop of Bath and Wells on the Society", *Our Waifs and Strays* V, 129 (1895): p. 6. See also T. J. Barnardo, "London Lodging Houses: Boys Found in Them", *Night and Day* I, 5 (1877): pp. 66–7.

60 Rev R. Bevan Shepherd, "Some Essentials to Our Work", *Highways and Hedges* XV (1902): p. 168.

61 "The London Shoe-Blacks", *Ragged School Union Magazine* 7, 74 (1855): p. 37; "Song for Our Little Servants", *Night and Day*, June 1878.

62 "Going Forth Unto the Springs", *Our Waifs and Strays* VII, 185 (1899): pp. 150–1.

63 Lord Bishop of Knaresborough, "Why It Appeals to Us", *Night and Day* XXXV, 263 (1912): p. 70.

64 Allen and Morton, *This Is Your Child*; L. Housden, *The Prevention of Cruelty to Children* (London: Cape, 1955); Ivy Pinchbeck and Margaret Hewitt, *Children in English Society: Volume II: From the Eighteenth Century to the Children Act 1948* (London: Routledge and Kegan Paul, 1973); Lionel Rose, *The Erosion of Childhood: Child Oppression in Britain, 1860–1918* (London and New York: Routledge, 1991).

65 A partial exception needs to be made at this point for the NSPCC which had a preference for disciplining parents in order that they would honour their obligations to their children. While this meant that the proportion of removals was much lower than for other child rescue agencies, the demonization of parents in much of the publicity did not act to strengthen family life.

Gender and Voluntarism in the Criminal Justice System: The Campaigning Activities of Women Magistrates in England, 1920–1960

ANNE LOGAN

This chapter focuses on some of the activities of the early women justices of the peace (JPs) or magistrates[1] and analyses reasons for their involvement with the prison system and their attitudes towards its policies and practices. It places special emphasis on the involvement of women magistrates in a network of voluntary bodies and pressure groups, especially the Howard League for Penal Reform (HLPR) and the Magistrates' Association, and their campaigning and voluntary work with prisoners. It challenges the assumption that penal reform organizations were "masculine" or "male-dominated"[2] pressure groups even at a time when women played a vital role in them and accounted for a large proportion of their active membership.

While in some respects the frontier between the state and voluntarism has moved since the late nineteenth century, in one crucial aspect of the criminal justice system it has remained fixed: the vast majority of criminal charges in England and Wales were and are brought to courts presided over by volunteer magistrates. However, in the period following the First World War there was a transformation of the magistracy. In 1919, as a direct result of the struggle for women's suffrage, the Sex Disqualification (Removal) Act permitted women to serve on juries, to train as legal professionals and to become JPs. But, whereas few women qualified for jury service before the 1960s and only small numbers became barristers or solicitors, within a few years a sizable group of women had begun to undertake the entirely voluntary role of JP and by the 1960s approximately 40 percent of JPs were women. Moreover, even at a time (in the 1920s and 1930s) when the proportion of women in the magistracy was still small, some women JPs were very active in a series of voluntary campaigns and pressure groups concerned with criminal justice. The introduction of women brought fundamental changes to the magistracy and to the criminal justice system. As one of the first women JPs, Eleanor Rathbone, emphasized, "Now that we have secured possession of the tools of citizenship, we intend to use them not to copy men's models but to produce out own".[3] One of the ways in which women magistrates, including Rathbone, accomplished this was through a network of women's organizations and penal reform pressure groups.[4] Through these they not only educated themselves about criminal justice and the penal system, but they also engaged in voluntary activity designed to promote change.

Women, Feminism and Penal Reform

The point has often been made that criminological study traditionally ignores women. What is less commonly recognized is the fact that it ignores not only women's involvement in crime but also their involvement in the formation of criminal justice policy, and it underestimates their (often voluntary) work in the criminal justice system and in the pressure groups associated with it. For example, David Garland analysed in some detail the relationship between social work and penal reform; pinpointed the alliance between the emerging social work project of the late nineteenth and early twentieth centuries and the pre-established world of philanthropy; and, importantly, located the penal reform groups in a discursive space between social work and criminology.[5] But he did not comment on or even identify the gendered characteristics of both philanthropy and social work in the late Victorian and Edwardian periods.[6] He identified a number of pressure groups that provided an "institutionalized" critique of policy and initiated proposals for reform, including the Howard Association, the Penal Reform League (PRL), the State Children's Association and the Wage Earning Children's Committee. These groups not only had strong links to the world of reforming philanthropy but were also closely allied to other "progressive" political forces, including, significantly, the women's suffrage movement.

The first full-length historical account of the penal reform lobby in Britain downplayed the significance of feminist activism in its development, despite recounting the circumstances of the formation of the PRL in 1907 in the wake of revelations concerning prison conditions made by a well-known suffragette, Mrs Cobden Sanderson. According to Gordon

Rose, the PRL had little interest in women's suffrage in the years before the First World War.[7] However, the PRL did comment about the forcible feeding of suffragette prisoners and the operation of the notorious Cat and Mouse Act by demanding the unconditional release of hunger-striking prisoners of conscience whose lives were in danger.[8] Moreover, members included a number of men and women involved in the suffrage campaign – for example, the magistrate, Cecil Chapman, and the suffragette, Lady Constance Lytton.[9] Even before the pro-suffrage Margery Fry took over as secretary of the PRL and brought about its merger with the Howard Association to form the HLPR in 1921, several women had played an active part in the PRL's work, and they took a particular interest in women prisoners, even though the latter represented only a small minority of the total prison population. The PRL also took part in joint lobbying activities with several philanthropic and women's organizations, ranging from the Salvation Army to the Women's Co-operative Guild.[10]

Neither Rose's nor any other account of the first thirty years of the HLPR could ignore the significance of Fry, and Rose eulogized her "talent, ability . . . charm, wit and kindness".[11] However, despite some references to their activities, Rose did not recognize the importance of a small group of women – mainly recruited by Fry herself – who worked voluntarily alongside her for the penal reform cause. These included Cicely Craven, Clara Dorothea Rackham, Theodora Calvert and Madeleine Robinson – all of whom were among the first women to become magistrates and who served on the HLPR's executive committee.[12] In addition, Rose and other criminologist commentators, despite their recognition of Fry's contribution to criminal justice policy, also overlooked the feminist influence on the penal reform lobby and Fry's and her colleagues' close relationship with the women's movement in the first half of the twentieth century. Only in his discussion of the establishment in the 1920s of the Committee on Sexual Offences against Young Persons did Rose sense feminist influence over reformers' policies, when he hesitantly suggested that its appointment could have been "a result of freer discussion of sexual matters, combined with the increasing participation of women in the public sphere".[13] In fact, the problem of the sexual abuse of children was a long-standing concern of the women's movement[14] and was widely discussed by feminists and penal reformers.

Recently, scholarship on penal policy in the immediate post-1945 period has suggested tentatively that the "metropolitan elite" that constituted the penal reform lobby may not have been as male-dominated as is often assumed.[15] An analysis of archival sources, including the records and journals of the HLPR, PRL and women's organizations, as well as accounts generated by women magistrates themselves, indicates that women activists played a major part in the policy networks formed around the criminal justice system during the era of penal welfarism. That is, they did not merely react to government initiatives but played a vital, creative role in the construction of policy, as they moved back and forth across the notional frontier between the state and the voluntary sector. While they did not restrict their concerns to issues relating to young and/or female offenders, women magistrates and their feminist allies concentrated especially on policy initiatives surrounding juvenile justice and the treatment of women in prison, perhaps because the prevailing gendered, maternal ideology enabled them to claim expertise in these areas.[16] They also focused on the needs of victims of crime, especially young victims of sexual abuse and female victims of male violence, decades before "the victim" became a mainstream concern of the politics of criminal justice. Fry even instigated discussion of compensation for victims of violent crime as a member of the government's Advisory Council on the Treatment of Offenders during the 1950s and continued to campaign for a compensation scheme until her death.[17] That having been said, women also gave due consideration to the treatment of adolescent and adult men, who made up the vast majority of prison inmates. This chapter will now briefly map some of the activities of women magistrates and volunteers in relation to prison reform and will conclude with a further consideration of the question as to why female activism in the penal reform lobby has been largely ignored.

Reforming Prisons – Women's Work?

Conditions in Britain's jails were inevitably a major concern of the penal reform lobby, although not its sole *raison d'être*. As already mentioned, the PRL, the younger and more radical of the two organizations that merged in 1921 to form the HLPR, was established as a direct result of the imprisonment of supporters of the Women's Social and Political Union following suffrage protests at the Houses of Parliament. The jailing of educated and articulate women and men posed an intermittent irritant for the prison service, and the suffragettes were soon followed to jail by the conscientious objectors of the First World War. As a result, liberal-minded social activists, even those who had no personal experience of life behind bars, became more aware of the deficiencies of the prison system and impatient with the Prison Commission's hesitant programme of reform.

Knowledge and understanding of the problems of the penal system were at first gathered and disseminated by an informal network of women's organizations, voluntary bodies and pressure groups. For women the tradition of prison visiting as an appropriate form of feminine philanthropy that stretched back nearly a century to Elizabeth Fry and Sarah Martin[18] was a vital stimulus to public concern about penal conditions and a spur to voluntary action. Although it seems that only a few of the first women magistrates appointed for England and Wales in 1920 had extensive acquaintance with the inside of the countries' penal establishments at that time,[19] the network of women's organizations to which many of them belonged encouraged them to make good the deficiency by visiting prisons as part of an informal justices' training programme developed by the women magistrates themselves (there was no formal education for JPs until the 1960s). Two of the former women's suffrage societies that were still in business in the early 1920s – the Women's Freedom League (WFL) and the National Union of Societies for Equal Citizenship (NUSEC) – took the new opportunities for women to exercise their citizens' rights in court as jurors and JPs exceedingly seriously. They organized conferences and summer schools for women magistrates and gave many column inches in their journals to discussions of criminal justice matters.[20] Readers of NUSEC's publication, *Woman's Leader*, were encouraged to read and digest official reports, including those of the Prison Commission, which were also summarized for readers by Rackham in the paper's regular "Law at Work" feature. Together with the WFL's newspaper, *The Vote*, and to a lesser extent, *The Labour Woman*, *Woman's Leader* provided a supportive and instructive forum of debate and information for existing, or even potential, women magistrates, as well as encouraging the emulation of best practice.

A key aspect of meetings of women magistrates was discussion of the most up-to-date methods of penal treatment – for example, the use of probation. But while activists promoted alternatives to prison at these gatherings, they also gave due consideration to a more pressing cause for concern, conditions within the jails. Some of their projects were merely palliative. For example, the Gloucestershire Women Magistrates' Society raised funds for a piano for Gloucester Prison and provided the jail with bedding plants.[21] Such seemingly small gestures were reminiscent of the charitable work of a Victorian "Lady Bountiful". However, attention to domestic detail in public institutions was not only a traditionally significant aspect of women's voluntary action, it was also undeniably important to those who had to endure what the composer and suffragette prisoner, Dame Ethel Smyth, described as the "unpleasant sensation when the iron door was slammed and the key turned".[22] Prison memoirs, which typically went into great detail about the mundane aspects of life "inside",[23] suggest that it was the apparently trivial minutiae which really mattered to those incarcerated in the country's jails. Fry, who urged women JPs at NUSEC's Summer School to be thorough in their inspections of prisons by tasting the food and inspecting the cells,[24] was, therefore, not only speaking in the tradition of women's philanthropy but also reminding her audience of the priorities for reform.

It should not, however, be assumed that women magistrates were only interested in day-by-day matters to the neglect of wider policy issues. Since the vast majority of the country's prisoners were men, it was inevitable that women JPs – who were, of course, sometimes unavoidably responsible for sending people to prison – would take an interest in the penal treatment of men as well as women. Their schemes were not restricted to improving food and hygiene or the provision of pianos. Two examples, both from the 1920s – Nottingham's "League of Honour" and the "women workers" scheme with young male prisoners in Wandsworth Prison – provide a good illustration of the involvement of women magistrates and volunteers in innovative prison policies: The following sections of this chapter examine these schemes, as well as some other developments in the reform of penal conditions for both men and women.

Nottingham's "League of Honour"

A remarkable programme of prison welfare was introduced in Nottingham Prison by Mrs. Helena Dowson – former suffragist, well-known philanthropist and JP – following her appointment as a visiting magistrate to the jail in 1922. Based on a "mutual welfare league" set up in Sing Sing Prison, New York, by the renowned reformer, Thomas Mott Osborne,[25] which Dowson had heard about on a visit to the United States, this scheme was at the cutting edge of modern penal treatment. Fourteen "star" prisoners (men with no previous convictions) were chosen by Nottingham's prison governor and chaplain to take part in the "League of Honour". The League was self-governing – effectively an early experiment in prison democracy – with the officers elected by the men and the rules agreed by members. Participants could engage together in recreational activities (such as games of chess and dominoes) and enjoy the company of what Dowson termed "decent people", presumably volunteers from outside the prison, since neither the governor nor any of his staff were involved. After a while a second league was launched for those Dowson termed "ordinary" prisoners (not first-time offenders). Dowson proudly asserted that the organisation gave the men "a public opinion and in addition to mental health, something to look forward to and a reasonable interest in the corporate life of the prison".[26] Soon the two leagues at Nottingham Prison had over 200 members between them.

Dowson's scheme was hailed by both feminist and penal reform journals.[27] This innovative project is indicative of the substantial impact feminist reformers were already having on the prison system. As the *Woman's Leader* pointed out, the Nottingham League of Honour was "one of the first fruits of the appointment of women magistrates".[28] Although opponents of penal reform might have argued the scheme was pampering offenders, the attempt at limited self-government represented a decisive rejection of the traditional degradation of prisoners and was arguably a precursor of later experiments with prison democracy, such as the therapeutic regime at Grendon Prison, opened in 1962. The League of Honour was launched at a significant moment, when penal reform had once again become a matter of public concern in the wake of the imprisonment of conscientious objectors during the First World War and the establishment of the Prison System Enquiry Committee (PSEC) in 1919.

Wandsworth's "Women Workers"

In another scheme established in 1922 and strongly supported by penal reformers, up to thirty women volunteers were recruited to visit young offenders in Wandsworth Prison in the hope that they would exert motherly influence over the young men (or "lads" as they were termed). Once again this was a prime example of women's voluntary action and innovation in the penal system, but, as the project's co-ordinator, Mrs Le Mesurier, stressed, there was "nothing of the amateur" about her team's work,[29] the style of which drew consciously on the nascent professionalization of social work taking place in the early twentieth century. Many of the volunteers had been to university at a time when only a tiny minority even of middle-class women had access to higher education, a fact that suggests that they turned to volunteer work at a time when professional openings for educated women were very limited.[30] Most of the women came to the work at Wandsworth as a result of recommendation, but they were first interviewed and then, if chosen, trained on the job.[31] In addition to talking to the young men in prison, and advising the authorities about them, the "women workers" were charged with the responsibility of visiting the lads' homes and interviewing their mothers.

Like Dowson's initiative in Nottingham, this scheme was well publicized by a supportive feminist press and widely discussed within the women's movement, particularly at meetings of women magistrates. While there were superficial similarities with the home-visiting practices of philanthropic ladies in the late Victorian era, it is significant that the volunteers at Wandsworth were styled "women workers" rather than "lady visitors", a term that re-enforced their quasi-professional status. Their charitably-funded, but professionally-run, project was supported not only by the penal reform lobby but also attracted the tacit support of Home Office officials and the Prison Commission. The organizer's salary was financed by a trust fund, and she was managed by a small, voluntary committee that included Fry, who worked strenuously behind the scenes for Le Mesurier's project to be placed on a proper, state-funded financial footing. Indeed, Fry emphasized in correspondence with the Prison Commission that the work was "non-charity" – that it was professionally organized and provided an essential, not a discretionary, service. [32]

Reforms to Prison Work and Education

Both the schemes outlined above were launched in the early 1920s and thereby coincided with the investigations of the PSEC, the launch of the Magistrates' Association and the formation of the HLPR. Fry played an important part in the last two developments, and she also received due acknowledgement in the PSEC report, *English Prisons Today*.[33] Another penal reform measure strongly backed by Fry and her colleagues was the introduction of wages for prison work. A strong case for this reform was made by the authors of *English Prisons Today*, Stephen Hobhouse and Fenner Brockway, who delivered a thorough condemnation of prison labour which they characterized as still mainly punitive, even though the notorious crank and tread-wheel had been done away with in 1896.[34] Once again English reformers took their creed from Mott Osborne, who argued that "prison labour is slave labour" and as such was "notoriously inefficient"[35] Activists agreed that prisoners needed some incentive to work: as Fry argued, prisoners should receive "the normal inducement [for their labour] – the expectation of some direct profit".[36] The wages scheme was first introduced in Wakefield Jail in 1928 with the co-operation of the HLPR, which donated £250 to cover the initial costs[37] and was gradually extended to other prisons, firstly Nottingham and later Maidstone.[38] But a full decade passed before women prisoners in Holloway were included in the scheme.

In the case of both Le Mesurier's project and the wages scheme voluntary funds were used financially to "pump prime" innovations in the penal system: the frontier between voluntary action and the state was, therefore, not at all clearly marked in this area. Moreover, despite some public apprehension that criminals were increasingly being pampered in the country's penal establishments, prison budgets remained very tight before, during and after the Second World War. As late as 1946 less than £38 was spent in a year on garden tools, entertainment, materials for needlework classes and radio licences/equipment for Holloway Prison.[39] Voluntary funds continued to provide many "extras", including educational facilities.

Women magistrates also played a major part in voluntary efforts to raise the educational levels of prison inmates, expose them to cultural influences and prepare them for citizenship. Once again Fry led the way when she became the first official, "honorary" education advisor at Holloway Prison in the early 1920s and began to recruit other volunteers to teach prisoners.[40] In 1945 Xenia Field, a London JP and former Labour councillor, organized the first "Field Lecture" at Holloway Prison, an address by Cicely Hamilton, the former suffragist, on the topic of "Votes for Women".[41] The "Field Lectures" programme, along with concerts and entertainments all organized by Field herself, was later offered to several of the men's prisons in the London area as well as Holloway. Voluntary action was once again not only "filling the gap" left by official parsimony but also initiating and developing policies to advance the humanitarian and rehabilitative agenda of penal reformers. As Dowson had remarked, prisoners did not want to be preached to or patronized but "just treated as human beings".[42] Wages and education were small steps towards achieving that aspiration.

Discharged Prisoners' Aid

Another area in which the voluntary action and policy vision of women JPs played a vital part was the provision of aftercare for discharged prisoners. Women magistrates often brought their experience of voluntary social work (in some cases gained in association with the Charity Organisation Society or Guilds of Help) to bear in adopting a "case work" approach to offenders by following up on the later careers of those who appeared before them.[43] The Birmingham magistrate and juvenile court chairman, Geraldine (Mrs Barrow) Cadbury was an outstanding proponent of this case work approach, and her quasi-professional methods were recommended to other justices.[44] However, aftercare for adult offenders was mainly a matter for the voluntary sector until the mid-1960s. Only former borstal trainees (who were catered for by the Borstal Association from 1908), corrective trainees and preventive trainees had any statutory provision. Other ex-prisoners could turn only to the voluntary Discharged Prisoners' Aid Societies (DPAS) for help, so once again philanthropic efforts provided a vitally important service.

Feminist penal reformers took special interest in the aftercare of female prisoners. Holloway's DPAS was established in 1922, shortly after the appointment of the first women magistrates. It was supported by volunteer funds from the thirteen counties (later raised to sixteen) for which the London jail was the "local" women's prison. In one of these counties, Hampshire, a local women magistrates' society provided financial support for Holloway's DPAS and sent a representative to its committee.[45] London women JPs who had been appointed as official visiting JPs for Holloway also helped to run the DPAS – for example, Florence Earengey, a solicitor and member of the WFL, who became the chairman in 1939.[46] The work of Holloway's DPAS was maintained until 1965 when it was disbanded and prison after-care became the responsibility of the probation service. The frontier between the state and voluntary action had moved as charitable efforts gave way to a statutory service. Yet it is interesting to note that Holloway's DPAS was soon reborn as the Griffins Society, which opened a new aftercare hostel for women in 1966.[47] To this day voluntary efforts continue to provide services for offenders both inside and outside prisons. As Fry surmised, "Even when laws are passed they are apt to fail in their full effect unless there is a group of citizens, ready to give time, money and work to their support".[48]

Conclusion

So far this chapter has attempted by way of a few examples to illustrate some of the voluntary work and penal reform campaigns undertaken by women magistrates. It must be stressed that prison reform was not the only interest of the women who devoted so much effort to the reform of criminal justice policy: for example, Fry is particularly remembered for her contribution to the recognition of the needs of the victim.[49] The question remains as to why women's activism and its significance in both the politics of penal reform and in the development of prison welfare has been so overlooked. The answer lies partly in the attitudes of the reformers themselves and their accommodation with the gender roles of their time, and partly in the tendency of commentators to dismiss women's voluntary work as limited and merely practical and to disassociate it from larger questions of policy vision, again largely as a result of discourses of gender.

Feminist penal reformers were by and large well-educated, but practical, women, and most were well-versed in the minutiae of voluntary social work. As mentioned above, many of Le Mesurier's workers were university-educated: this is true also of the HLPR activists, and it seems likely that graduates were over-represented among the early women JPs as well.[50] Educated women lacked alternative, more formal, avenues for their talents such as employment in universities or professional work – including law – and were therefore attracted by the possibility of useful labour in voluntary organizations. Although the discipline of criminology developed rapidly in this period and was becoming institutionalized in the universities by the 1950s, the criminological research of women such as Fry still took place largely outside the academy.[51] Professional social work also developed rapidly after 1945, but budget restraints restricted full-time employment opportunities before that time, and women's employment in the penal system was largely restricted to routine work in female institutions. Even Holloway, England's main women's prison, was run by a man until 1944, despite the protests of penal reformers and the women's movement.[52] With the exception of the war years opportunities for women in the higher grades of the Civil Service were highly circumscribed, but perhaps significantly, several of the university-educated HLPR activists had occupied such roles during the First World War. Feminist groups worked hard to promote equality of opportunity and women's employment, but many well-educated women seem to have accepted that their access to professions remained restricted and instead put their energy into voluntary work such as the magistracy.[53] By instigating their own training programmes through women's organizations and the newly-founded Magistrates' Association they effectively began to professionalize unpaid roles such as that of JP and were able to build their expertise in issues of criminal justice.[54] In doing so, they no doubt gained a great deal of personal fulfilment and satisfaction, and they performed valuable roles within both the criminal justice system and in the pressure groups that developed around it.

While much of the voluntary work of women in the penal system might appear to have been mundane and routine, it had major policy implications in a period when official action was constrained both financially and in its scope. HLPR activists were not content to leave so many reforms to the vagaries of voluntary action but lobbied for their initiatives to be adopted officially. Practice and policy were not separated but closely linked. Nevertheless, the tendency has been for both contemporary and subsequent commentators to regard women's voluntary work in the criminal justice system as "welfare" work and to ignore its significance in terms of policy. Due to their knowledge, understanding and expertise as well as their excellent connections in political and official circles, women magistrates took their place on a variety of official committees and enquiries between the 1920s and 1950s. This gave them, along with their lobbying activities, the opportunity to have an impact on policy at the national level. A prime example of the this was Fry's criminal injuries compensation scheme, a version of which was enacted a few years after her death in 1958.[55]

Arguably, a general tendency to dismiss or downplay the significance of voluntary work lies at the heart of the generally poor understanding of women's work in the criminal justice system between 1920 and 1960. Fry was self-deprecating about her role and referred to herself as "the essential amateur".[56] But she and her colleagues in the HLPR combined a professional understanding of criminology with campaigning zeal: for them theory and practice were united. Many of the women magistrates from the 1920s to the 1960s belonged to a generation of women schooled in voluntary social work and bloodied politically in the campaign for women's votes. They believed in the efficacy of political campaigning and hoped to influence policy. Through their involvement with the magistracy and in working for changes in the penal system such as those covered by this chapter, they were expressing their right to be equal citizens and to engage in practical and political strategies to improve the treatment of all prisoners, male and female, young and old.

Notes

1 The terms "justice of the peace", "JP" (its abbreviation) and "magistrate" are used interchangeably in this chapter. There are two kinds of magistrates – 'lay" or volunteer magistrates (the subject of this chapter) and "stipendiary" (or paid) magistrates (not considered in this chapter).

2 For example, Helen J. Self, *Prostitution, Women and Misuse of the Law: The Fallen Daughters of Eve* (London: Frank Cass, 2003), p. 183. It should be noted in fairness to Self that, by the time of the Wolfenden Inquiry which is the focus of her book, feminist influence on the HLPR had waned somewhat.

3 Quoted in Cheryl Law, *Suffrage and Power: The Women's Movement 1918–28* (London: I.B. Tauris, 1997).

4 Anne Logan, *Feminism and Criminal Justice: A Historical Perspective* (Basingstoke: Palgrave Macmillan, 2008), p. 17.

5 David Garland, *Punishment and Welfare* (Aldershot: Gower, 1985), p. 124.

6 Among many accounts of women's involvement in philanthropy and social work is Frank Prochaska, *Women and Philanthropy in Nineteenth Century England* (Oxford: Clarendon Press, 1980).

7 Gordon Rose, *The Struggle for Penal Reform* (London: Stevens, 1961), p. 75.

8 *Times*, 21 July 1913, p. 10. For the controversy surrounding forcible feeding and the Cat and Mouse Act, see J. F. Geddes, "Culpable Complicity: the Medical Profession and the Forcible Feeding of Suffragettes, 1909–14', *Women's History Review* 17, 1 (2008): 79–94.

9 Warwick University Modern Records Centre, MSS16C/6/P/6: *PRL Annual Report* (1911).

10 Logan, *Feminism and Criminal Justice*, p. 14.

11 Rose, *Struggle for Penal Reform*, p. 96.

12 Craven was Fry's successor as secretary of the HLPR, and Calvert was one of Britain's first women barristers. For the work and ideas of Rackham and Robinson, see Anne Logan, "Feminist Criminology in Britain circa 1920–60: Education, Agency and Activism outside the Academy" in Jean Spence, Sarah Jane Aiston, and Maureen M. Meikle (eds), *Women, Education, and Agency, 1600–2000* (New York: Routledge, 2010).

13 *Ibid.*, p. 156.

14 Sheila Jeffreys, *The Spinster and her Enemies: Feminism and Sexuality 1880–1930* (London: Pandora Press, 1985).

15 Mick Ryan, *Penal Policy and Political Culture in England and Wales* (Winchester: Waterside Press, 2003), p. 18.

16 For the impact of the women's movement on youth justice policy, see Anne Logan, "'A Suitable Person for Suitable Cases': The Gendering of Juvenile Courts in England, *c.*1910–39", *Twentieth Century British History* 16, 2 (2005): 129–45. Feminists were also interested in the reform of the criminal law with regard to prostitution, but on this question the leading pressure group was the Association for Moral and Social Hygiene, which worked in co-operation with the HLPR. See Julia Ann Laite, "The Association for Moral and Social Hygiene: abolitionism and prostitution law in Britain (1915–59)", *Women's History Review* 17, 2 (2008): 207–23.

17 Logan, *Feminism and Criminal Justice*, pp. 140–7.

18 Prochaska, *Women and Philanthropy*, pp. 163–71. Prochaska argues (p. 172) that there was a subsequent decline in women's prison visiting in the mid-Victorian period, with a revival taking place in the 1890s which culminated in the formation of the Duchess of Bedford's Association of Lady Visitors in 1901.

19 Only four of more than 200 women whose appointments as JP were announced in July 1920 had their experience as prison visitors cited in support of their nomination. The full list of appointments is in London Metropolitan Archives ACC/3613/03/002/B. For a detailed analysis, see Anne Logan "Making Women Magistrates: Feminism, Citizenship and Justice in England and Wales, 1918–50" (unpublished PhD thesis, University of Greenwich, 2002).

20 Anne Logan, "Professionalism and the Impact of England's First Women Justices", *Historical Journal* 49, 3 (2006): 833–50.

21 Gloucestershire County Record Office, 06156/1: minute book of Gloucestershire Women Magistrates' Society.

22 R. Crichton (ed.), *The Memoirs of Ethel Smyth* (Harmondsworth: Penguin, 1987), p. 299.

23 For example, Kathleen Lonsdale, *Account of Life in Holloway Prison for Women* (Chislehurst: Prison Reform Council, 1943).

24 *Woman's Leader*, 8 September 1922, p. 248.

25 Osborne, a former governor of Sing Sing, visited England in the summer of 1922 and lectured at NUSEC's Summer School for women magistrates (mentioned in the *Woman's Leader*, 3 December 1926). Dowson may have been involved in inviting him to the event. His address was printed in *Howard Journal* I, 1 (1921).

26 Helena B. Dowson, "The League of Honour at Nottingham", *The Magistrate* VII (1925).

27 *Howard Journal* I, 4 (1925), pp. 192–4; *Woman's Leader*, 21 March 1924, p. 114.

28 *Ibid.*

29 L. Le Mesurier, *Boys in Trouble* (London: John Murray, 1939), p. 96.

30 For a discussion of the employment opportunities for women graduates, see Carol Dyhouse, *Students: A Gendered History* (London: Routledge, 2005).

31 Le Mesurier, *Boys in Trouble*, p. 97.

32 National Archives, PCOM9/409.

33 Stephen Hobhouse and Fenner Brockway (eds), *English Prisons Today* (London: Longman for the Labour Research Department, 1922), p. ix.

34 *Ibid.*, p. 113. The Report stated that prisoners were still made to pick oakum.

35 *Ibid.*, p. 119.

36 Quoted in Enid Huws Jones, *Margery Fry: the Essential Amateur* (Oxford: Oxford University Press, 1966), p. 170.

37 *Ibid.*

38 B. D. Grew, *Prison Governor* (London: Herbert Jenkins, 1958), p. 86.

39 H.C Deb., vol. 433, col. 90, Written Answers, 13 February 1947, reply by James Ede, Home Secretary, to Mrs Ayrton Gould.

40 Huws Jones, *Margery Fry*, p. 120.

41 Xenia Field, *Under Lock and Key: a Study of Women in Prison* (London: Max Parrish, 1963), p. 209.

42 Dowson, "League of Honour".

43 For the importance of case work in the development of the Charity Organisation Society, see Kathleen Woodroofe, *From Charity to Social Work in England and the United States* (London: Routledge & Kegan Paul, 1962), Chapter 2.

44 Geraldine Cadbury, *Young Offenders Yesterday and Today* (London: Allen and Unwin, 1938).

45 Hampshire Record Office, 23M57/1: Minutes of Hampshire Women Magistrates Association.

46 Mary Size, *Prisons I Have Known* (London: Allen & Unwin, 1958), pp. 115–16.

47 Judith Rumgay, *Ladies of Lost Causes: Rehabilitation, Women Offenders and the Voluntary Sector* (Cullompton: Willan, 2007) p. 20.

48 Quoted in Huws Jones, *Margery Fry*, p. 223.

49 Paul Rock, *Helping Victims of Crime: the Home Office and the Rise of Victim Support in England and Wales* (Oxford: Clarendon Press, 1990).

50 Logan, "Making Women Magistrates".

51 Logan, "Feminist Criminology".

52 The authors of *English Prisons Today* recommended in 1922 that Holloway should have an all-female staff, from the governor downwards.

53 Pat Thane, "Girton Graduates, Earning and Learning 1920s–1980s", *Women's History Review* 13, 3 (2004): 347–61.

54 Logan, "Professionalism".

55 Logan, *Feminism and Criminal Justice*, pp. 153–7.

56 Huws Jones, *Margery Fry.*

PART III

Organizational Challenges

Success and Failure in Scottish Convalescent Homes, 1860–1939

JENNY CRONIN

In terms of growth and sustainability convalescent homes were one of the most successful types of charitable institutions established during the nineteenth century. The majority of these establishments grew in size and remained open until at least the beginning of the Second World War. There were, however, a few that closed down long before then, even at the height of their popularity as institutions. As a means of explaining the success or failure of convalescent homes – and perhaps that of other charities – this chapter explores the history of the Glasgow Convalescent Home (Glasgow CH) and the Dundee Convalescent House (Dundee CH). Part of the rationale for selecting these particular case studies was the fact that they were independent charities, and therefore reliant upon their own resources for their sustainability. They also opened around the same time, in the 1860s, and both began as relatively small establishments. These similarities should have subjected them to comparable social and economic influences and they might have been expected to follow a similar course of development. However, the Glasgow CH flourished until after the Second World War whereas the Dundee CH experienced minimal growth and eventually closed in 1911. This chapter examines factors that could explain the differing fortunes of the two homes, including the motivation of the founders; finance; governance and management; the other individuals involved; expansion and decline; and admission policies. In the process it will make a contribution to two of the key themes of this book – its discussion of the motivations of the founders of the two convalescent homes informs our understanding of the "springs of voluntary action" while its analysis of the factors making for comparative success and failure helps us to explore the nature of the organizational challenges faced by voluntary agencies then and now.

Convalescent Homes

Since World War II, the history of convalescence and convalescent homes has for the most part been included in larger works on health or philanthropy such as Abel-Smith's *The Hospitals*.[1] Olive Checkland also refers to the importance of convalescent homes in her highly respected survey of Victorian charitable institutions in Scotland,[2] as does Jacqueline Jenkinson's more recent work, *Scotland's Health*.[3] A number of hospital histories also mention the role played by their own convalescent homes. Two examples of these are the history of the Glasgow Royal Infirmary (Glasgow Royal), *The Royal*, by Jenkinson et al and A. Logan Turner's *Story of a Great Hospital, The Royal Infirmary of Edinburgh*, but there are many more. The inclusion of convalescent homes within hospital histories has contributed to a common misconception that most convalescent homes were attached to voluntary hospitals. Steven Cherry goes some way to correcting this misunderstanding in *Medical Services and the Hospitals in Britain, 1860–1939*, where he notes that the voluntary hospitals in Britain provided only one-third of total nursing and convalescent care.[4] Similarly, Cronin's thesis on *the Origins and Development of Scottish Convalescent Homes*, 1860–1939 estimated that, in Scotland, voluntary hospitals provided even less, at 23%. This illustrates the importance of understanding the mechanism of the success or failure of convalescent homes established by non-hospital charities, such as the Dundee CH and the Glasgow CH. Cronin's thesis also provides a fuller introduction to the medical and social literature on convalescent home.

When the Dundee and Glasgow CHs opened in Scotland in 1860 and 1865 respectively, they were seen as a unique type of institution. Yet in the same decade, another four opened, one at Edinburgh and three in the West of Scotland. Moreover, they were not alone but formed part of a far wider movement that established similar institutions in many other Western countries.[5] In 1842 the first English convalescent home, the Metropolitan Convalescent Institution, opened at Walton-on-Thames. In France, the Convalescent Hospital of Vincennes opened slightly later in 1859.[6] The introduction of convalescent homes was one of the ameliorative responses to the appalling social and environmental conditions found in mid-nineteenth century towns and cities that not only exacerbated ill health amongst the poor but also impeded the recovery of survivors.[7] The main objective of these institutions was to provide the poor who were recovering from illness, trauma or surgery with two to four weeks of respite care in an institutionalized but healthy environment. Although these institutions came under a general heading of convalescent homes, "hospital" or "house" often appeared in their title; these variations in title did not, however, necessarily signify any difference in function.

During the mid-nineteenth century, charitable organizations, rather than the infirmaries, established the majority of convalescent homes, particularly in the West of Scotland. The Glasgow Royal and Western Infirmary of Glasgow, therefore, had no immediate need to establish their own specialist convalescent institution. This was the situation until the 1890s, when increased demand led the Glasgow infirmaries, and many others elsewhere in Scotland, to establish their own convalescent homes at the seaside or in the country.[8] From the turn of the twentieth century onwards, as a further response to their growing popularity, trade organizations, benefit and co-operative societies also opened convalescent homes for their members. By 1900, Scottish convalescent homes were caring for over 20,000 patients annually. In 1939, there were more than sixty such institutions in Scotland owned or run by independent charities, infirmaries, religious organizations and self-help groups. The homes varied in size from as few as eight beds with an annual admission of fewer than a hundred patients, to homes with more than 300 beds, admitting over 2,000 patients per annum. For the purposes of this chapter, homes considered small were those with fewer than thirty-five beds. When they first opened, the Dundee CH and the Glasgow CH had fewer than this number.[9]

The Dundee Convalescent House

The mid-nineteenth century was a critical period in the history of Dundee – with the population rising from 45,355 in 1841 to 90,658 in 1861.[10] Overcrowding, poor sanitation and a frequentlyly polluted water supply led to regular outbreaks of infectious diseases such as cholera, typhus, typhoid and smallpox. Poverty, inadequate nutrition and poor social conditions compounded the effects of ill health. Through their charitable works, the two founders of the Dundee CH observed the difficulties encountered by the poor following illness, particularly amongst the extraordinarily high workforce of women in the town. The first founder was Lady Jane Elizabeth Ogilvy (1809–1861) and the second was the Scottish Episcopal Bishop of Brechin, Alexander Penrose Forbes (1817–1875). In 1860, they opened this first permanent institution for convalescents in Scotland in a rented house in Union Place, near the centre of Dundee. They called it the Dundee Convalescent Hospital but, after the first year, it was renamed with a more homely title of Dundee Convalescent House. During the first year, it admitted seventy-seven patients.

Unfortunately, Jane Ogilvy died only eight months after the Dundee CH opened, leaving Alexander Forbes as the sole manager.[11] In 1866, after several years of high demand for admission, Alexander Forbes and other supporters began fundraising for larger premises. In 1870, the Dundee CH moved into converted villas in nearby William Street where it continued to flourish until 1875 when Alexander Forbes also died. Thereafter, financial support declined and the Dundee CH admitted fewer patients. Although it stayed open until 1911, it remained very small and attracted little public attention. After this time, it disappeared from the records.

Glasgow Convalescent Home

When the Glasgow CH opened in July 1865 at Bothwell, just south of Glasgow, the poor social conditions in the city equalled those of Dundee and the need for a convalescent home was, therefore, just as great. The Glasgow CH was the second convalescent home established in Scotland and it came about mainly through the never-ending enthusiasm of philanthropist Beatrice Clugston (1817–1886). Although initially the Glasgow CH was exclusively for patients from the Glasgow Royal, their managers had little input in establishing the home. Nevertheless, they rapidly became aware of the huge benefits it offered by allowing doctors to discharge patients earlier with less risk that they would relapse and return to the infirmary. As in Dundee, demand exceeded supply and in 1869 the Glasgow CH managers decided it was time to find new, larger premises. Beatrice Clugston again took command of the fundraising and by 1870 sufficient funds had been raised to buy a site at Lenzie, a pleasant suburb to the north of Glasgow. Lenzie also had a railway station, enabling easier access for patients. On 28 August 1871, the Earl of Shaftesbury laid the foundation stone for the new premises.[12] It opened on 31 January 1873 with sixty-two beds; thirty of which were allocated to the sick poor within the general public and the rest to the infirmary.[13] Expansion continued, even after the death of Beatrice Clugston in 1886. In 1893, a further building programme provided the Home with eighty-five beds[14] and, in 1922, the managers organized the funding and construction of a day room for mothers and children.[15] The Glasgow CH then enjoyed a brief spell as a military hospital during World War II before returning to its function as a convalescent home. In 1948, the Western Region Hospital Board took it over and it became part of the NHS. The Glasgow CH entered a new era in June 1973 when it became a geriatric unit and was renamed Lenzie Hospital. This hospital is now closed.

Motivation of the Founders

Historians of philanthropy, such as Prochaska and Finlayson, provide several explanations for the growth of charitable enterprise, particularly among middle class women, which include religious obligation, altruism, civic pride, social mobility, social control and self-fulfilment.[16] Eleanor Gordon noted that, "It provided them with the opportunity to carve out a public space, and to push back the boundaries of their lives, as well as providing training in organizational and administrative skills".[17] Olive

Checkland also argued that "much charitable work, especially in the first phase, lay in the evangelical movement". Checkland also divided philanthropists into activists who "forced people to consider the needs of society", and those who took a more passive role and "waited to be solicited".[18]

Jane Ogilvy, daughter of Thomas, Sixteenth Earl of Suffolk and Berkshire (1776–1851) and wife of Sir John Ogilvy (1803–1890), was sufficiently wealthy and well connected to have no need for social advancement or to work, either inside or outside her home, although she may have wished to, in Gordon's words, "push back the boundary of her life". The author of Jane Ogilvy's obituary remarked that that "a tale of distress never failed to be attended by her", suggesting that she was at least partly motivated by a strong social conscience. She had a number of private charities, but her main charitable credits were a home for "fallen women" which opened in 1848 and the "Baldovan Orphanage and Asylum for Idiot Children" which opened in 1855. In common with the Dundee CH, the Baldovan Asylum was also the first of its kind in Scotland and led the way for many other similar institutions. Moreover, as the driving force behind two innovative institutions, Jane Ogilvy clearly falls into Checkland's philanthropic model of an "activist". Although she was a key figure in setting up the Dundee CH, her untimely death meant that she was less significant in its subsequent history.

Since his death in 1875, the prominent ecclesiastical life of Dundee CH's second founder, Alexander Forbes, has attracted the attention of numerous biographers. He was born into a privileged and aristocratic family. His parents were a leading lawyer, John Hay Forbes, Lord Medwyn (1776–1854), and Louisa Gordon Cumming (1770–1845). As a young man with a potentially promising career with the East India Company, Alexander Forbes spent several years in Madras but returned to Britain in 1840 due to ill health. After furthering his education at Brasenose College, Oxford, he became a clergyman with the Scottish Episcopalian Church and in 1847 was consecrated as Bishop of Brechin. He remained unmarried, devoting most of his life to charity and the Scottish Episcopal Church. Interest in Alexander Forbes has remained, partly because of his controversial religious views but also because he resurrected the Scottish Episcopal Church in Dundee following a period of decline as a result of its alliance with the Jacobites.[19] Alexander Forbes' most recent biographer, Rowan Strong, argues that he "worked to develop a congregation that was inclusive of the urban poor. Forbes also set a powerful example to his own clergy and to the Episcopal Church of responsiveness to the labouring poor and civic involvement."[20] Although this – and his own lengthy illness – may partly explain his charitable interest in the sick poor, all his biographers emphasize his compassionate nature. For example, a contemporary biographer who was also his cousin, Felicia Skene (1821–1899), noted that he "not only personally attended to the wants of the poor, and sought them out in the crowded lanes and alleys of the town, but he visited with untiring zeal the sick in the hospitals". She went on to describe how "he used to be seen at all hours of the day and night, hurrying along the street on his way to some of the numerous victims, with his Prayer Book in one hand and a bottle of cholera mixture in the other".[21] Alexander Forbes' biographers also point out that he did not wish to change society, but believed that it was the duty of the rich to help the poor.[22] This could account for his focus on obtaining financial support from a narrow band of wealthy members of his congregation and his aristocratic connections. His other charities included a model lodging-house, an agricultural school and an institution for training teachers, as well as the Baldovan Asylum, founded together with Jane Ogilvy in 1855.

A strong biographical trail also exists for Beatrice Clugston. She was the daughter of a factory owner, John Clugston (1800–1850), who left her with sufficient means to live without resorting to paid employment.[23] John Clugston's commercial shrewdness may well have rubbed off on to his daughter since Beatrice also had good business sense – a useful asset for a philanthropist. Her father was also reputed to have encouraged his daughter's philanthropy, although contemporary commentators also suggest that she was drawn towards charity through genuine concern for the sick poor. For instance, her mother, Mary Clugston (1796–1881), was believed to have commented that she was "pleased to leave Glasgow as Beatrice was constantly bringing in the halt, the lame and the blind to be fed and clothed".[24] Beatrice was also motivated by a strong sense of Christian evangelism and did not hesitate to remind the rich of their Christian duty towards the poor. For example, in the 1870s she wrote to Sir Archibald Orr Ewing (then Member of Parliament for Dunbarton-shire), appealing for donations to her second convalescent home at Dunoon, requesting that she "might she be favoured, since God had blessed him with wealth, with a subscription as a token of thankfulness for past mercies".[25] She also adorned the walls of one of her fundraising bazaars with bible-quoting banners that read "I was sick and ye visited me, naked and ye clothed me".[26] When it came to soliciting support, Beatrice did not stop at the wealthy; she also sought or cajoled support from church leaders, businessmen, employees and even children. She was particularly keen on soliciting support from working men as evidenced in a promo-tional paper written in 1881 specifically "for circulation among the working classes to induce the giving of a day's pay for endowing Broomhill Home for Incurables".[27]

Beatrice began her public philanthropic career first as a prison visitor and then as founder of the Glasgow Royal Dorcas Society, a charity that provided discharged patients with clothing and small sums of money.[28] The Dorcas Society may have given Beatrice valuable insight into the workings of the Glasgow Royal which could be used as a model for the Glasgow CH. Following its opening in 1871, she later established the largest convalescent home in Scotland on the West Coast at Dunoon. Although called the West of Scotland Seaside Convalescent Home, it was commonly known as the Dunoon Home. Her final charitable project was the Broomhill Home for Incurables, opened at Kirkintilloch in 1875. Her good works made her a popular figure in the West of Scotland. In a short contemporary biography, the Scottish theologian and social reformer, Reverend W. G. Blaikie (1820–1899), reported that he had observed this popularity first-hand when he accompanied her on a visit to the Dunoon Home. He noted that patients lined the pier to greet her and that "a ready work of inquiry for every one shows the tenderness of her interest and the secret of her power".[29] Beatrice Clugston never married and spent her life working tirelessly to raise money for her charitable projects.

The biographies of the three founders suggest that their entrepreneurial approach to voluntary action led them to establish these first two Scottish convalescent homes. They appeared to be motivated by compassion and their own understanding of sickness. In addition, their religious beliefs encouraged them to pursue the rich to support their charities. However, Beatrice also sought financial support from a wider social level of support that laid the foundations for further growth of the Glasgow CH.

Financial Support, Governance and Management

During the first year, Jane Ogilvy and Alexander Forbes used their own resources to finance the Dundee CH supplemented by "the kindness and liberality of a few friends".[30] Although the Medical Superintendent, the Matron, the Secretary and the Treasurer donated their services, other expenses such as rent and tradesmen's bills were not covered by kindness. Alexander Forbes did not expect either the patients or the Dundee Infirmary to make contributions towards their keep but appealed successfully to the public for financial support through donations and subscriptions. By 1863, the finances of the home were on a firmer footing with income that amounted to £207 – sufficient to meet expenditure during the second year of £179. Despite the need for public support, a personal statement in 1867 revealed that Alexander Forbes deliberately kept the management of the Dundee CH to himself. This statement said, "for obvious reasons, I kept the general management in my own hands".[31] Unfortunately, during the intervening 150 years, these "obvious reasons" have become less clear. Alexander Forbes may have recognized that single-handed management was far easier than reconciling the differing views of a sixteen-member Board of Directors such as that at the Glasgow CH.

The quiet, privately funded beginnings of the Dundee CH contrasted with the high profile fundraising undertaken by Beatrice Clugston to establish the Glasgow CH.[32] She embarked on her mission to fund the new

Home with unstoppable enthusiasm, organising meetings and activities in and around Glasgow in support of the new venture. She raised the bulk of the funds with a well-publicized bazaar held in the Glasgow City Halls in December 1864 over a period of four days. The Town Council supported the venture by not charging any rent and even donated money for decorations. The *Glasgow Herald,* reporting on the general level of excitement, observed that "the crowds were so great that locomotion around the Halls was difficult".[33] The bazaar raised £6,520 in four days, and by the standards of the day, this was an excellent result. Frank Prochaska has estimated that, while nineteenth-century bazaars took in between £100 and £10,000, most were nearer to the lower figure.[34] Within 10 months, Beatrice Clugston had raised an astonishing £10,000. This, together with subscriptions and donations, was sufficient to rent and maintain the Home. As with the Dundee CH, because the Glasgow Royal was itself funded by voluntary subscriptions, the Infirmary made no payments towards the upkeep of patients.

Despite her proactive role in fundraising for the Glasgow CH, Beatrice Clugston did not take on a direct managerial role. She worked with the system, rather than attempting to change it. As such, she worked within the established gender division common to nineteenth-century Scottish voluntary hospitals with a "ladies committee" that took on the fundraising and a "committee of gentlemen" that formed the Board of Managers, who managed the Home and its finances.[35] This was similar in structure to the Glasgow Royal and other voluntary hospitals in Britain. As with the Glasgow Royal, there were no female members on the Glasgow CH Board of Directors until the 1920s.

The Board of Management consisted of sixteen directors. These included, the Lord Provost of Glasgow and representatives from the Glasgow Town Council (one), Glasgow University (one), Directors of the Royal Infirmary (two), medical officers of the Glasgow Royal Infirmary (two), Glasgow Trades House (one), Glasgow Merchants House (one) and the Royal College of Physicians, as well as the Surgeons of Glasgow (one). Six subscribers were also elected to the Board, thus ensuring a continual supply of influential directors. For example, during the first four years, the representative from Glasgow University was Professor Joseph Lister. His name on the Board ensured the credibility of the Home within the medical profession. When Lister went to Edinburgh, another eminent Glasgow doctor, Professor William Tennant Gairdner, who later became the first Medical Officer of Health for Glasgow, succeeded him. This lineage of distinguished professors on the Board continued until 1939 with Professor George Buchanan, Professor Walter K. Hunter and Professor J. A. G. Burton. Another influential name amongst the managers during the early years of the Glasgow CH was Dr George Macleod, a surgeon at the Glasgow Royal and successor to Joseph Lister. Before he joined the Glasgow CH Board, he established his interest in convalescent homes with an article published in the *Glasgow Medical Journal* in 1859 on "Reasons Why Sanatoria should be established on the Clyde for the Sick Poor of Glasgow". He was, therefore, most likely not very difficult to recruit. The non-medical composition of the Board was drawn from influential members of Glasgow trade and business communities.

Despite the fact that both homes were managed independently of any infirmary, in many other respects they were administered quite differently. The organization of a strong influential Board of Managers, with a similar structure to that of the Glasgow Royal and links to wider medical, trade and business communities, proved to be a major strength of the Glasgow CH. By contrast, Alexander Forbes chose a vastly different, single-handed management style, relying on financial support from his aristocratic connections. Although this was initially successful, it later proved to be a major reason why the home failed to thrive after his death.

Staffing Issues

Although both homes enjoyed the voluntary services of their managers, the Glasgow CH also benefited from the work of several paid employees, including their medical officers. Nineteenth-century doctors often agreed to take unpaid posts, either from a sense of obligation or because it provided access to more lucrative private patients.[36] However, most convalescent homes, including the Glasgow CH, paid their doctors. It was often a welcome addition to what could be an uncertain income from private practice and was particularly important to Scottish doctors. As Anne Digby points out, "Medical incomes in Scotland were notorious for their meagreness and for the hard work that was needed to win them."[37] The benefit of appointing a salaried doctor was that it gave a wider choice of applicant; and. once appointed, they often stayed for long periods. The Glasgow CH had two medical officers, one for visiting patients while in the home, and the second for examining patients prior to admission. Between 1865 and 1936, the post of visiting medical officer changed only four times and the examining medical officer three times. By contrast, the Dundee CH had just one – honorary – medical officer,and, although the first to be appointed, Dr Crockett, stayed with the Dundee CH for fifteen years, he was difficult to replace.[38]

Apart from the Dundee CH's first year, both homes employed salaried matrons. The post was popular because it provided income and accommodation, although until the later nineteenth century a matron was regarded as more of a housekeeper than a nurse.[39] Initially, however, neither of the homes engaged staff with specific nursing responsibilities. By the 1880s, trained nurses became common in hospitals and in 1889 the directors of the Glasgow CH agreed to employ a trained nurse

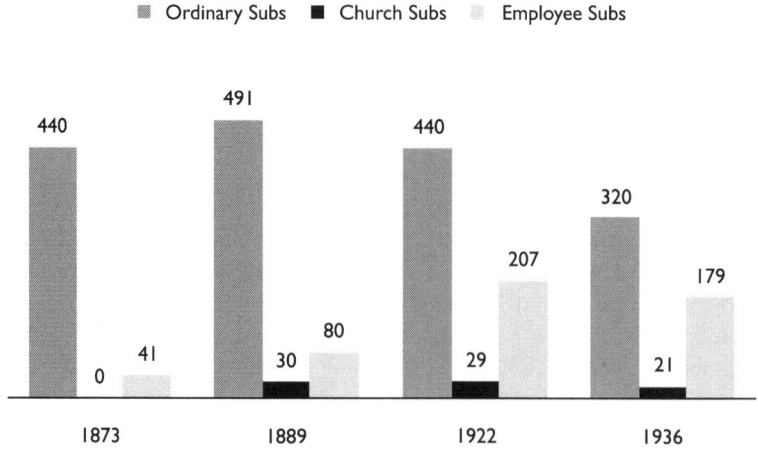

■ Ordinary Subs   ■ Church Subs   Employee Subs

Sources: Annual Reports for Glasgow CH, 1873, 1889, 1922 and 1936.

Figure 10.1 Glasgow CH Subscriptions, 1873–1936

to allow patients recovering from surgery "whose complaints only required such attention and dressing as in hospital". To support the viability of this proposal they added "to allow patients to return to their work more quickly".[40] There is no evidence of any trained nurses at the Dundee CH.

Another key employee at the Glasgow CH was the subscriptions collector who was paid on commission. Not all convalescent homes employed collectors and there is no evidence that the Dundee CH ever did. The use of collectors was frowned upon by some of the homes. For example, James Smith, one of the founders of the Mission Coast Home (located at Saltcoats on the Ayrshire Coast), published a letter in the *Ardrossan and Saltcoats Herald* expressing his disapproval with the statement: "I shall take it kind of friends not to press the very objectionable work of canvassing upon me."[41] However, the Mission Coast Home had underlying support from the Glasgow City Mission. Subscribers were far more important for independent charities such as the Glasgow and the Dundee CH. Figure 10.1 illustrates the overall growth of subscriptions at the Glasgow CH during the twentieth century. Table 10.1 translates the subscriptions into their monetary value and although indicating a slight downturn in 1936 demonstrates that there was nevertheless an overall rise in subscriptions during the twentieth century. This may have been due to employing a collector. By contrast, the lack of a collector at the Dundee CH may have contributed to the decline of subscriptions after 1875, illustrated in Table 10.2.

Table 10.1 Glasgow Convalescent Home: income, capital subscriptions and patients, 1867–1936

Year	Income £	Capital £	Subscriptions £	Number of Patients
1867	1,380	10,454	958(inc.donations)	345
1873	1,668	13,670	957	633
1889	2,099	24,928	1,389	1,381
1922	4,461	24,404	2,626	1,399
1936	3,823	33,866	2,231	1,330

Sources: Annual Reports for Glasgow CH, 1867–1936.

Table 10.2 Dundee Convalescent House: income, capital, subscriptions and patients, 1863–1883

Year	Income £	Capital £	Subscriptions £	Number of Patients £
1863	318	N/A	54	59
1866	222	N/A	98	94
1870	263	N/A	110	119
1877	281	2,323	94	88
1883	234	2,723	67	68

Sources: Annual Reports for Dundee CH, 1863–1883.

This historical perspective on volunteering supports a modern view that in many circumstances the benefits of employing paid staff outweigh those of involving volunteers.[42] It supports Charles Handy's argument that "giving professional services for free runs up against the requirements of the professional core, namely that they are fully committed, flexible and available".[43] Salaried medical officers not only had greater commitment but were easier to replace. In addition, a fully-committed collector was also vital to an organization such as the Glasgow CH without a parent organization since it ensured a healthy supply of subscriptions. Furthermore, employing a trained nurse enhanced the status of the institution. This all suggests that the use of paid employees was a better strategy than relying entirely on volunteers.

Expansion and Decline

In 1867, with increased demand for admission, Alexander Forbes found himself fundraising for larger premises. With the patronage of Princess Mary Adelaide (mother of the future Queen Mary and consort to George V) and thirty-four aristocratic ladies, he held a bazaar that raised over £2,300.[44] This was his major source of revenue and the funds were sufficient to purchase a house on William Street. Although this cost £800, plus £200 in additional expenses, there was still sufficient left over to increase the endowment. Before moving to William Street, the Dundee CH annual report for that year also indicated a visit to the Glasgow CH with the optimistic conclusion that "it is gratifying to know that as regards the economy of management, and the size of the institution, that of Dundee, even in its present state, may challenge a favourable comparison with it".[45] The visit to the Glasgow CH may have encouraged Alexander Forbes to broaden his management, particularly as the Dundee CH now owned property and substantial capital of over £2000. Consequently, in 1870, Alexander Forbes set up a trusteeship that included himself, David Small, a solicitor, Lord Kinnaird and Jane Ogilvy's husband, Sir John Ogilvy. Forbes continued to make personal appeals for public funding. In 1874, he also persuaded prominent Dundee doctors to write letters of endorsement for the Home.[46] Yet despite all of this, when Alexander Forbes died in 1875, although the new Bishop of Brechin vowed to continue his work and took his place as a trustee, both subscriptions and the number of patients admitted declined thereafter (see Table 10.2).

In 1870, Beatrice Clugston also launched another fundraising programme to fund larger premises for the Glasgow CH and raised a further £5,000 with her second bazaar. This, together with a special building fund, provided over £18,000 that was sufficient to purchase an eighty-three acre site at Auchinloch Farm at Lenzie, just north of Glasgow. The managers decided to use some of the land for building the new convalescent home, but rented out the farm as extra income. After the move to Lenzie, public subscriptions rose as patients were admitted from the general public and subscribers were allowed to sponsor patients. This was usually one patient per £1.1s subscribed, although there were some variations, particularly for subscriptions from larger organizations. During the twentieth century, the Glasgow CH responded to the widely acknowledged growth in national concern over the welfare of mothers and children and opened special facilities for them.[47]

Both homes faced challenges during the latter part of the nineteenth century in the form of competition from new convalescent homes. In 1876, the Dundee Royal Infirmary opened an impressive new convalescent home at the fashionable seaside resort of Broughty Ferry. This new Infirmary even gave it the similar name of the Dundee Convalescent Home. Although it was mostly funded by a wealthy businessman, David Baxter, the Infirmary also made public appeals for donations and subscriptions that may have diverted funds away from the Dundee CH. With a wider pool of subscribers, the Dundee CH could have remained unaffected but the arrival of a rival estabishment also coincided with the loss of Alexander Forbes and there was a decline in subscriptions, overall income and patients following his death (see Table 10.2).

The Glasgow CH experienced a similar problem to that in Dundee when, in 1896, the Glasgow Royal opened the Schaw Convalescent Home at Bearsden, an affluent suburb of Glasgow. The new home was a far grander building than the plain and functional structure that housed the Glasgow CH at Lenzie and was also exclusively for Glasgow Royal patients. These factors could have drawn patients away from occupying beds that the Glasgow CH had always reserved for Glasgow Royal patients – with potentially disastrous effects on their admissions, subscriptions, donations or legacies. Yet this did not happen and there was no noticeable effect from the opening of the Schaw Home. Table 10.1 shows that there were only marginal changes in patient admissions during the twentieth century.

The strong financial position of the Glasgow CH together with its continued popularity helped it to meet further challenges during the twentieth century such as the general decline in subscriptions to charities and hospitals that Cherry has identified as a reflection of the development of National Insurance.[48] By 1936, the Glasgow CH had a healthy capital sum of £33,866 that, together with land and buildings, made it a relatively wealthy charity. This buoyant financial position supports the reappraisal of the finances of medical institutions in Britain by Cherry, Gorsky et al, in that their general financial position during the inter-war period was less gloomy than previous thought.[49]

Following a promising expansion for both homes, financial support for the Dundee CH declined together with patient admissions. This coincided with the death of Alexander Forbes and the opening of a new convalescent home by the Dundee Royal Infirmary. However, there was no such decline at the Glasgow CH when Beatrice Clugston died and the Glasgow Royal opened its own convalescent home. While this resilience can be explained by progressive staffing policies and management, the admissions policies of the homes also help to explain the different experiences of the two organizations.

Admissions Policy

Gosling has identified policy changes in some voluntary hospitals during the Inter-War period to introduce payments by patients.[50] There were no such policy changes at either the Dundee or Glasgow CH and, as with most Scottish convalescent homes, they restricted their intake to patients unable to pay for themselves. Even as late as 1929, the Glasgow CH rules clearly stated that "no patient should be admitted unless they are in poor circumstances and considered unable to pay for themselves".[51] On the other hand, while patients made no direct payments there was a rise in subscriptions from benefit societies and employees schemes. Gosling also refers to the increased number of contributory schemes during the inter-war period that gave patients rights of admission to voluntary hospitals. While the

Glasgow CH had always encouraged subscriptions through employee contributions, Figure 10.1 illustrates the dramatic increase from this source during the twentieth century.[52] Patients admitted through employee schemes might well have been poor, but their membership gave them entitlement rather than admission through charity and they were, therefore, contributory. By contrast, in 1883 the Dundee CH annual report revealed that subscriptions had dwindled from around eighty subscribers who provided £110 in 1870 to just forty and a corresponding £67 in 1883 (see Table 10.2). The remaining subscriptions were from individuals with no employee organizations.

Aside from issues of entitlement, neither the Glasgow nor the Dundee CH – in common with other Scottish convalescent homes – accepted patients recovering from all types of illnesses or conditions. The rules of the Glasgow CH excluded those recuperating from infectious diseases, the chronic sick, epileptics and persons suffering from copious ulcers. And, once medical authorities had established the infectious nature of tuberculosis, these patients were also ineligible. They also banned "persons of immoral character or of intemperate habits".[53] In practice this meant that they only admitted patients unlikely to be troublesome and sufficiently recovered to be up and about all day. This was important as ambulatory patients required less supervision and nursing care. Although there were similar exclusions at the Dundee CH, surprisingly they did not exclude patients recovering from infectious diseases. The unease that this could cause amongst potential patients might well have had a negative effect on admissions.[54] Support at the Dundee CH was probably further reduced by the female-only policy. There was no gender restriction at the Glasgow CH. Most of the patients at the Glasgow CH were of working age, as they were most likely to have access to a subscriber.

Although therefore, both homes only admitted patients well on the road to recovery and those in poor circumstances, the Glasgow CH benefited from an increased number of patients admitted through organizations, wherein membership gave them entitlement to admission. As the Dundee CH closed in 1911, it was not able to take advantage of this new trend in subscription contributions, whereas it enabled Glasgow CH to increase in strength.

Conclusions

In conclusion, although both convalescent homes are now closed, there is much to learn from them and their particular histories. A recent report commissioned by OSCR (Office of the Scottish Charity Regulator) noted that the resilience of charities with a small number of trustees was lower than that of larger organizations.[55] Although Dundee CH did indeed have fewer trustees than its counterpart in Glasgow, their developmental history reveals wider issues which help to explain the success of one and the early retirement of the other.

Both homes benefited from dedicated and pioneering founders motivated by compassion and the Christian belief that was the duty of the rich to help the poor and sick. However, whereas Alexander Forbes focussed attention on his congregation and aristocratic connections, Beatrice Clugston sought support from a wider range of the population – anyone with funds or time to spare was acceptable. And their management style was very different. Following the death of co-founder Jane Ogilvy, Forbes managed the Dundee CH at first alone – and then with only four trustees. When he died, there was no effective replacement for his energy and drive, and the home failed to develop further. By contrast, Beatrice set up a self-renewing board containing sixteen directors with links to leading Glasgow medical and commercial organizations, which meant that the organization had the potential to attract even further support.

There were, however, other factors that contributed to the success of the Glasgow CH. One was the decision to employ paid staff rather than to rely entirely on volunteers. They employed salaried medical officers who were able to make a stronger commitment to the work and were far easier to replace than the voluntary doctors at the Dundee CH. Glasgow CH also employed a trained nurse, thus enhancing its credibility as a medical institution. Another paid employee, the Collector, proved central to its financial viability and stability since subscriptions were particularly important to independent charities such as these two homes. The absence of a collector at Dundee may have contributed to the fall in subscriptions after 1875. By contrast, a dedicated collector together with general management from their influential Board of Directors gave the Glasgow CH a healthy bank balance by 1936.

Admission policies also affected the development of the homes. Despite Alexander Forbes' intention to eventually admit male patients, the Dundee CH remained for females only and specifically for those over the age of ten years. Although the Glasgow CH had no age restriction, until the nineteenth century, in practice most patients were of working age since they were more likely to have access to subscribers. Changes only occurred in the Inter-War period when the Glasgow CH responded to the growing concern over mother and child welfare, by providing special facilities for this group.

In summary, the success of the Glasgow CH compared to its counterpart in Dundee can be explained in good measure by the greater breadth of support – both financially and in terms of its governing body – which had been secured by its founders. This comparative advantage was then reinforced and consolidated by two key sets of managerial decisions – the nature of the admissions policy which meant that many patients attracted financial support and the employment of paid staff to perform key medical, nursing and fund-raising functions. Without these advantages the Dundee

CH struggled and closed. The Glasgow CH grew into a large organization because it had sustainable management and attracted a far higher level of support than the Dundee CH, despite the similar aims of their respective founders.

Notes

This chapter is based on research undertaken for my PhD thesis and I therefore wish to acknowledge the generous sponsorship of Glasgow University, major support from my supervisors, at the Centre for the History of Medicine in Glasgow, Professors Marguerite Dupree and Eleanor Gordon, Dr Alastair Durie and the invaluable assistance of archivists, Alastair Tough (Glasgow) and Fiona Watson (Dundee).

1 Brian Abel-Smith, *The Hospitals* (London: Heinemann, 1964).
2 Olive Checkland, *Philanthropy in Victorian Scotland* (Edinburgh: John Donald, 1980).
3 Jacqueline Jenkinson, *Scotland's Health, 1919–1948* (New York, London: Peter Lang, 2002).
4 Steven Cherry, *Medical Services and the Hospitals in Britain 1860–1939* (Cambridge: Cambridge University Press, 1996), p. 47.
5 E. G. Gardiner, *Convalescent Care in Great Britain* (Chicago: University of Chicago Press, 1936), pp. 30–4.
6 John Bryant, *Convalescence, Historical and Practical* (New York: Burke Foundation, White Plains, 1927), pp. 12–26.
7 For example: R. A. Cage, "Health in Glasgow", in *The Working Class in Glasgow 1750–1914* (London: Croom Helm, 1987), pp. 56–76; M. A. Crowther, "Poverty, Health and Welfare", in *People and Society in Scotland, Vol. II, 1830–1914* (Edinburgh: John Donald, 1990), pp. 265–89; D. Hamilton, *The Healers (Edinburgh*: Canongate, 1987), pp. 146–7.
8 Glasgow's third major voluntary hospital, the Victoria Infirmary, opened in 1890 – and its own convalescent home, the Brooksby at Largs, in 1897.
9 Jenny Cronin, *The Origins and Development of Scottish Convalescent Homes, 1860–1939* (Glasgow: Unpublished PhD Thesis, 2003).
10 Christopher Whatley, *The Industrial Revolution in Scotland* (Cambridge: Cambridge University Press, 1997), p. 85.
11 "Lady Jane Ogilvy", Obituaries, Lamb Collection, Dundee City Library, p. 199.
12 *Glasgow Herald*, 5 September 1871.
13 *Annual Report*, Glasgow Convalescent Home (*A/R*, GCH), 1871, p. 3.
14 *A/R*, GCH, 1893, p. 4.
15 *A/R*, GCH, 1922, p. 7.
16 Frank Prochaska, *Women and Philanthropy in Nineteenth-Century England* (Oxford: OUP, 1980), pp. 5–17; Geoffrey Finlayson, *Citizen, State and Social Welfare in Britain 1830–1990* (Oxford: OUP, 1994), pp. 49–63; Olive Checkland, *Philanthropy in Victorian Scotland* (Edinburgh: John Donald, 1980), pp. 4–6.
17 Eleanor Gordon, "Women's Spheres" in *People and Society in Scotland, Vol. II, 1830–1914* (Edinburgh: John Donald Publishers, 1990), pp. 224–6.

18 Checkland, *Philanthropy*, pp. 5–6.
19 F. Goldie, *A Short History of the Episcopal Church in Scotland* (London: St Andrew's Press, 1976) p. 60.
20 Rowan Strong, *Alexander Forbes of Brechin* (Oxford: Clarendon Press, 1995), p. 49.
21 Felicia Skene, *A Memoir of Alexander, Bishop of Brechin* (London: J. Masters and Co., c. 1875), p. 7.
22 W. Perry, *Alexander Penrose Forbes* (London: SPCK, 1939), pp. 74–5; Donald Mackay, *Bishop Forbes, A Memoir* (London: Kegan, Paul Trench and Co., 1888); J. D. Mowat, *Bishop A. P. Forbes* (Edinburgh: Robert Grant and Co. 1925).
23 Olive Checkland, "Beatrice Clugston" in *Oxford Dictionary of National Biography* (Oxford: OUP, online ed. 2004).
24 Andrew Morrison, *The Story of Free St David's* (Kirkintilloch: D. Macleod, 1926), pp. 85–6.
25 Robert Hillhouse, *Bygone Years of the West of Scotland Convalescent Seaside Homes, Dunoon* (Glasgow:1909), pp. 14–15.
26 *Glasgow Herald*, 15 December 1864.
27 Beatrice Clugston, *Speak to the Clock* (Glasgow: David Bryce and Son, 1881).
28 *Glasgow Herald*, 5 September, 1871.
29 William Blaikie, *Miss Clugston and her Work* (Glasgow, 1875).
30 *Annual Report*, NNNN, Dundee Convalescent Home (*A/R*, Dundee CH, 1861).
31 *Ibid.*, 1867.
32 "Clugston, Beatrice" in *Biographical Dictionary of Scottish Women* (Edinburgh: Edinburgh University Press, 2006), p. 77.
33 *Glasgow Herald*, 15 December 1864.
34 Prochaska, *Women and Philanthropy*, p. 54.
35 Jane Lewis, "The Boundary between Voluntary and Statutory Social Service in the Late Nineteenth and Early Twentieth Centuries", *Historical Journal*, 39 (1996): 165.
36 Anne Hardy, *Health and Medicine in Britain since 1860* (Basingstoke: Palgrave, 2001), p. 165.
37 A. Digby, *Making a Medical Living: Doctors and Patients in the English Market for Medicine, 1720–1911* (Cambridge: Cambridge University Press, 2002), p. 165.
38 *A/R*, Dundee CH,1877.
39 Monica Baly, *Nursing and Social Change* (London: William Heinemann Medical Books, 1973), pp. 176–7.
40 *A/R*, GCH, 1889.
41 *Ardrossan and Saltcoats Herald*, 18 November 1871.
42 For example, David Billis and Margaret Harris, Taking the Strain of Change: UK Local Voluntary Agencies Enter the Post-Thacher Period, *Nonprofit and Voluntary Sector Quarterly*, 21, 3: (1992); 211–25.
43 Charles Handy, *Understanding Voluntary Organisations* (Harmondsworth: Penguin, 1988), p. 119. I am grateful to Colin Rochester for suggesting this and other references relating to paid employees versus volunteers.
44 *A/R*, Dundee CH, 1867.
45 *Ibid.*, p. 6

46 *A/R*, Dundee CH, 1874 and *Dundee Advertiser*, 23 April 1875.
47 For example see: H. Hendrick, "Child Labour, Medical Capital and the School Medical Service", c. 1890–1918' in R. Cooter, ed., *The Name of the Child* (London: Routledge, 1992), p. 45.
48 Steven Cherry, Before the National Health Service: Financing the Voluntary Hospitals, 1900–1939. *Economic History Review* (1997), p. 317.
49 Martin Gorsky *et al*, "The Financial Health of Voluntary Hospitals in Interwar Britain", *Economic History Review*, LV, 3 (2002), 533–57.
50 G. Gosling, "The Patient Contract in Bristol's Voluntary Hospitals, c. 1918–1929", *University of Sussex Contemporary History*, 11 (2007).
51 *A/R*, Glasgow CH, 1936.
52 *A/R*, Glasgow CH, 1936.
53 "Rules", *A/Rs*, Glasgow CH, 1867–1936.
54 "Rules", *A/Rs*, Dundee CH, 1861–1883.
55 Alastair McCrae and Izabella Nowak, *A Short Study of Resilience in Scottish Charities* (Glasgow: OSCR, 2010).

Change or Decay: The House of Charity for Distressed Persons in London, 1919–2000

PAT STARKEY

The survival of any charity depends on its ability to convince donors of the urgency or importance of its cause. But as economic and social environments change so do the needs of those who ask for help, and the imperative to survive and to continue to raise sufficient funds may force an alteration in the focus of the work or a reconsideration of its fundraising strategies. This chapter will consider the history of the House of Charity for Distressed Persons in London, particularly in the period from 1919. Its original mission had been to provide assistance to men and women in poverty through no fault of their own. However the ability to apply this criterion began to be challenged when, just a few years after the House opened its doors, altered economic conditions left it no option but to accept requests from less desirable applicants. At the same time, in order to encourage the continued support of benefactors, it was believed necessary to give the impression publicly that help continued to be offered to those men and women who fitted the founders' criteria for admission. The period between the two world wars saw an increase in the number of applicants whose backgrounds more nearly approximated to those for whom the charity had been designed, but this did not last, and social and economic changes after 1945 finally weakened the hold of the founders' intentions and forced the House to undertake major changes in direction in order to survive.

Origins and Early Challenges

The House of Charity for Distressed Persons in London was founded in 1846 in Rose Street, Soho by members of the Engagement, a group of eminent Anglo-Catholic Christians intent on works of charity.[1] They counted amongst their number W. E. Gladstone; his brother-in-law Lord Lyttelton; the future Lord Chancellor Roundell Palmer; the principal of King's College, London, R. W. Jelf; the theologian F. D. Maurice, and the physician of Bethlem Hospital, Dr Henry Monro.[2] Their aim was to aid the "deserving poor" at a time of national economic difficulty. The description "deserving" is, of course, a slippery one. The founders of the House had in mind those men and women who were able to equip themselves with proof of their good character from clergy or other professional men and to use profitably the support and opportunities presented to them during a short period of residence, before returning to lives of self support. Those unable to meet the criteria for admission were refused; Templeton, a man who applied three times in 1848 but was not admitted "because he brought his poverty on himself" was not untypical.[3] The House was anxious to distinguish itself from the workhouse or anything that might resemble a common lodging house.[4] Those who were admitted were helped to solve their various needs, whether that was employment and child care for a recently widowed woman; assistance in the process of finding work for a man whose employer's business had failed; or temporary care for children attending hospitals in London.[5] Whole families, many of whom were in the process of emigrating and waiting for their ships to sail, were admitted on a regular basis, allocated family rooms and supported as a unit.

No clear indication is given of the numbers that could be housed at any one time, but incidental references in the Minutes of the Council suggest that, when full, the House had at least 50 residents, possibly more. At the Annual Meeting in 1912, it was claimed that more than 28,000 men and women had been helped since 1846; this figure must include applicants who were given forms of outdoor relief, including money, as well as those who needed residential accommodation.[6]

By the last quarter of the nineteenth century, when the "hungry forties" were just a memory and fewer requests were received from suitable applicants, qualifications for residence had been relaxed to include many of the sort for whom the House had not been intended, a development that the Council noted with regret. For example, Eliza White and her child were admitted in August 1879. A situation as a cook was found for Eliza but the day before she was due to take up the appointment her prospective employer discovered, though we are not told how, that Eliza had shown herself to be unsuitable in a previous post, that her child was illegitimate and that she was bad-tempered and disobliging and an inveterate drunkard.[7] And some whose respectability might have been taken for granted proved to be a disappointment. In October 1899, the minutes note requests for admission from three clergymen – one "bibulous", the second "an imposter convert from many religions" and the third "amenable to the criminal law".[8]

That such unsuitable applicants were even considered for admission illustrates the difficulties faced by the charity by the end of the nineteenth century. The interval since its foundation had seen various attempts to manage the tension between the need to keep beds full and ensure a steady income while attempting to maintain an unchanged public image and discussions about ways to raise money had been routinely recorded in the minutes of late-nineteenth century Council meetings — something that changes little in the following decades.[9] Publicity for the House of Charity, therefore, continued to allow its supporters to believe that the principal recipients of its generosity were the respectable poor who had fallen on hard times. The speaker at the Annual Meeting in 1910 was to argue that the House was worthy of support because:

> It deals so largely with the middle class. Long experience had taught him that the working man had no special claim beyond others and that the Church ought to do more for the middle class who suffered silently, without either official or unofficial assistance . . . he did not speak against the work to be done for the poor but would like to see such work as the House of Charity was doing for the middle class very largely extended in London.[10]

Supporters may have applauded, but in the period to the outbreak of war the casebooks of the charity told a rather different story.

Inter-war London: The Rediscovery of the Respectable Poor?

Few applications for admission were received during the early months of the First World War. The Annual Meeting of 1915 drew attention to figures from the Local Government Board that demonstrated a marked decrease in unemployment and vagrancy and, although the House did not formally close, its normal activities were curtailed;[11] on occasion, money was given to applicants or rooms were rented to individuals or organizations needing temporary accommodation.[12] Because his services were not required, the Warden was given leave of absence "to proceed to service" in September 1915.[13]

After 1918 and the cessation of war, discussions about the future appeared to be based on the assumption that applications for admission might continue to come from those deemed to be socially undesirable and that to avoid having to admit them it might be necessary to alter the focus of the work. Suggestions for a fresh approach included using the House as a hostel for "educated women, where they could reside while undergoing training for the professions" and "advising people about the best place to go in their circumstances".[14] So radical a change in direction, however, proved to be unnecessary. During the inter-war years, and particularly between 1929 and 1939, the case books increasingly record the admission of those whom the original benefactors would have welcomed. For example, several entries for 1933 record that temporary accommodation was given to chartered accountants, lawyers, several managers of various sorts, university graduates and public school men.[15] It is not surprising, therefore, that attempts were made to recover the original function of the House of Charity, to re-establish admission criteria that approximated to those of the mid-nineteenth century and to serve the needs of respectable men and women temporarily in financial difficulty.[16] At the Annual Meeting in 1934, echoing the speaker in 1910 but this time with more reason, the Archbishop of Canterbury spoke approvingly of the House's work "among the black-coated gentry as they are entirely outside all schemes for unemployment relief".[17]

Although the records are not explicit about how many places were available, the minutes suggest that during the inter-war period, up to 20 women and as many as 16 men could be resident at any one time. This is fewer than during the nineteenth century and reflects improvements to the accommodation involving the introduction of cubicles and separate rooms in place of dormitories. Informal systems evolved which enabled the House to work towards meeting its founders' aims. For example, in 1935 Lord Halifax, a long-term supporter of the House, left £220 to charity. His son's decision to give it to the House, to facilitate work with London County Council and the Public Assistance Committee (PAC) in order that suitable persons might be referred by a central office for investigation and assistance was, in effect, a filter system which allowed the PAC to send socially acceptable people to the House while those less acceptable would be sent from the House to the PAC. The Chaplain was given the task of liaison.[18]

A similar filter operated as a result of links with Rowton House, a housing charity which provided accommodation for working men. (George Orwell described their establishments as amongst the best common lodging houses available, where for one shilling a night a man had a cubicle to himself and the use of excellent bathrooms.[19]) From early in 1932 applicants for admission who had been rejected by the House of Charity began to be sent by them to Rowton House hostels.[20] There is no explanation about why this decision was taken, although it is likely that this was an option used as a temporary measure when there were no free beds for men in Greek Street. For instance, in June 1933, it is suggested that applicants referred to Rowton House should re-apply to the House of Charity in a few days.[21] But that does not explain those occasions when some were chosen and others rejected. For instance, on 21 September 1933 when only 13 women, one child and three men were resident --

suggesting that there was a number of empty places for men – six of the eight male applicants were sent to Rowton House.[22] Given the confident expectation that the beds could be filled by men from the professional or managerial classes, it must be assumed that those encouraged to apply to Rowton House were considered, for reasons that are not stated, to have failed the test of acceptability.

Moreover, although Rowton House appears to have been the most commonly used source of alternative accommodation, similar arrangements were made with other hostels, such as those run by the Church Army, the Salvation Army, and that dedicated to St Martin of Tours in Penzance Place, suggesting that a well-recognized selection process weeded out those deemed to fit less well with the admission criteria.[23] So successful was the application of this policy that a note in September 1933 claimed that the "quality of applicants" to the House of Charity was up – of the admissions on that day, one was an insurance broker, one a manager in a house purchase and insurance company and a third was a chartered accountant.[24] At the outbreak of war in 1939, therefore, the House had every reason to believe that it was at least as successful as its mid-nineteenth century predecessors in providing accommodation for those whose credentials would have satisfied the founders.

London After 1945: Meeting New Challenges

The Second World War and its aftermath forced inescapable change in the life of the House.[25] If the national economic problems of the 1930s had allowed it to revert to some extent to the selection procedures laid down by its founders, this was less true after 1945. Low levels of unemployment in the late 1940s dramatically reduced the numbers of people needing emergency accommodation. Moreover, the inauguration of new welfare legislation appeared to allow a greater openness in addressing the longer-term mismatch between ideal and reality in the House of Charity admission policy. Discussions about how to adjust to the post-war situation can be dated to April 1945 when the Council minutes state:

> In view of Government proposals of social insurance it was important to consider reviewing the normal functions of the Charity and the advisability of providing for necessitous cases not covered by the Beveridge scheme. The chairman referred to elderly persons and the infirm needing a home.[26]

However, although there was no agreement to make major changes some adjustments were made and it was decided that the House should re-open "on the old lines" but that for the time being only women should be admitted,[27] a decision prompted by the recognition that during the 1920s and 1930s more women than men had applied for and been given accommodation in the House. The resolution that a matron or superintendent should be in charge of housekeeping, thus displacing the previous arrangement whereby sisters of the Community of St John Baptist managed the daily life of the House, marked a further shift. [28]

The new arrangements enjoyed only partial success. An interim period, during which accommodation was offered on a temporary basis to the staff of the Hospital for Women in Soho and sundry other residents[29] while discussions about the future of the House continued and work was undertaken to repair wartime damage and improve the standard of accommodation, finally came to an end in May 1951.[30] It was then resolved that rooms should be made available to the "educated in distress" and "young, low-income working girls."[31] A further significant change was the agreement that those who had hitherto been accommodated free should in future be asked to make a financial contribution towards their keep and may well owe something to the anxiety common to many charities which feared that the inauguration of new statutory welfare arrangements would discourage erstwhile donors from continuing their financial support.[32] It is also a recognition that applicants, even if not in employment, may well have been entitled to some sort of statutory benefit and could be expected to pay something towards their keep. The decision to change its name from the House of Charity to the House of St Barnabas in Soho was taken on 26 September 1951, after nearly half a century of discussion.[33]

That such a name-change was essential in the era after the legislation inaugurating the welfare state is unsurprising. Retention would have been more remarkable. But it was more than a change of name. The months and years of uncertainty about whom to admit, and on what basis, inaugurated a period of short-term arrangements with hospitals and other bodies, including an ambitious scheme for turning the House into an annexe of the Middlesex Hospital.[34]

The new situation gave rise to dissension among those who managed the House. Between November 1950 and March 1951 the warden and at least three of the four trustees required by the Constitution of the House resigned because they were unable to agree to the Council's new policy.[35] The full details of this new policy are not spelled out, but in addition to the requirement that guests should be female and contribute to the cost of their accommodation (the figure of 25/- a week had been agreed in 1950 and was increased to two guineas a few months later[36]) a sub-warden was to be appointed to help with their pastoral care and spiritual follow-up.[37] The work of a resident chaplain, hitherto essential to the running of the House, appears to have devolved -- at least temporarily – on the non-resident Cowley Fathers (the Society of St John the Evangelist, whose base was in Oxford).[38]

If, during the mid-nineteenth century and the first half of the twentieth, it had been possible to assert that the House met the acute needs experienced by respectable people who only needed short-term assistance, this was manifestly less often the case after 1945. Moreover, "the educated in distress" and "young, low-income working girls" whom the Council had identified as being well-suited to what it had to offer were either too thin on the ground or choosing other sorts of accommodation. Nevertheless, the Annual Meeting in 1954 affirmed its conviction that charities such as St Barnabas were still needed, and that the State did not, and could not, meet all needs.[39] But a letter from the Chairman of the Council to a number of hospital almoners in March 1957, outlining the characteristics of the "women we most like to receive",[40] brought few extra applicants, and the minutes begin to hint that the type of person most in need of help was to be found, not among young women needing temporary accommodation, nor even convalescent patients from nearby hospitals, but within the walls of the House among the "larger number of residents . . . suffering from some mental illness".[41]

It had become clear that the survival of the House would be dependent on admitting those whom it had previously wished to reject, supported by some form of public assistance. Attempts to adjust to changing fashions in welfare, changing legislation and changing definitions of "homelessness" (like "deserving", another slippery concept) and financial pressure had been reflected in the sorts of people arriving at the door of 1 Greek Street. Dr Dennis Brinton, speaking at the Annual General Meeting of the charity in June 1966, attempted to boost support for the change in direction as well as to give public expression to the new focus of its work. With skilful reference to one of the original benefactors, the Bethlem Hospital physician Dr Henry Monro, he made a rather disingenuous link to the charity's nineteenth-century origins, neglecting to mention that the provision of care for the mentally ill had not been part of Monro's intentions in the foundation of the House. Nevertheless, Brinton called attention to Monro's realization that "mental illness was not always determined by heredity, but that the stresses and strains of the hungry forties were bringing a great spate of mental breakdown". He linked this observation with the inability of the welfare state to provide "compassion and consolation" which he averred, "depend upon personal relationships of trust and affection between men and women". Applying those intangible qualities to the care of the mentally ill was, he implied, the new task of the House.[42]

Some attempt was made to ensure that the care provided was on the right lines. For example, the appointment of a consultant psychiatrist from the Tavistock Clinic in May 1968 proved useful as a support to the staff, none of whom appears to have had any training to deal with people with mental health issues.[43] But this arrangement was terminated after the appointment of a warden whose CV recorded that she had been a prison visitor at Pentonville Prison and had worked for Blackfriars Settlement and for Alcoholics Anonymous.[44] She lacked any sort of professional qualification but her experience was thought to provide the necessary basis for the care of those residents, possibly the majority, who were psychiatric patients, drug addicts or alcoholics.[45] Although it was decided that 19 of these were unsuitable and should be asked to leave,[46] a couple of years later it was acknowledged that it was impossible to keep all beds full unless what were described as "other undesirable" residents were admitted.[47]

The last third of the twentieth century was characterized by both insecurity and constancy. There were difficulties in staffing at every level although the sort of resident for whom the charity provided valuable support remained unchanged. That this coincided with the passing of the 1959 Mental Health Act, the phasing out of locked wards, the closure of large psychiatric hospitals and the advent of "care in the community" from the 1980s can be no accident especially, as the National Association for Mental Health pointed out, many local services vital to the support of patients being cared for in the community were not in place.[48] The House of St Barnabas, almost by default, had become a refuge for women whose mental health issues made it difficult for them to live independent lives.

This, then, was the background to the statement issued by the House of St Barnabas in 2005 that the work of 160 years, and more particularly the last half-century, was to come to an end. It was prompted by the realization that the premises – a Grade One listed building – were no longer up to standard for residential accommodation, but also by changing patterns in health and social care. Readers of the House web site were alerted to moves that were being taken to find a new way of serving people in need in central London. It claimed that:

> ... always at the forefront of meeting homeless persons' needs, the House is in the process of changing from a residential hostel for homeless women to a state of the art centre offering essential life skills, training, personal development and career paths for London's homeless people and those in crisis.[49]

The future work of the charity would be directed towards the development of a well-equipped day centre, designed for homeless people and equipped with opportunities for health care and training for employment. While stressing the continuity of its history, the authors neglected to mention that this change in activity was the latest of many. After all, the House had only been a hostel for homeless women since the early 1950s, and it had spent much of its 160-year history trying to reconcile the realities it found around itself with the philanthropic aims of its founders.

The Challenge of a Changing Religious Climate

There is a further twist. The House was founded with a strong religious purpose by members of the Engagement –– a group devoted to high Anglicanism and good works –– and instilling religious values in those who sought its help was one of its aims and one which, it must be assumed, its supporters approved. Residents were expected to attend church services and to obey rules which included allowing members of staff to determine which books and newspapers were permitted in the House.[50] These and similar rules had been difficult to enforce in the 1840s – by the twenty-first century, the thinking that lay behind them was no more than a feature of the organization's history. To survive, it needed to access funds greater than those offered by individual Christian donors and to tap into the resources of statutory provision.

The advent of the welfare state affected all voluntary agencies providing personal services. Most people in need had some sort of financial support as of right and needed no longer to tailor their requests for assistance to the constitutions of charitable organizations in order to avail themselves of basic support. Inevitably the effects were considerable. By the last decades of the twentieth century, many voluntary agencies were themselves in receipt of money in order to perform tasks and run projects on behalf of, and under the direction of, the local or the national state. As Frank Prochaska and others have argued, the provision of particular services turned "the intermediary institutions of civil society into agencies of the state through contracts and financial control".[51] Although such arrangements may have provided a degree of stability, it is claimed that the embrace of the welfare state denied Christian charity its opportunity for influence and undermined what had hitherto been the essentially personal relationship between donor and recipient.[52] Supporters of the House of St Barnabas would argue that this has not been the case; the House had always prided itself on its close relationship with those it had called at various times inmates, clients, guests or service-users. That relationship, however, was no longer freighted with the religious ambitions of the founders. Like other organizations with a Christian foundation it found itself operating in an increasingly secular society where too close an association between religion and service had become unacceptable, both to funders and to service users.

Although they differ in both chronology and interpretation, historians like Hugh McLeod and Callum Brown have shown how profoundly British civil society has been influenced by the decline of religion in recent decades.[53] None would disagree with Prochaska's observation that Christian child rescue societies like Dr Barnardo's Homes (now Barnardo's), the Church of England Central Home for Waifs and Strays (now the Children's Society) and other humane organizations have abandoned their once overt evangelical mission, for which their co-religionists would have been prepared to give generously, and now depend on funding from government sources in exchange for specific activities in order to survive.[54] But as Robert Skidelsky has recently argued, although Britain is no longer a Christian country, it is a christianized one; the retention of what may be described as a Christian moral and ethical base alongside the abandonment of overtly religious daily practice in agencies such as these can be said to illustrate his claim. [55]

Conclusion

The plot of this story will be familiar to those with interests in charity and the voluntary sector. It demonstrates the urge to continue to exist, even after the original purposes for which the organization was founded have ceased to obtain, giving rise to the necessity for it regularly to reinvent itself in order to survive. It also illustrates the changing nature of need in the light of shifting social and economic conditions and increased state intervention. The necessity to compete for limited funds, whether charitable or statutory, forces responses to changing patterns of funding based on public understanding of need. Some may applaud this as demonstrating the invaluable flexibility, and versatility, of the voluntary sector – others may agree with the member of one organization overheard describing it as 'Next Thing-ism'.

As well as its change of name, the erstwhile House of Charity for Distressed Persons in London has much in common with other religiously-based organizations. Its original ambition was to provide temporary care for, and to instil religious values in, those who availed themselves of its help — men and women who, in the twentieth century, would have been labelled middle class. Discussion about providing help for a particular class of person fades rapidly after 1945 and gradually evolves into an admission that those most in need of its assistance had little in common with those of the 1840s or even the 1930s. The expectation that the House would be in a position to demand, or even encourage, religious observance among its clients also fades. There is a tacit acceptance that, although still a charity with Christian foundations and a Christian ethos, its purpose is to provide practical assistance to those in need but not to engage in overtly religious activity.

Although it has taken on a different shape, homelessness is still a feature of life in London, but provision at the House for those who find themselves on the streets has recently changed again. The greater part of its Grade One listed building has recently been taken over by Quintessentially, "The world's leading luxury lifestyle group", as a private members club.[56] Work with and for the homeless at the House of St Barnabas has been restricted to rooms at the top of the House and the plans for helping homeless people develop new skills, described so enthusiastically in 2005, have been modified. The Quintessentially web site claims that:

> Revenue generated through Membership, Event Sales, the restaurant, lounge and bars, finances the charity in the delivery of its programme, while the operation itself acts as a unique resource for training and work experience opportunities.[57]

Some commentators fear that future funding for the work of the House of St Barnabas is as uncertain as it has been for most of its history.

Notes

I am grateful to Jacqueline Turton for allowing me to consult her thesis, *Christian charity and social control: attitudes to the poor at the House of Charity for Distressed Persons in London 1847–49* (MA, University of Liverpool, 1995) and to Linda Morris for permission to use her unpublished research on the House of Charity.

1 Now Manette Street. The House moved to its current premises at 1 Greek Street in 1860.
2 Flintshire Record Office (hereafter FRO) Glynne Gladstone MSS 1688, Prospectus, 11 June 1846. Members of the Monro family have been associated with the House since 1846.
3 Westminster Archive Centre (hereafter WAC) ACC 2091 House of Charity Minute Book (hereafter HCMB), 31 October 1848.
4 FRO, Glynne Gladstone MSS 1688, Prospectus, 11 June 1846.
5 See P. Starkey, "Club feet and charity: the experience of children at the House of Charity, Soho, 1848–1914" in A. Borsay and P. Dale (eds), *Disabled Children: Contested caring, 1850–1979* (London: Pickering and Chatto, 2010).
6 WAC ACC 2091 HCMB, 7 March 1912. From the mid-1890s the minutes record details of those who had been rejected, but in spite of some unease unsuitable applicants were often given the given the benefit of the doubt and admitted.
7 WAC ACC 2081 HCMB, 2 August 1879. See .Starkey, "Temporary relief for specially recommended or selected persons": the mission of the House of Charity, Soho, 1846–1914" *Urban History*, 38 (2005), 112.
8 WAC ACC 2091 HCMB, 13 October 1899.
9 See Starkey, "Temporary relief", 112.
10 WAC ACC 2091 HCMB, 8 March 1910.
11 WAC ACC 2091 HCMB, 17 March 1915.
12 WAC ACC 2091 HCMB, 17 March 1915; 6 May 1915, 23 September 1915.
13 WAC ACC 2091 HCMB, 3 September 1915. He was taken prisoner two months later and repatriated in 1916.
14 WAC ACC 2091 HCMB, 3 October 1918, 4 April 1919.
15 See, for example, WAC ACC 2091, HCMB, 21 September 1933, 5 October 1933, 12 October 1933, 23 November 1933.
16 WAC ACC 2091 HCMB, 3 October 1918.
17 WAC ACC 2091 HCMB, 16 March 1934.
18 WAC ACC 2091 HCMB, 7 November 1935.
19 G. Orwell, *Down and out in London and Paris* (London: Penguin, 2001), ch. 37.
20 See, for example, WAC ACC 2091 HCMB, 15 June 1933, 22 June 1933, 30 June 1933.
21 WAC ACC 2091 HCMB, 15 June 1933; 30 June 1933.
22 WAC ACC 2091 HCMB, 21 September 1931.
23 For example, WAC ACC 2091 HCMB, 14 December 1933. 11 January 1934.
24 WAC ACC 2091 HCMB, 21 September 1933.
25 It had been agreed before the outbreak of war that the House should close for the duration. The building was damaged by the bombing, although some parts of it were rented from time to time to various organizations, including the

YWCA and TocH. WAC ACC 2091 HCMB, 28 November 1939; 9 January 1940; 19 March 1940, 30 April 1941, 27 August 1942, 9 November 1943.

26 WAC ACC 2091 HCMB, 17 April 1945.

27 WAC ACC 2091 HCMB, 20 March 1946.

28 The Community had played an important part in managing the housekeeping and some of the pastoral functions of the House since 1860, when they moved into the property in Rose Street vacated by the House of Charity. The sisters ran a penitentiary for "fallen women" in Rose Street. V. Bonham, *A Place in Life. The Clewer House of Mercy, 1849–83* (Windsor: Thameslink Publishing, 1992), passim.

29 WAC ACC 2091 HCMB, 6 July 1949.

30 See, for example, WAC ACC 2091 HCMB, 7 September 1949; 5 October 1949; 2 November 1949, 7 December 1949.

31 WAC ACC 2091 HCMB, 2 May 1951.

32 For example, Sir Robert Waley-Cohen, a supporter of Toynbee Hall, had argued in 1946 that " . . . a totalitarian government is robbing the individual so that he can no longer enjoy the immense pleasure of supporting beneficent causes" quoted in N. Deakin, "The perils of partnership: the voluntary sector and the state, 1945–1992", in J. Davis Smith, C. Rochester and R. Hedley (eds), *An Introduction to the Voluntary Sector* (London: Routledge, 1995), p. 84. See also, F. Prochaska, *Christianity and Social Service in Modern Britain: The disinherited spirit* (Oxford: Oxford University Press, 2006), pp.148ff; P. Starkey, *Families and social workers: The work of Family Service Units, 1945–1985* (Liverpool: Liverpool University Press, 2000), pp. 175–6.

33 WAC ACC 2091 HCMB, 26 September 1951. A change was first mooted on 29 November 1909, because the name gave rise to confusion about whether it referred to a "refuge" or, perhaps, an off-shoot of the Charity Organization Society and had the potential to disadvantage inmates seeking employment or emigration.

34 WAC ACC 2091 House of St Barnabas Minute Book (hereafter HSBMB), 13 October 1953; 10 November 1953.

35 WAC ACC 2091 HSBMB, 1 November 1950, 7 February 1951, 7 March 1951.

36 WAC ACC 2091 HCMB 5 July 1950, 26 September 1951.

37 WAC ACC 2091 HCMB, 1 November 1950.

38 WAC ACC 2091 HCMB, 5 April 1950, 3 January 1951.

39 WAC ACC 2091 HSBMB, 10 June 1954.

40 WAC ACC 2091 HSBMB, 11 March 1957.

41 WAC ACC 2091 HSBMB, 8 December 1959.

42 WAC ACC 2091 HSBMB, 14 June 1966.

43 WAC ACC 2091 HSBMB, 25 February 1969.

44 The Blackfriars Settlement had been founded as the Women's University Settlement in 1887 and had changed its name in 1961.

45 See 22 April 1969, when a laconic entry records that it is difficult to resist "entry of unsuitable cases".

46 WAC ACC 2091 HSBMB, 23 September 1969.

47 WAC ACC 2091 HSBMB, 23 March 1971.

48 WWW.MIND.org.uk/information. Accessed 25 May 2008.

49 www.Atthehouse.org.uk. Accessed 29 April 2008.

50 WAC ACC 2091 HCMB, 19 January 1847.
51 F. Prochaska, *Christianity and Social Service in Modern Britain* (Oxford: Oxford University Press, 2005), p. 165.
52 *Ibid.*, pp.148ff.
53 H. McLeod, *The Religious Crisis of the 1960s* (Oxford: Oxford University Press, 2007), pp. 215ff; C. Brown, *The death of Christian Britain* (London and New York: Routledge, 2001), passim; but see J. Cox, "Master narratives of religious change", in H. McLeod and W. Ustorf (eds), *The Decline of Christendom in Western Europe, 1750–2000* (Cambridge: Cambridge University Press, 2003), pp. 201ff for a discussion of theories of secularization.
54 Prochaska, *Christianity and Social Service*, p. 170.
55 R. Skidelsky, "Twentieth-century Britain: A success story?" in J. Clark (ed.) *A World by Itself. A history of the British Isles* (London: William Heinemann, 2010), p. 590.
56 www.quintessentially.com (accessed 26 June 2010).
57 www.hosb.org.uk. (accessed 30 August 2010).

PART IV

Change and Continuity

Scientific Philanthropy and the Society for Bettering the Condition and Increasing the Comforts of the Poor, 1796–1824

JONATHAN FOWLER

In the late eighteenth century Britons increasingly perceived poverty as a social problem. "The 'annals of the poor' ceased to be 'short and simple'" and, according to historian Gertrude Himmelfarb, "became long and complicated."[1] The problem of poverty was complicated by intermittent war with France, population growth, the first wave of industrialization, and periods of dearth brought on by poor harvests. Throughout the period, but especially during the crises of 1795–96 and 1800–1, a dramatic rise in the numbers of laboring poor drove poor rates up and threatened to overwhelm the entire poor law system. In *A Dissertation on the Poor Laws* (1786), Joseph Townsend claimed that the security afforded by parochial aid actually worsened the problem of poverty and thus abolition, or at least reform, was needed. Similar criticism was leveled at privately funded charities that frequently coordinated their efforts with poor law officials in what Joanna Innes and others have described as a mixed economy of welfare. While emergency almsgiving and food charity during periods of dearth drew particular criticism, the very roots of charity seemed at stake.[2]

Riding this tide of reform, Thomas Bernard, philanthropist and Treasurer of the London Foundling Hospital, presented a proposal for a new philanthropic organization to a trio of like-minded gentlemen, William Wilberforce, E.J. Eliot and Shute Barrington, the Bishop of Durham.[3] Its remarkable scope would be "every thing that concerns the happiness of the poor – every thing by which their comforts can be increased" and thus was it christened *The Society for Bettering the Condition and Increasing the Comforts of the Poor* (hereafter SBCP).[4] For the most part, the SBCP eschewed providing direct relief, opting rather to serve the cause by publishing news and accounts of friendly societies, savings banks, schools of industry, fever hospitals and other welfare measures. By specializing in publicity the founders set out to answer critics but, more importantly, to address the core problem of poverty by making philanthropy a science.

This chapter explores how the SBCP's development of "scientific philanthropy" appeared in its philosophy of poor relief, the tone and structure of its printed materials, and finally in the Society's development of a close working relationship with members of the scientific community. What follows also makes clear that the SBCP's quest for a science of philanthropy grew from its complex relationship with administrators of statutory forms of relief and from the unique organizational challenges associated with developing a coordinating charity. Serving as a clearing house for charitable projects allowed the Society to interact with and influence both parish officers and local philanthropists without falling into jurisdictional and territorial disputes that sometimes impeded the introduction of new ideas and reforms. It is true that the life of the SBCP spanned only the years 1796–1824; nevertheless, many of the projects it championed and the scientific principles it helped establish endured well into the Victorian era, demonstrating, in fact, a remarkable continuity with the Charity Organisation Society founded in 1869. In this and other ways, the history of the SBCP echoes the major themes of this book, specifically the 'moving frontier' between state and voluntary action, the springs of voluntary action, the organizational challenges facing volunteer groups, and, finally, the roots of modern philanthropic practices.

Toward a Scientific Investigation of Poverty and Its Relief

In the Society's *Preliminary Address to the Public*, the founders boldly asserted: "Let us therefore make the enquiry into all that concerns the POOR, and the promotion of their happiness, a SCIENCE; let us investigate *practically* and upon *system*, the nature and consequences, and let us unite in the extension and improvement, of those things which experience hath ascertained to be beneficial to the poor."[5] This call to arms made clear that the best way to wage war on poverty was through systematic investigation of root social causes, followed by a comprehensive collection of information respecting proven relief methods. Rather than sponsor its own relief projects, the SBCP would collect "information respecting the circumstances and situation of the poor, and the most effectual means of meliorating their condition; in order that any comforts and advantages which the poor do now actually enjoy in any part of England, may eventually be extended to every part of it". The intelligence collected was to be "*useful* and *practical* information, derived from experience, and stated *briefly* and *plainly*, so as to be generally read and understood".[6] Information as relief stood at the heart of the SBCP vision, a vision shaped in part by early setbacks for its four founders. In April 1796 Marylebone workhouse officials rejected a proposal, fully funded by Bernard, Wilberforce, Eliot, and Barrington, that would have introduced the latest cookery technology of Count Rumford whose stoves would become somewhat legendary for their efficiency. Bernard for one attributed such failed initiatives to the resentment of parish officers and private charity governors to what they perceived as outsider interference. In the months that followed, he articulated the idea of an information clearing house as a way to overcome such territorialism.[7]

The SBCP's formation of a clearing house for information for philanthropists reflected three basic premises regarding poverty and its relief: that poverty resulted from environmental conditions; that it was both a moral and material issue; and that the problem was societal, not simply a dysfunction of the poor.[8] Of the first, Bernard, who served as both society secretary and editor of all publications, once wrote, "the vices and faults of the poor must be deemed the vices and faults of an unfavourable situation rather than of individual delinquency. Remove those disadvantages, and you add as much to moral character as to personal conduct".[9] Addressing the poor's social environment, however, required a combination of moral and material aid. "No plan for the improvement of the condition of the poor, will be of any avail, – or in any respect competent to its object," he wrote elsewhere, "UNLESS THE FOUNDATION BE LAID IN THE MELIORATION OF THEIR MORAL AND RELIGIOUS CHARACTER."[10] Despite the Evangelical tone of Secretary Bernard, the SBCP's focus was to encourage social virtue and moral well-being rather than religious conformity. In its first public statement the Society declared: "Let useful and practical information be offered to them [the poor]; give them time to understand; and the choice of adopting it; and I am mistaken, if they do not show as much good sense on the subject, as any other class of men in the kingdom."[11] In other words, an effective plan for relief depended on a mixture of material assistance for immediate concerns and education for the purpose of effecting long-lasting change. The Society, for instance, sponsored Rumford-style soup kitchens which distributed hot meals to urban poor. These kitchens, however, also sought to alter the poor's diet permanently by teaching them to make the soup for themselves. Self-help became a guiding principal as the poor were expected to help themselves by hard work, discipline, and thrift and by taking advantage of the material, educational, medical and other opportunities presented by the Society. Self-help, of course, applied primarily to the able-bodied, or "laboring poor" who had, the Society believed, a moral obligation to work toward their independence. Throughout its existence the SBCP also supported the application of the self-help principle to collective action and collaboration among the poor, most notably via friendly societies, savings banks, and chapel societies in which the poor could help one another as a group.[12]

A Scientific Journal of Philanthropy

The SBCP's role as a coordinating charity rested on its voluminous printed materials which took three primary forms. The most basic publication was called an *account*. It focused on a specific project and, according to Society guidelines, had to "consist of, first, a concise and correct statement of the fact which is the subject of the communication; and, secondly, practical observations and deductions arising out of that fact, and applicable, either to the particular object, or to the poor generally".[13] The SBCP occasionally published such an *account* individually; however, typically they grouped four to seven *accounts* together along with associated appendices in a numbered periodical labeled a *report*. Once five to six *reports* had gone to press, the Society republished them in a collected volume known simply as *The Reports*. From the late 1790s through the 1810s the SBCP produced 184 accounts and 132 appendices in six complete volumes and an unfinished seventh, distributing as many as 24,000 publications in one year. Given that some accounts subsequently appeared in literary magazines or pamphlets such as John Coakley Lettsom's *Hints Designed to Promote Beneficence, Temperance, and Medical Science* (1801), the circulation of the Society's printed materials was impressive.[14] As a result *The Reports* became, if only for a time, a public space where Britons encountered a variety of philanthropic projects which they were encouraged to imitate and supplement by creating and conducting experiments of their own, and, when a project proved effective, by submitting a written account to the SBCP editor for possible publication. This process made the SBCP in London a focal point for a national welfare network that extended to bettering societies throughout Britain: Clapham, Sheffield, Kimbolton, and Liverpool in England; Oswestry in Wales; Edinburgh in Scotland, and Cork, Dublin, Sligo, Carrick, Kilkenny, Donamyne, and New Ross in Ireland.

While ultimately unique, *The Reports* did draw from existing scientific literary models. SBCP accounts, for instance, shared basic characteristics with the journals of scientific societies such the Royal Society for the Improvement of Natural Knowledge, better known as the Royal Society. In general, such science periodicals published articles from members of the scholarly community. Decisions for adoption often rested on the reputation of the correspondent but consideration, too, was given to readability and writing style. In similar fashion, the SBCP depended upon professional correspondence from parish officials, philanthropists and others considered experts in the field of welfare measures. Another model from which the SBCP drew inspiration was Frederic Eden's *History of the State of the Poor* (1797). Of particular influence was its systematic and copious collection of information and details from parishes throughout England. "It has been a principle of Sir Frederic Eden", Bernard observed, "that enquiries respecting the state of the Poor should precede any great alteration in the system; the result of those enquiries being formed into well abstracted and perspicuous Reports".[15] The SBCP secretary highly esteemed Eden's use of concise, clear and useful intelligence as a basis for action and it definitely influenced Bernard's editorship of *The Reports*. He went so far as to advise his audience to read *State of the Poor* on their own as it would be "useful for abridging labour, and for directing enquiry".[16]

Building upon the tenor of these earlier models, Bernard used editorial license and a consciously scientific tone to create a sense of authority for the parish officials, clergy, physicians, and philanthropists who were the primary contributors to *The Reports*. Meeting this challenge was crucial because readers tended to associate the reliability of an account with the prestige and reputation of its author. While many correspondents were locally known and respected, *The Reports* aspired to a national audience and so needed to reach thousands of readers for whom these authors were basically anonymous. It fell to the SBCP secretary to convince a regionally diverse readership that these men and women not only were knowledgeable experts, but most importantly that their plans were worthy of imitation.

Bernard's strategy rested first upon drawing readers' attention to the unifying themes of *The Reports* rather than the authorial personae. Since he was the Society's most prolific contributor, in addition to being editor, Bernard could draw on his experience to transform the raw submissions of others into concise five to seven page accounts, replete with explanatory footnotes, and a separate concluding commentary labeled "Observations". In these concluding remarks the editor outlined what basic principles or lessons readers might glean from the plan before them. In similar fashion Bernard composed an introductory essay for each collected volume of *The Reports* in which he articulated recurrent motifs, such as self-help, that bound the individual accounts together.[17] When framing these themes, the editor logically made explicit connections to noted contemporary social theorists Thomas Malthus, Adam Smith, and others. In this fashion an unknown Yorkshire magistrate's plan for a spinning school became an object lesson in the political economy of Adam Smith. The juxtaposition of established thinkers and faceless correspondents cultivated a mental association designed to elevate the credibility of SBCP contributors thereby creating an authoritative voice for *The Reports*. Bernard reinforced this association with the specific language he used. When commenting on William Pulteney's *Extract from an Account of a Cottager's Cultivation in Shropshire,* for example, the SBCP secretary asserted that the account contained "not vague and unsupported theory; but practical and experimental truth; for the evidence of which we may refer not only to this account of the family of Richard Millward, but to a succession and variety of facts, stated in the four preceding volumes of the Society's Reports".[18] Bernard's direct diction, specifically his use of the phrase "practical and experimental truth", staked out for this account the authority and credibility of science.

The SBCP secretary added substance to the scientific tone and rhetoric of *The Reports* by educating his readers in contemporary social theories and philanthropic practice. The goal was clear – to develop a new legion of scientific philanthropists. To this end Bernard published a digest of two hundred years of British philanthropy entitled *A short View of different Proposals which have been made respecting the Poor, during the two preceding Centuries* (1804). Here he categorized previous relief measures under the headings of: benefit clubs or friendly societies, employment schemes, and workhouses. This literature review cross-referenced established plans by Baron Maseres, Joseph Townsend, Sir Josiah Child, Sir Matthew Hale, Henry Fielding, Thomas Gilbert, Daniel Defoe, Bernard Mandeville, and Frederic Eden with the new projects that appeared in *The Reports*. This process of association naturally served to put the SBCP plans in a broader context but it also provided direction for the Society's readers who one day might conduct their own local experiments. An audience well-versed in past charitable plans and theories would, it was hoped, avoid redundant plans, and, more importantly, be better positioned to conceive projects that were theoretically sound and ultimately "scientific".

Would-be scientific philanthropists benefited, too, from the statistical information that accompanied many SBCP accounts. Empirical data informed readers precisely how to reproduce an experiment, what results could be anticipated, and what costs were involved. After readers had tried their hand at a charitable experiment, they could compare their own results and submit them to the Society as a new account, or in support of an existing one. In order to make updates more accessible, Bernard added extensive footnotes for new data, to reference other accounts on the same subject, or, occasionally, to direct readers to another account by the same author. The SBCP's collected volumes, moreover, included a topical and geographical index, allowing readers to quickly find articles on education, workhouses, soup kitchens, or whatever topic they wished to investigate. In short, *The Reports* became a ready-reference for British and possibly continental philanthropists that pioneered a scientific approach to relief.[19]

In assessing *The Reports* as a scientific journal of philanthropy, it appears that SBCP founders, especially Bernard, consciously synthesized existing publishing methods and models, but in a way that created something new. On the one hand, the Society's accounts echoed the reliance of the Royal Society's *Philosophical Transactions* on a scientific scholarly correspondence. Yet, Bernard's extensive introductory essays and observations gave *The Reports* a thematic unity that the Royal Society's journal lacked. As for Frederic Eden's *State of the Poor*, its coherence of thought as well as its basis in empirical data served as a model for the SBCP. Eden's work, however, presented a largely static picture of England during the crises of the mid-1790s. Moreover, the exhaustive statistics and copious detail found in *State of the Poor* potentially overwhelmed readers. The functional design of *The Reports*, by contrast, emphasized accessibility as a tool for effecting philanthropic reforms. They needed to be useful and imminently readable and Bernard's editorial skill, his succinct "Observations" and his utilitarian reference system ultimately created a user-friendly publication. The fact that he updated accounts regularly to reflect the latest innovations made *The Reports* much more fluid than any contemporary publication dealing with poverty and relief measures. They truly represented a novel and innovative literary form after which later generations of philanthropists modeled their own works.

Building a Bridge to the Scientific Community

In addition to its effort to produce a scientific journal of philanthropy the SBCP also fostered a close relationship with innovators from the British scientific and medical community. The Society, for example, strongly advocated on behalf of Edward Jenner, developer of smallpox vaccination. Many physicians and practitioners of inoculation were sceptical of Jenner's discovery and in 1798 the Royal Society considered his work too controversial to publish in *Philosophical Transactions*. Bernard, who was quite convinced of vaccination's public utility, subscribed to and became Vice President of the Royal Jennerian Society to vaccinate the poor and used *The Reports* as a promotional vehicle for Jenner's ideas.[20] SBCP accounts in support of vaccination included committee reports of the Jennerian Society, observations from the Royal College of Physicians of both Ireland and Great Britain, a government report from Spain and several testimonials from individual physicians including William Hassey from South Africa, Dr. Grey from Chichester, and Sir Gilbert Blane.[21] Jenner obviously welcomed this support, but the SBCP benefited, too, because it was publicly linked to an important, if controversial, scientific discovery.

The Society also contributed to the spread of fever hospitals at the turn of the century. In general, eighteenth-century hospitals had been all-purpose facilities, but true to their name fever hospitals specialized in the treatment of contagious fevers. Since hospitals shared a deadly reputation, fever-hospital founders frequently named their facilities "houses of recovery". The SBCP vigorously promoted this first wave of the fever hospital movement by publishing two accounts of the Manchester Fever Hospital as well as an instructional tract entitled *Dr. Haygarth's Rules to Prevent Infectious Fevers*.[22] Haygarth, a pioneer of fever wards at the Chester Infirmary in the 1780s, was one of several experts cited in *The*

Reports. In 1801 several SBCP members, in collaboration with influential London physicians William Babbington, Robert Willan and Thomas Murray, took the initiative of opening a new fever hospital in the metropolis. The London Fever Hospital, which followed the provincial example of Manchester and Liverpool, served the city for more than a century, although it changed its name to the Royal Free Hospital in later years.[23] Direct involvement with the London Fever Hospital entailed important contacts in London's medical community, leading to several reports and pamphlets featuring expert medical opinions and professional advice from prominent physicians Thomas Bateman and W. P. Dimsdale.[24] Publicity in *The Reports* for the London and other fever hospitals was so effective that in 1804, when Parliament voted to issue a grant of £3000 for the prevention of contagious fevers, the award did not go to a hospital or public health charity but to the SBCP.[25] Although other factors undoubtedly were at play, winning this grant validated the Society's reputation for supporting scientific innovation in the realm of public health, a reputation that it had carefully cultivated and nurtured through the philosophical approach to philanthropy that resounded in the pages of its printed materials, especially *The Reports*.

Conclusion

As this chapter has shown, the SBCP was created to establish a science of philanthropy. To that end the founders articulated a comprehensive approach to the relief of poverty that recognized the complexity of the problem and the inadequacy of existing welfare measures, both statutory and voluntary. What was necessary, they maintained, was an empirical evaluation of relief methods and the social causes of poverty. Science was to provide the guiding principle for this investigation, but the SBCP founders had to decide how they, as a single group of volunteer citizens, could best lead this process. From a logistical perspective the Society opted to serve primarily as a publicist for philanthropic plans across Great Britain. Of course, only "scientific" projects would grace the pages of *The Reports*. In this way the gospel of scientific philanthropy could be broadcast far and wide with readers possessing the freedom to choose which plans might work in their locality. This tact had an additional benefit of reducing turf wars with parish officials and philanthropists. Thomas Bernard's editorial skill in establishing a scientific tone for the Society's publications, moreover, elicited submissions from scientific experts from a variety of fields, but especially from the realm of public health. As a result, *The Reports* served as a scientific journal of philanthropy from the late 1790s to the 1810s.

The SBCP facilitated a more systematic and scientific approach to welfare at the turn of the century; however, the work of late nineteenth-century voluntary organizations suggests that the battle was far from won. "While vast sums are expended annually for charitable purposes," the members of the Association for the Prevention of Pauperism and Crime in the Metropolis observed in 1868, "the want of system and co-operation in the distribution of relief but too often tends to the increase of the very evil which that relief was intended to remedy."[26] Although separated by half a century, these observations make it clear that Victorian philanthropists faced many of the same challenges as their late eighteenth-century counterparts. Interestingly, several groups, most notably the Charity Organization Society, adopted strategies pioneered by the SBCP. The COS, for example, published a weekly periodical, the *Charity Organisation Reporter*, to which they added in 1882 the *Charities Register and Digest*, a massive thousand-page annual on London charities to which the editor added an introductory review of significant alterations from year to year. The COS used these publications to coordinate welfare efforts into a system and to promote a more discriminating and scientific approach to the distribution of relief. [27]

The common attributes of the COS and the SBCP reflect continuity over the years; but they also point to a significant disjunction. Given their shared philosophy and approach to philanthropy, the need to create a new coordinating charity in the 1860s would have been largely moot if the SBCP had survived. The reasons for the Society's demise and the resulting chasm are too complex to address here but one factor was the waning of the pressure to make philanthropy systematic and scientific during periods of economic prosperity. The SBCP remains largely a product of its era, born at a time when dearth, industrialization, and war pushed the eighteenth-century mixed economy of welfare to the brink of collapse. Amid calls for reform, and even abolition, of the poor laws and open criticism that charity had become a problem rather than a solution, Thomas Bernard turned to that shining beacon of the Enlightenment era, science. And, although the SBCP was a product of that age, its promotion of a scientific approach to social problems and the central role it carved out for a charity coordinating organization of private citizens continues to inform modern debate. The attempt to understand the roots of voluntary action, as represented in this book, must therefore, acknowledge a debt to the SBCP and its establishment of scientific philanthropy.

Notes

1 Gertrude Himmelfarb, *The Idea of Poverty* (New York: Alfred A. Knopf, 1984), p. 18.

2 Joanna Innes, "The 'mixed economy of welfare' in early modern England: assessments of the options from Hale to Malthus (c.1603–1803)" in Martin Daunton (ed.) *Charity, Self-Interest and Welfare in the English Past* London: University College London Press, 1996, especially pp. 139–80.

3 E. J. (Edward James) Eliot, 1758–1797, M.P. and philanthropist; Shute

Barrington, 1734–1826, bishop of Durham from 1791 to 1826, noted for promoting philanthropy and education; William Wilberforce, 1759–1833, M.P., philanthropist, anti-slavery champion, and leader of the Evangelical Clapham Sect.

4 "Account of the Society", *The Reports of the Society for Bettering the Condition and Increasing the Comforts of the Poor* (hereafter *The Reports*) London: I (1797): 282–4. Harvard University's Kress Library has six complete volumes. HOLLIS No. 007314342. The British Library holds the four individual reports of the incomplete *Volume VII*, Shelfmarks, 1027.h.7.(3.), 1027.i.4, and 8289.11.

5 Thomas Bernard, "Preliminary Address", *The Reports* I (1797): 1–2.

6 "Account of the Society", *The Reports* I: 285.

7 Jonathan A. Fowler, *Adventures of an "Itinerant Institutor": The Life and Philanthropy of Thomas Bernard* (unpublished dissertation, University of Tennessee, 2003), pp. 157–64.

8 Himmelfarb, *The Idea of Poverty*, p. 18; Donna T. Andrew, *Philanthropy and Police: London Charity in the Eighteenth Century* (Princeton University Press, 1989), pp. 164–9.

9 Thomas Bernard, "Prefatory Introduction to the Second Volume", *The Reports* II (1799): 13.

10 Thomas Bernard, "Introductory Letter to the Fifth Volume, Addressed to William Wilberforce, Esq. M.P." *The Reports* V (1805):44–5.

11 Bernard, "Preliminary Address", *The Reports* I: 5.

12 Rowland Burdon, "Extract from an account of a friendly society at Castle-Eden, in the county of Durham", *The Reports* I (1797): 23–6. John Kingston, Jr., "Extract from an account of the Provident Institution for Savings, established in the Western part of the Metropolis", *The Reports* VII (1817): 93–113; Thomas Bernard, "Extract from an account of a Society in West-street, for the relief of their Poor Neighbours in Distress", *The Reports* IV (1803): 63–71.

13 "Account of the Society", *The Reports* I: 289.

14 Society for Bettering the Condition and Increasing the Comforts of the Poor, *Report of the Society for 1810* (London: 1810).

15 Thomas Bernard, "A short View of different Proposals which have been made respecting the Poor, during the two preceding Centuries", *The Reports*, IV (1804): A84-100. For *Volume IV* and *V* of *The Reports* an 'A' has been added to indicate location in the appendices.

16 Bernard, "A short view of Proposals", *The Reports*, IV: A99.

17 Volume VI of *The Reports* had no introductory essay.

18 William Pulteney, "Extract from an Account of a Cottager's Cultivation in Shropshire", *The Reports* V (1804): 78n.

19 The first volume of *The Reports* was translated into French and published in 1798. It is unclear how it was received or used in France.

20 Wellcome Library for the History of Medicine, Western Manuscripts (WMS) 4302–4306. Minutes of the Royal Jennerian Society.

21 "Report of the Medical Committee of the Jennerian Society", *The Reports* V (1805): A59-65; "Extract from an account of the measures taken by the Spanish Government, to extend the benefits of Vaccination to their foreign dominions, and to other countries", *The Reports* V (1806): A100-5; "The Report of the Royal College of Physicians of London on Vaccination: with the

opinions of the Royal Colleges of Physicians of Dublin and Edinburgh; and of the Royal Colleges of Surgeons of London, Edinburgh, and Dublin", *The Reports* V (1807): A142-68; "Case of the small pox, after variolous Inoculation. In a letter from Dr. Grey, of Chichester, dated June 24th, 1811", *The Reports* VI (1811): 290–1; Sir Gilbert Blane, M.D., "On the Practice of Vaccination", *The Reports* VI (1811): 305–10; "Extract from a letter on Vaccination, from William Hussey, M.D. dated Cape of Good Hope, 1st September, 1812", *The Reports* VI (1812): 379–82.

22   Thomas Bernard, "Extract from an account of the house of recovery, established by the Board of health at Manchester", *The Reports* I (1797): 86–97; Thomas Bernard, "Extract from a further account of the house of recovery at Manchester", *The Reports* II (1799): 158–64; "Dr. Haygarth's rules for the prevention of infectious fevers", *The Reports* II (1800): 265–6.

23   Royal Free Hospital Archives Centre, Minutes of the London Fever Institution, 1801–1818. The seminal history is William Bynum, "Hospital, Disease, and Community: the London Fever Hospital, 1801–1850" in Charles E. Rosenberg (ed.), *Healing and History: Essays for George Rosen* (Dawson, 1979), pp. 95–115.

24   Thomas Bernard, "Extract from an account of the institution to prevent the progress of contagious fever in the metropolis", *The Reports* III (1801): 202–15; "Certificate of several physicians of hospitals and dispensaries in London, as to the prevalence of the infectious fever in the metropolis", *The Reports* III (1801): 307–9; Thomas Bateman M.D., "Statement of the medical reports of the London House of Recovery, for the year 1805", *The Reports* V (1805): A74-80; W.P. Dimsdale, M.D., "Cases of Typhus Fever, in which the Affusion of cold water has been applied in the London House of Recovery", *The Reports* V (1802): A169-77.

25   *Report on the Petition respecting the Fever Institution*, 5 July 1804; Minutes of the London Fever Hospital, 16 August 1804.

26   Michael J. D. Roberts, "Charity Disestablished: The Origins of the Charity Organization Society Revisited: 1868–1871" *Journal of Ecclesiastical History*, 54.1 (January 2003): 42.

27   Discussions of COS and SBCP similarities appear in David Owen, *English Philanthropy 1660–1960* (Belknap Press, 1964), esp pp.105–6 and 234–8; Frank Prochaska, *The Voluntary Impulse: Philanthropy in Modern Britain* (London: Faber and Faber, 1988), p. 31; M. E. Jersey, "Charity a Hundred Years Ago" in *The Nineteenth Century and After* LVII (1905): 668; and Andrew, *Philanthropy and Police*, p. 174.

Is There a "New Philanthropy"?

BETH BREEZE

This chapter examines the current consensus that there is something distinctively "new" about philanthropy at the start of the twenty-first century. It addresses two of the book's overall themes: the dominance of continuity or change in the development of voluntary action and the historical evidence for the "springs" of voluntary action in the UK. Specifically, this chapter explores the widespread suggestion that contemporary philanthropic activity constitutes a radical break from the past, and argues that there is insufficient historical evidence to support claims regarding the existence of a distinctively "new philanthropy" at the start of the twenty-first century.

The Rise of "New Philanthropy" and "New Philanthropists"

The phrases "new philanthropy" and "new philanthropist" first appeared in common usage towards the end of the twentieth century and a sixteen-fold increase in their usage in UK newspapers occurred between 2001 and 2007.[1]

Foremost amongst those promoting the suggestion that a radical break has occurred in the practice and practitioners of contemporary philanthropy is Charles Handy whose book *The New Philanthropists* seeks to describe and exemplify "the new enthusiasm for giving that seems to have infected many of the seriously rich in Britain today".[2] Handy insists that "these givers are different"[3] and argues that, "we are certainly seeing a a new kind of philanthropic movement in Britain".[4] Belief in a "new philanthropy" is not restricted to the United Kingdom and a discussion of this phenomenon at the global level appears in a supplement to *The*

Economist magazine,[5] which analyses various aspects of new philanthropy.

The idea of new philanthropy implies a paradigmatic change in the charitable giving of rich people, and a review of its usage in both academic and non-academic literature indicates that this alleged paradigm shift has three different manifestations. Firstly, it is used to refer to new types of donors. New philanthropists are said to be younger, richer, more likely to be self-made and living a cosmopolitan lifestyle. They are, "in the prime of life, with goals still to achieve, passions to satisfy, and the energy that is needed to start something new".[6] The youthfulness of new philanthropists is often cited as a defining feature: "Many of the new breed of philanthropists have made their money in the City or computing. Some are still in their thirties".[7] The emergence of new sources of wealth from industries such as information technology and the financial sector, notably hedge funds, have also been cited as factors behind the creation of new multi-millionaires who are able to make significant philanthropic commitments at a younger age. As a media report on 'new philanthropists' claims, "most of them are self-made . . . they are hedge funders, bankers, corporate raiders, venture capitalists, dot-com millionaires, fashion tycoons or global magnates".[8]

Secondly, the term "new philanthropy" refers to support for new types of causes. Prominent new philanthropists are said to support emerging issues such as global health problems, notably HIV/AIDS, and the environmental crisis, especially climate change. For example, in 2006 the person most often named in UK media coverage of new philanthropy,[9] Sir Tom Hunter, donated £55 millions to fund poverty alleviation in Africa,[10] whilst another contemporary UK philanthropist, also described as being of the new breed, Richard Branson, funds a world council called "The Elders" which is, "a kind of United Nations of the great, the good and the rich to tackle issues such as conflict and global warming".[11]

Thirdly, new philanthropists are said to conduct their giving in new ways by setting up their own foundations and projects instead of funding existing charities. They are alleged to be distinctive in terms of being catalysts, rather than just responding to requests for money to support established charities.[12] They are said to use their power to leverage money from other funders (especially the government) and claim to pay far greater attention to how their money is spent, by demanding targets, performance indicators and measurable outcomes. It is this aspect of new philanthropy that lies behind the synonymous label of "philanthrocapitalism" which refers to the application of businesslike skills to the charity sector. As the authors who coined that phrase explain, they are, "businesslike in the sense of a serious focus on results"[13] and their preference for operating in this way is said to be due to their background in the private sector. As Handy explains "New Philanthropists have all been successful, most of them in business . . . They look at their philanthropic projects in a businesslike way."[14] New philanthropists are also said to be distinctive in their preference for intensive personal engagement with the causes that they fund,[15] a trait said to be found on both sides of the Atlantic:

> Britain's new philanthropists share with [Warren] Buffet and [Bill] Gates a mixture of impatience and business acumen that is shaking up the charity world. Reluctant to sign away their money to traditional [charities], they are adopting a hard-nosed approach that insists on looking at the bottom line. They want to make a difference, but balk at feeding the maws of self-perpetuating bureaucracies that squander money on administration and promotional campaigns. If charities don't cut the mustard, they are prepared to go it alone.[16]

Recent research into contemporary UK philanthropy found that the vast majority of significant contemporary UK philanthropists (82 percent) do conduct their giving through personal foundations and the UK's richest donors are concerned with offering leadership and personal engagement as well as money, and often use the language of business to emphasize their outcomes-oriented approach.[17] On the other hand, despite offering some support for all three aspects of new philanthropy (new donors, new causes and new methods of giving), a review of the historical literature, and of wider claims about changes in behaviour that are characterized as "new", indicates there is insufficient evidence to suggest that these variables are wholly new, particularly widespread or a result of changes that are specific to philanthropic behaviour.

Some Historical Evidence

This section of the chapter examines the three elements that constitute the idea of new philanthropy – new types of donors, new types of causes and new approaches to giving – in the light of historical studies on philanthropy.

The first suggestion, that new philanthropists are distinctively younger, entrepreneurial and "first-generation" rich, was found to be historically typical rather than exceptional. The historic roll call of donors includes many self-made entrepreneurs who began giving before retirement, notably Andrew Carnegie and John D. Rockefeller. In the UK, Thomas Guy, Isaac Wolfson and Joseph Rowntree all fit this description. Indeed one of the standard historical explanations of Victorian philanthropy is that it offered an opportunity for "new money" to buy the status required to be integrated into the elite.[18] Other types of "new donor" emerged as a result of changes in the sources and distribution of wealth. Rubinstein's studies of the patterns of wealth-creation in nineteenth- and twentieth-century Britain demonstrate a long-standing experience of constantly newly emerging means of becoming rich such that, "men of every type and of high and low degree could amass a fortune".[19] In her 1934 book *The New Philanthropy* (a title which demonstrates the currency of this phrase long before the present era), Elizabeth Macadam suggests that "new philanthropists" emerged after the Great War as "The class accustomed to generous giving gave place to a different class – the 'new rich', not bred in the same tradition".[20] Having surveyed the philanthropic terrain in the first third of the twentieth century, Macadam concluded it was no longer "the prerogative of the 'older families' or the 'upper class'".[21]

Macadam's account of the way in which the profile of the rich had altered over time offers an explanation for possible changes in the profile of philanthropists: as a sub-set of those possessing wealth, philanthropists reflect the characteristics of the group from which they are drawn. Within the UK's richest people there has been a shift from a majority that have inherited wealth to a majority that are self-made.[22] If a distinctive feature of the new philanthropists is that they are likely to be self-made entrepreneurs, this could be due to the changing composition of the rich rather than the changing nature of philanthropists. The types of people who are drawn to philanthropy can also be seen to change over time; Shapely's study of charity and power in Victorian Manchester, for example, found that being associated with philanthropy became a crucial, if unwritten, criterion for parliamentary candidates in that era.[23]

The second suggestion is that new philanthropists support "new causes", such as global health and the environment, yet similar shifts in the focus of philanthropic attention have occurred throughout history as the most urgent social problems changed over time. AIDS and climate change are prevailing concerns at the start of the twenty-first century just as, for example, it was popular to help poor maids to marry in the fifteenth century; to pay ransoms for people captured by pirates in the sixteenth century; and to make contributions to rebuild London after the Great Fire in the seventeenth century.[24] Clearly, the social problems facing sixteenth-century philanthropists, such as the loss of the contribution made by the monasteries to the relief of poverty following their dissolution by Henry VIII and the consequences of epidemic disease, were not the same as those faced by donors living during the Industrial Revolution which "posed problems for philanthropists different in degree and kind from those they had faced in the past".[25]

Given that philanthropy can be seen as part of a mixed economy of welfare, the role it plays in any given period will depend to a large extent on the kinds of needs which the private or public sectors are failing to address. It will also be shaped by the wider cultural context and prevailing social norms that affect every aspect of public life. In the seventeenth century, for example, factory schools which set children to work in a factory by day and taught them by night were considered an appropriate response to the challenge of educating poor children who needed to contribute to the family budget[26]. Factory schools would be viewed as unacceptable child labour today but received enthusiastic support from prominent philanthropists at the time. As different social problems emerge in different ages, it is to be expected that the philanthropic individuals of the time will offer what seems to them to be new and appropriate solutions. As Macadam observed:

> The worthy citizen of the eighteenth century relieved his conscience by a gift to an orphanage; the benevolent lady of the nineteenth century distributed soup and blankets. Her daughter 'taught the orphan boy to read and the orphan girl to sew'; her grand-daughter went 'slumming'. The twentieth-century lady is on the committee of the village institute; her daughter is a guide captain and her son helps at an unemployment centre.[27]

Any perceived "newness" in terms of causes is therefore more a consequence of external forces, notably changes in social need, social norms and provision by other sectors, than the result of internal decisions made by individual to seek out and support new types of recipients. The concerns of philanthropists living at the start of the twenty-first century are undoubtedly affected by contemporary issues, but a historical perspective highlights the inappropriateness of describing the constant evolution of privately-funded solutions to emerging social problems as "new', given how quickly these "new" issues will, in turn, become "old". Indeed, the ability of philanthropy to keep up with changing times is one of its most under-rated assets, as Macadam noted:

> This emphasis on the provision for new needs that may arise, rather than the bolstering up of old-established schemes, shows imagination and wisdom. The garden of charity needs constant pruning and weeding and replanting. Schemes which have outworn their usefulness must be allowed to die; others showing fresh shoots must be strengthened, and new growths must be tended and nurtured.[28]

The third suggestion is that new philanthropy involves new approaches to giving. New philanthropists are said to emphasize their "hands on" engagement with the causes they support, for example by sitting on charity boards and interacting with staff and beneficiaries. But again, a review of the historical literature shows that giving time, skills and energy as well as money is not a new approach. In Victorian England, for example:

> the dispensers of charity . . . were expected to give generously of their time and resources and to have a sustained personal involvement in their work. This was not 'checkbook philanthropy' satisfied merely by the contribution of money.[29]

The rise of "scientific philanthropy" in the late eighteenth century, which is discussed by Fowler in chapter twelve of this book and its importance in the nineteenth century and beyond which is documented by Lewis in her history of the Charity Organisation Society[30] provide further evidence that new approaches have arisen throughout the history of philanthropic activity.

Another facet of the newness claimed for contemporary philanthropic approaches is the implementation of businesslike models in the charity world, such as providing venture capital and using key performance indicators to monitor the impact and progress of donations. Yet the transfer of techniques from the business world into charities has a long history. For example, accounts of seventeenth-century philanthropy note the emergence of "associational philanthropy", based on the private sector model of joint-stock principles, which was frequently used to fund schools and hospitals.[31] The introduction of associational philanthropy was as revolutionary in its day as the introduction of "venture philanthropy" (a method commonly associated with new philanthropists) is today, and exemplifies how "old" philanthropists "pioneered a range of new forms in which aid could be delivered".[32] Another idea developed by philanthropists in previous centuries (yet often assumed to be a modern innovation) was the use of loans to provide funding to hospitals in need of cash injections. Loans were often necessary due to the proclivity of founders for providing the capital but not the running costs of such institutions.[33] This was clearly a major difficulty before the introduction of the state-funded National Health Service.

The concept of "Five Per Cent philanthropy", pioneered in the second half of the nineteenth century by advocates of the social housing movement, offers a further example of the historic transfer of business approaches into the philanthropic world.[34] This concept combined commercial and philanthropic responsibilities by offering investment opportunities in house-building companies that built dwellings for the labouring and artisan class; tenants paid an affordable rent and investors' returns were capped at a maximum rate of five percent, with any surplus re-invested in efforts to tackle the shortage of decent housing.[35] Five percent philanthropy demonstrated the long-standing compatibility of altruism with business acumen as investors sought to make a profit (albeit restricted) whilst doing good. This model also demonstrates a pre-existing concern with something often assumed to be a contemporary philanthropic obsession: that of sustainability. The policy of "philanthropy and five percent" was implemented as a concerted attempt to ensure the self-perpetuation of the social housing movement, "so that future generations might gain some benefit".[36] Pursuing sustainability through revenue-generating schemes is revealed as yet another *leitmotiv* of the "new philanthropy" that does not withstand scrutiny. Despite claims that contemporary major donors have a new appetite for funding "new entrepreneurial approaches",[37] earned income was a significant source of income for some charities in the early twentieth century, exemplified by residential institutions, such as homes for the blind, in which residents produced goods for sale.[38]

In addition to the idea that strategies such as pursuing sustainability are unique to the modern philanthropic era, it is also suggested that the approaches taken by new philanthropists are more innovative, bolder and "cutting edge" than their predecessors. For example, Handy claims that "they like to fill gaps and to meet needs neglected by others".[39] Yet some "old philanthropists" tackled the difficult issues of their times with ground-breaking initiatives, a prime example being London's Lock Hospital, which opened in 1747 to treat people with venereal diseases. This has been described as: "a courageous attempt on the part of mid [18th]-century philanthropists to grapple with one of the more noisome evils of their time".[40] Also in the health field, philanthropists were early supporters of contentious issues such as birth control, as well as backers of pioneering work in the new field of maternal health.[41]

Finally, an archetypal feature of new philanthropy is said to be a desire for impact or "value for money" which involves calculating the precise consequences achieved by philanthropic donations. For example, it is suggested that effective philanthropy involves, "being confident that your gift will make a difference, and being assured that your donation is an efficient use of your money".[42] Yet there is no basis for the suggestion that all old philanthropists indulged in careless benevolence without concern for outcomes, and the historical evidence reveals that concerns about ineffective philanthropic acts are not new.[43] An example of a careful approach to philanthropic spending can be found as far back as 1758 when one of the life-governors of the Foundling Hospital, Jonas Hanway, resigned after calculating that it cost £60 to raise a foundling in the institution, which was more than twice the £25 needed to raise a child within their own family.[44] Similarly, proponents of the Five Percent movement deployed research to demonstrate the effectiveness of their approach, publishing a report showing that mortality rates fell by two-thirds as a result of better housing, and that infant mortality in "model houses" was just a fifth of that found in the metropolis generally.[45] A concern with measuring need and demonstrating the effectiveness of philanthropic interventions is therefore clearly not the sole preserve of new philanthropists.

This review of historical precedents for the allegedly defining characteristics of new philanthropy indicates that previous generations of givers demonstrated similar properties, and therefore might equally have been perceived to be as "new" and "ground-breaking" in their time as those who live and give at the start of the twenty-first century. It appears that "newness" is a feature of every successive era, rather than the preserve of any specific generation. This begs the question, explored in the next section, as to why the idea of new philanthropy has gained so much ground.

Why Have Claims of a "New Philanthropy" Gained Credence?

If there is nothing especially new about contemporary philanthropy, why has the idea of a new philanthropy gained widespread adherence? Three explanations are proposed: an ahistorical approach amongst contemporary commentators that might be deemed a "loss of historical memory"; a "preference for novelty" which is a defining feature of late modernity; and a desire by contemporary givers to appear distinctive and to distance themselves from the negative connotations of the traditional meanings of philanthropy.

Loss of historical memory

As this chapter has demonstrated, the conclusion that twenty-first century philanthropists are "a breed apart from their forerunners"[46] can only result from taking an ahistorical approach. An historically-grounded study of the development of the philanthropic tradition suggests that what may seem to be innovations are rarely new departures from "traditional" philanthropy and frequently have much in common with what came before.[47] Despite contemporary claims of newness, historical studies largely emphasize continuity over change. Such differences that are identified tend to be differences in degree rather than in kind[48] because few donors funded "anything particularly venturesome or imaginative [and] money went, on the whole, to maintain established institutions or to create new ones of the same sort".[49] When change does occur, as for example with the introduction of associational philanthropy in the seventeenth century or the new arrangements between private funding and the welfare state in the mid-twentieth century, it occurs as a process of adaptation rather than as a paradigmatic shift or sharp dividing line between old and new philanthropy, thus enabling philanthropy and philanthropists to remain relevant to changing circumstances.

Those who promote the idea of new philanthropy[50] are not historians and do not bring historical knowledge to bear on their conclusions. The interests of those advocating the idea of new philanthropy lie purely in the present, and they are primarily driven by a desire to promote philanthropy and encourage more rich people to give. Most studies of new philanthropy therefore constitute examples of "advocacy research" in which conclusions are pre-determined and in which there is no room for inconvenient historical truths. Furthermore, the mid-twentieth century side-lining of philanthropy in the UK, as a result of firstly the creation of the Welfare State and subsequently the age of Thatcherite reforms, means that the longstanding and relatively unchanging nature of philanthropy is outside the memory and personal experience of contemporary commentators. The recent "discovery" of a "new philanthropy" is in fact a return to historical norms that has gone unrecognized.

The "preference for novelty"

A second explanation for the widespread acceptance of the existence of something called new philanthropy, is found in the concept of a "preference for novelty" which scholars from a range of disciplines, including economics, psychology and sociology, have identified as a defining feature of late modernity. The idea of "novelty" contains two implications: that it is both newly created and that it is improved or better. The intrinsic favourability of the term "new" is reinforced by the fact that its antonyms are generally pejorative, for example: "obsolete", "old fashioned" and "out of date". This desire for the new was well documented at the end of the nineteenth century when the sociologist Veblen wrote that:

> A fancy bonnet of this year's model unquestionably appeals to our sensibilities to-day much more forcibly than an equally fancy bonnet of the model of last year; although when viewed in the perspective of a quarter of a century, it would, I apprehend, be a matter of the utmost difficulty to award the palm for intrinsic beauty to the one rather than to the other of these structures.[51]

Recent sociological literature notes that a preference for novelty is a distinctive mark of modern consumerism, and that "the desire for the new" is continuously created and disseminated through all social classes. For example, Avner Offer's central argument in *The Challenge of Affluence* is that novelty is the driving force behind the pursuit of affluence.[52]

Historic studies of philanthropy also note the attraction of novelty. Gorsky's account of the declining attraction of endowed trusts as the preeminent vehicle for giving during the nineteenth century, for example, suggests that "the displacement of endowed charity was not simply the result of the inadequacy of the old forms, but also of preference for the new".[53]

The idea of "newness" being intrinsically "better" can also be found in cultural critiques of Britain's economic decline during the twentieth century which claim that "old" families and "old" institutions held Britain back. As Rubinstein notes, with reference to the version of this thesis contained in Sampson's *Anatomy of Britain:*

> Confidence was almost always placed in the "new men", the new knowledge, the new technology, and the new institutions to right Britain's deteriorating position.[54]

New philanthropists might thus be viewed as simply another manifestation of the widespread social approval for things that are "new". Claims of "newness" may be a result of a wish on the part of both donors, and those who observe donors, to associate themselves with novelty and its positive implications, even where there is little substantive basis for such claims.

The desire for distinction

A third explanation for the widespread promotion of the concept of a new philanthropy is a desire by contemporary givers to be distinctive and to distance themselves from negative connotations of the traditional meaning of philanthropy. Being new and different is part of distinguishing oneself as better, because people gain cultural cachet by displacing the authority of the past.

As an influential strand of sociological thinking has argued, people often seek to distinguish themselves by proving they possess greater quantities of cultural capital[55] which can be demonstrated through philanthropic acts that offer opportunities to display refined cultural tastes and appropriate mores. In the past, simply being philanthropic may have served as a sufficient display of cultural capital and generated enough distinction to justify an elevated status. However, in a society where almost everyone can afford to make donations, elites will seek to distinguish themselves further by making donations in ways that differentiate them from people in lower social strata.[56] They may, for example, give to high-status organizations such as universities and cultural institutions, or pursue what they perceive to be distinctive approaches to giving, such as being emphatically "strategic" or "highly engaged".

The fact that only famous and wealthy donors are described as new philanthropists lends support to the suggestion that new philanthropy is a recent facet of the quest for distinction, as this label is restricted to the economic and social elite. This scenario is hardly new: historic studies show that philanthropy has always been connected with mechanisms of exclusion and inclusion[57] and has consistently been "a vital means of acquiring or reinforcing [donors'] symbolic capital and social position."[58] Gorsky's analysis of the rise of associational philanthropy in nineteenth-century Bristol notes that this new form of giving, with donors' names publicized in subscriber lists, "provided an alternative means of registering social standing".[59] Nor is this situation unique to any one country or era, as a study of voluntary activity in seventeenth to nineteenth-century Italy notes: "charity had a crucial role in defining and reproducing the external and internal boundaries which characterized the body social in a particular period".[60] In support of the notion that a novel approach to philanthropy can be part of a strategy of differentiation, the same study goes on to note that philanthropy "became a means to distinguish oneself from others – from the poor but also from one's peers".[61]

The distinction gained by acquiring the label "new philanthropist" is a means of distinguishing oneself not only from "inferior" social contemporaries but also from givers in the past. In the words of one adviser to new philanthropists: "This is not your father's philanthropy; this is a whole new world of charitable giving."[62] The cultural distancing apparent in such comments is noteworthy. Whilst the "golden age" of nineteenth-century philanthropy is often referred to with approval, the donors of that era suffer from a poor image, as a contemporary commentator notes: "The reputation of Victorian philanthropists as interfering, paternalistic busybodies has deterred generations of successful Britons from setting off on the philanthropic path."[63] The re-branding of philanthropy as new philanthropy may be, at least in part, an attempt to alter its entrenched, negative public image and shed the connotations of "bewhiskered Victorian do-gooders"[64] in order to appeal to younger, predominantly self-made people who have the capacity to make major donations. Therefore, the idea of new philanthropy may well be less concerned with documenting substantive changes than it is concerned with re-branding philanthropy as a more attractive lifestyle choice for the potential major donors of the twenty-first century.

Conclusion

This chapter has argued that proponents of the idea of a new philanthropy appear to be unaware of historical precedents that undermine claims that a recent radical break has occurred in relation to the type of donors, causes and approaches that characterize philanthropy. Yet, given the changing economic, social and cultural contexts, none of the alleged characteristics of new philanthropy is particularly new. It has also been suggested that advocates of the idea of new philanthropy are likely to be influenced by the general disenchantment with things that are old in contemporary society, which leads to a self-conscious distancing from the past and the rise of a cult of novelty. Finally, it has been argued that contemporary wealthy donors wish to distance themselves from traditional notions of philanthropy, which lack cultural affirmation in contemporary UK society. By this account new philanthropy is primarily a presentational trope and a strategy to make philanthropy more appealing to both potential donors and the observing public.

This chapter has explored the suggestion that there is something distinctively new about philanthropy at the start of the twenty-first century, and concluded that there is no historical evidence to support the notion of a recent and radical break in the way philanthropy is carried out in the UK. Widespread acceptance of the idea of a new philanthropy is attributable to the loss of historical memory, a "preference for novelty" and a desire by contemporary givers to be distinctive and to distance themselves from negative connotations of the traditional meaning of philanthropy.

Philanthropy has undergone continual processes of change and has appeared "new" at many points in its history. The role of the philanthropist is continually being re-invented to reflect contemporary needs, dominant values, available wealth, technological developments and the broader socio-political context. Philanthropy is now, as it always has been, a product of its time.

Notes

1 This data is presented in Beth Breeze, *More than Money: The social meaning of philanthropy in contemporary UK society* (unpublished PhD thesis, University of Kent, 2010), chapter 5.

2 Charles Handy, *The New Philanthropists* (London: William Heinemann, 2006), p. 8.

3 *Ibid.*, p. 3.

4 Handy is quoted in an article entitled "Celebrity and the new philanthropy" published in *The Independent* newspaper on 26 September 2006

5 Matthew Bishop, "The Business of Giving", *The Economist*, February 2006.

6 Handy, *The New Philanthropists*, p. 9.

7 This quote is from an article entitled "Bill Gates: the designer-trousered philanthropist" published in the *Daily Telegraph* on 17 June 2006.

8 This quote is from an article entitled "The new face of philanthropy", *The Times* Saturday magazine, 24 February 2007.

9 This finding appears in a media analysis in Breeze, *More than Money*, chapter 5.

10 http://www.thehunterfoundation.co.uk/news/?news_id=16 [accessed 30/07/09].

11 This quote is from an article entitled 'Losing his virginity', in the *Daily Mail*, 21 August 2006.

12 Handy, *The New Philanthropists*, p. 3.

13 Matthew Bishop and Michael Green, *Philanthrocapitalism: how the rich can save the world* (New York: Bloomsburg Press, 2008), p. 272.

14 Handy, *The New Philanthropists*, p. 15.

15 Joel Fleishman, *The Foundation: A Great American Secret* (New York: Public Affairs, 2007), p. 271.

16 "Giving away billions is hard business", *Sunday Times*, 2 July 2006.

17 Breeze, *More than Money*.

18 See, for example: David Owen, *English Philanthropy 1660–1960* (London: Oxford University Press, 1965), p.165 and Keir Waddington, "Grasping Gratitude": Charity and hospital finance in late Victorian England, in Martin Daunton (ed.), *Charity, Self-interest and Welfare in the English Past* (London: UCL Press, 1996), p. 183.

19 William D. Rubinstein, *Men of Property: The very wealthy in Britain since the industrial revolution* (London: Croom Helm, 1981), p. 248.

20 Elizabeth Macadam, *The New Philanthropy* (London: George Allen and Unwin Ltd, 1934), p. 245.

21 *Ibid.*, p. 286.

22 As noted by Philip Beresford, author of the annual *Sunday Times Rich List*, in the 2006 edition, p. 10.

23 Peter Shapely, *Charity and Power in Victorian Manchester* (Manchester: The Chetham Society, 2000), p. 20.

24 See, for example, W. K. Jordan *Philanthropy in England 1480–1660: A Study of the Changing Pattern of English Social Aspirations* (London: George Allen and Unwin, 1959) and Owen, *English Philanthropy 1660–1960*.

25 Owen, *English Philanthropy 1660–1960*, p. 91.

26 *Ibid.*, p. 17.

27 Macadam, *The New Philanthropy*, p. 191.

28 *Ibid.*, pp. 259–60.

29 Gertrude Himmelfarb, *The Demoralization of Society: from Victorian virtues to modern values* (New York: Vintage, 1995), p. 148.

30 Jane Lewis, *The Voluntary Sector, the State and Social Work in Britain: The Charity Organisation Society/Family Welfare Association since 1869* (Aldershot: Edward Elgar, 1995).

31 B. Kirkman Gray, *A History of Philanthropy: From the dissolution of the monasteries to the taking of the first census* (London: Frank Cass and Co., [1905], 1967), p. 124.

32 Hugh Cunningham and Joanna Innes, *Charity, Philanthropy and Reform: from the 1690s to 1850* (Basingstoke: Macmillan, 1998), p. 7.

33 Gray, *A History of Philanthropy*, p. 226 and Waddington "Grasping Gratitude", p. 190.

34 John Nelson Tarn, *Five Per Cent Philanthropy: An account of housing in urban areas between 1840 and 1914* (Cambridge: Cambridge University Press, 1973).

35 Tarn, *Five Per Cent Philanthropy*, pp. 22–3.

36 *Ibid.*, p. 46.

37 The Social Investment Consultancy, *Financing Revenue Generation in the Third Sector* (London: The Social Investment Consultancy, 2010), p. 1.

38 Macadam, *The New Philanthropy*, p. 266.

39 Handy, *The New Philanthropists*, p. 9.

40 Owen, *English Philanthropy 1660–1960*, p. 53.

41 Macadam, *The New Philanthropy*, p. 129.

42 Susan Mackenzie, *A Guide to Giving*, 3rd edition (London: Association of Charitable Foundations, 2008), p. 13.

43 Macadam, *The New Philanthropy*, pp. 34–7.

44 Betsy Rodgers, *Cloak of Charity: Studies in Eighteenth-Century Philanthropy* (London: Methuen & Co. Ltd, 1949), p. 38.

45 Tarn, *Five Per Cent Philanthropy*, p. 24.

46 As suggested in an article entitled 'Let's leave it to the super-nerds to make poverty history', in *The Herald*, 30 June 2006.

47 Robert L. Payton and Michael P. Moody, *Understanding Philanthropy: Its meaning and mission* (Bloomington, Indianapolis: Indiana University Press, 2008), p. 153.

48 Owen, *English Philanthropy 1660–1960*, p. 75.

49 *Ibid.*, p. 474.

50 Such as Handy, *The New Philanthropists* and journalists writing about "new philanthropy" and "new philanthropists" including those referenced in this chapter in footnotes 7, 8,11, 16 and 44.

51 Thorstein Veblen, *The Theory of the Leisure Class* (New York: Dover,1994, first published 1899), pp. 80–1.

52 Avner Offer, *The Challenge of Affluence: Self-control and Well-Being in the United States and Britain since 1950* (Oxford: Oxford University Press, 2006), p. vii.

53 Martin Gorsky, *Patterns of Philanthropy: Charity and Society in Nineteenth-Century Bristol* (Woodbridge, Suffolk: The Boydell Press, 1999), p. 19.

54 William D. Rubinstein, *Capitalism, Culture, and Decline in Britain 1750–1990* (London and New York: Routledge, 1993), p. 18.

55 Pierre Bourdieu, *Distinction: A Social Critique of the Judgement of Taste* (London: Routledge, 1984).

56 Francie Ostrower, *Why the Wealthy Give: The Culture of Elite Philanthropy* (Princeton, NJ: Princeton University Press, 1995).

57 Thomas Adam, *Philanthropy, Patronage and Civil Society: Experiences from Germany, Great Britain and North America* (Bloomington, Indianapolis: Indiana University Press, 2004), p. 3.

58 Peter Shapely, "Charity, Status and Leadership: Charitable image and the Manchester man" in *Journal of Social History*, Vol. 32, No. 1 (Autumn, 1998), p. 157.

59 Gorsky, *Patterns of Philanthropy*, p. 123.

60 Sandra Cavallo, 'Charity as Boundary Making: Social stratification, gender and the family in the Italian states (Seventeenth – Nineteenth centuries)' in Cunningham and Innes, *Charity, Philanthropy and Reform*, p.110.

61 Cavallo, "Charity as Boundary Making", p. 119.

62 Eric Kessler of Arabella Advisers, Washington DC, cited in the *Financial Times*, 1 December 2007.

63 This comment appears in an article entitled 'The new philanthropists', in the *Sunday Telegraph*, 15 January 2006.

64 This description appears in an article entitled 'A continued charity of giving' in the *Daily Post*, 26 December 2006.

Index